Good times, bad times

The welfare myth of them and us

John Hills

To Tony, Howard and Julian

Contents

List of figures   viii

Glossary and acronyms   xii

Acknowledgements   xvi

1. Introduction: 'Them and us'   1

2. Are the poor too expensive?
   Redistribution and the welfare state   15

3. The long view: Social policies and the life cycle   47

4. It's complicated: High frequency living   75

5. Good years, bad years: Reacting to change   111

6. The long wave: Wealth and retirement   145

7. The longest wave: From generation to generation   181

8. A moving backdrop: Economic crisis, cuts,
   growth and ageing   217

9. Conclusion: Britain's misunderstood welfare state   249

Endnotes, figure sources and figure notes   269

References   311

Index   324

List of figures

2.1 'Should government redistribute income from
the better-off to those who are less well off?'   20

2.2 'Would you say the gap between those with high incomes
and those with low incomes is too large, about right or too small?'   21

2.3 'Should it be the government's responsibility to reduce income
differences?'   22

2.4 'Should government spend more money on welfare benefits
for the poor, even if it leads to higher taxes?'   23

2.5 Pen's parade of incomes in the UK, 2010–11   26

2.6 Inequality in disposable incomes in industrialised
countries, 2010 (Gini coefficients, %)   27

2.7 Distribution of household incomes, 2010-11   29

2.8 Inequality of market incomes in industrialised countries,
2010 (Gini coefficients, %)   31

2.9 Inequality before and after redistribution in the UK
and Sweden, 2010 (Gini coefficients, %)   32

2.10 Taxes and benefits by household income group, 2010–11   34

2.11 Preferences for taxation and cash benefits, 2008 (%)   37

2.12 The poor cost more? Benefits and taxes going to poorest
fifth of all households, 1979, 1996–97 and 2010–11   40

2.13 Net gain to poorest fifth of all and of non-retired
households as a percentage of average market income   41

2.14 Shares of income going to each fifth of distribution,
1979 to 2010–11   43

3.1 Seebohm Rowntree's 'cycles of want and plenty' in a
labourer's life, York, 1899   50

3.2 Schematic effects of Beveridge's social insurance over
the life cycle   51

3.3 Schematic effects of Beveridge's social insurance and
short-term income changes   51

3.4 Market income by age of household, 2005–06   53

3.5 Taxes and benefits by age of household, 2005–06   55

3.6 Market and disposable incomes by age of household, 2005–06   56

3.7 Poverty rates for different population groups   57

3.8   Net incomes by age, 1997–98 (GB) and 2010–11 (UK)   58
3.9   Difference in median net income for each age group
      from overall median, 1997–98 and 2010–11   59
3.10 Range of net incomes by age, 2010–11   60
3.11 Overall balance of cuts and reforms after 2010 by age   63
3.12 Lifetime social benefits and taxes by income group
      (1991 tax and social security systems)   66
3.13 Projected lifetime receipts from health, education and social
      security, and taxes paid towards them by year of birth,
      1901–1960, GB   70
4.1   Example case with regular weekly income: one-earner couple
      with two children and mortgage, 2003–04   80
4.2   Example case with unchanging circumstances but varying
      income: lone parent with one child and mortgage, 2003–04   81
4.3   Example case with changing circumstances: lone-parent
      tenant with one child, 2003–04   82
4.4   Highly stable cases: incomes in four-week periods, 2003–04 84
4.5   Highly erratic cases: incomes in four-week periods, 2003–04 85
4.6   Income trajectories followed by 93 families, 2003–04   86
4.7   Unemployment rate in the UK by duration   89
4.8   Proportion of claimants remaining on Jobseeker's
      Allowance, spells starting in April 2007, 2009 and 2011   91
4.9   Components of income for a couple with one child, 2010–11 98
4.10 Combined tax and benefit withdrawal rates for a couple
      with one child, 2010–11   100
4.11 Net income by hours worked under current system and
      Universal Credit, lone parent with two children   101
5.1   Income-age trajectories for women born in 1966 from 1991 to 2007 116
5.2   Income trajectories in the first 10 years of BHPS compared to
      random patterns   117
5.3   Age-earnings profiles by gender, private sector employees
      with high and low education, UK (gross hourly wages
      in 2000 terms)   121
5.4   Average hourly wage-age trajectories for men and
      women born before 1955 by qualifications   122
5.5   Proportion of claimants remaining on Incapacity Benefit
      or Severe Disablement Allowance, spells starting in April 2004
      and April 2007   123
5.6   Positions in income distributions of 1992 and 2006 of those
      who started in top and bottom tenths of distribution in 1991 125

5.7   Where people starting in different fifths of the income
      distribution spend their time over following years   126
5.8   Length of spell of poverty starting in one year   129
5.9   Patterns of poverty persistence over nine-year periods   130
5.10 Persistent low income 1991–94 to 2005–08   131
5.11 Total effective marginal tax and withdrawal rates on
      £1,000 differences in parental income – average for 27 universities   139
6.1   Pen's parade of household wealth (excluding pensions), 2008–10, GB   150
6.2   Pen's parade of household wealth (including pension rights),
      2008–10, GB   151
6.3   Wealth by age of household, 2008–10, GB   153
6.4   Wealth in 1995 and 2005 by initial age of household   159
6.5   Projections for remaining years of life for men reaching 65
      between 1955 and 2055   163
7.1   Six-year survival rates (%) for men and women aged over 60
      by wealth   185
7.2   Differences in 'school readiness' (average position out of 100)
      by parental income   186
7.3   Factors related to differences in teachers' assessment of
      children at the start of primary school   188
7.4   Children's test scores (aged 5–16 in 2004) by parents'
      socio-economic position and parents' test scores in childhood
      (aged 10 in 1980)   189
7.5   Attainment gaps between children receiving free school meals
      (FSM) and other children at different ages, 2011–12, England   192
7.6   Trends in attainment gaps between children by background,
      by year of birth   194
7.7   GCSE results for girls (rank in national distribution) by
      area deprivation, 2010, England   196
7.8   University attended by background, UK-born students,
      UK universities   197
7.9   Class of degree achieved by background, UK-born students,
      UK universities   198
7.10 How much of the variation in children's earnings is
      associated with parental income? (Men born in 1958 and 1970)   204
7.11 The Great Gatsby curve   208
7.12 Education earnings premiums and earnings mobility   209
8.1   Losses from general cuts in social benefits and services
      or general tax increases averaging £1,000 per household   224

8.2   Distributional effects of Labour's tax and benefit reforms
from 1997 to 2009 compared to systems adjusted with prices
or incomes   226

8.3   Institute for Fiscal Studies estimates of effects of tax and
benefit reforms, January 2010 to April 2015   229

8.4   Institute for Fiscal Studies estimates of effects of tax and
benefit reforms, January 2010 to April 2015, by household type   231

8.5   HM Treasury estimates of distributional effects of tax,
benefit and public service changes by 2015–16   232

8.6   Distributional effects of direct tax and benefit changes in
six countries, 2008–13   235

8.7   Effects of fiscal drag and benefit erosion over 20 years,
if real earnings grew by 2 per cent per year   239

8.8   Effects of fiscal drag and benefit erosion if part of revenue
used for tax cuts or benefit increases   240

8.9   ONS projections for percentage of population in each
age range, 2011 and 2051   242

8.10   OBR long-term public spending projections   245

9.1   Spending on the welfare state, 2014–15 (£ billion)   260

9.2   Agreement that 'social benefits and services make
people lazy', 2008   262

9.3   Commitment to work and benefit levels in different countries   263

Glossary and acronyms

BENEFIT EROSION
Situation where benefits fall in value relative to average incomes, for instance, because they are increased each year in line only with prices, when incomes are growing in real terms

CASH TRANSFERS
Cash benefits and tax credits from government

DECILE GROUP
One tenth of a population divided up in order of income, wealth, etc

DEFINED BENEFIT
Kind of pension where the amount paid depends on final salary (or other measure of earnings) rather than on investment returns

DEFINED CONTRIBUTION
Kind of pension where the amount paid depends on how much is paid in and on subsequent investment returns

DISPOSABLE INCOME
Income after direct taxes

DIRECT TAXES
Taxes paid by an individual or a household where the amount paid depends on their circumstances; they include Income Tax and National Insurance Contributions

EFFECTIVE MARGINAL TAX RATE (OR DEDUCTION RATE)
The proportion of any increase in earnings or other earnings that is taken in direct taxes and reduced means-tested benefits

EQUIVALISED INCOME
Income adjusted for family size

FISCAL DRAG
Situation where tax takes a greater proportion of people's income because tax allowances and brackets grow more slowly than average incomes

GINI COEFFICIENT

Index of inequality (equal to zero
if all households or individuals have
the same and 1 or 100 per cent if
one person has everything and the
rest nothing)

INDEXATION

Adjustment each year of benefits,
tax allowances, etc, for inflation
or to keep in line with earnings or
income growth

INDIRECT TAXES

Taxes where the amount paid
does not depend on an individual's
income, but on things such as
spending on particular goods, and
often collected via businesses, such
as Value Added Tax

MARKET INCOME

Income from wages, private
pensions, interest and other
investment income, before taxation
or state benefits

MEDIAN

The middle level of income, wealth,
etc, in a population, with half
having more and half having less

NET INCOME

Income after direct taxes

PEN'S PARADE

Way of showing income or wealth
distribution, with the height of
each column in proportion to the
amount received by each group
in order

PERCENTILE

Value separating each 1 per cent
of a population arranged in order
of income, wealth, etc

POVERTY TRAP

Situation where people on low
incomes gain little from any
increase in gross income because
of combined effects of taxes and
reduced means-tested benefits

PROGRESSIVE TAXATION

Tax system where those with higher
resources pay taxes that are a greater
proportion of those resources

QUINTILE GROUP

One fifth of a population divided
up in order of income, wealth, etc

REGRESSIVE TAXATION
Tax system where those with
higher resources pay taxes
that are a lower proportion of
those resources

TRIPLE LOCK
Guarantee that pensions rise
each year by the *higher* of prices,
earnings, or 2.5 per cent

WELFARE STATE
Public spending on and provision
for healthcare (such as NHS),
education, housing, personal care,
pensions and cash benefits of all
kinds (as opposed to 'welfare', as
used in the US, referring narrowly
to means-tested cash benefits for
out-of-work working-age people)

AHC	After Housing Costs
BHC	Before Housing Costs
BHPS	British Household Panel Survey
BSA	British Social Attitudes survey
CPI	Consumer Prices Index
CTC	Child Tax Credit
DCLG	Department for Communities and Local Government
DfE	Department for Education
DWP	Department for Work and Pensions
EMA	Education Maintenance Allowance
ESA	Employment and Support Allowance
EUROMOD	Essex University tax and benefit microsimulation model
FSM	Free School Meals
GDP	Gross Domestic Product
HB	Housing Benefit
HBAI	Households Below Average Income
HMRC	Her Majesty's Revenue and Customs
IFS	Institute for Fiscal Studies
ILO	International Labour Organization (which measures unemployment in terms of those looking for work, not just those claiming unemployment benefits)
IS	Income Support
ISA	Individual Savings Account
JSA	Jobseeker's Allowance
LAs	Local Authorities
LFS	Labour Force Survey
LHA	Local Housing Allowance
NMW	National Minimum Wage
NAO	National Audit Office
NSP	National Scholarship Programme
OBR	Office for Budget Responsibility
OECD	Organisation for Economic Co-operation and Development
ONS	Office for National Statistics
PAYE	Pay As You Earn
PEP	Personal Equity Plan
RPI	Retail Prices Index
SERPS	State Earnings-Related Pension Scheme
TESSA	Tax Exempt Special Savings Account
UC	Universal Credit
VAT	Value Added Tax
WFP	Winter Fuel Payment
WTC	Working Tax Credit
WFTC	Working Families' Tax Credit

Acknowledgements

The time to research for and prepare this book was generously supported by a fellowship from the Economic and Social Research Council (ESRC) (on 'Dynamics and design of social policies', RES-05127-2034). I am very grateful for this support, and for the flexibility of the Council in adjusting the fellowship's timing, so that I could take on some other unexpected responsibilities. I am also very grateful to the Social Policy Department of the London School of Economics (LSE) for providing some sabbatical time to allow the writing of the book to be completed.

One aim of the book was to draw together in one place the results of some of the research carried out in recent years at the Centre for Analysis of Social Exclusion (CASE) at LSE. The book therefore draws on research that has been supported by a range of funders to all of whom I am indebted, including the ESRC, the Nuffield Foundation (for work used in Chapters 6 and 7 on wealth inequality), the Joseph Rowntree Foundation, the Trust for London, the Government Equalities Office, HM Treasury, and HM Revenue and Customs. None of these bodies is in any way responsible for the views expressed here.

Most of the research reported here draws on joint work with colleagues within and outside CASE. Among those whose work I draw on particularly are: Fran Bennett, Jack Cunliffe, Ludovica Gambaro and Polina Obolenskaya (Chapter 2); Jane Falkingham, Julian Le Grand, Rachel Smithies, Holly Sutherland and Frances Woolley (Chapter 3); Matt Barnes, Ben Baumberg, Jon Hales, Abigail McKnight and Rachel Smithies (Chapter 4); Tania Burchardt, Stephen Jenkins, Ben Richards, John Rigg and Tom Sefton (Chapter 5); Francesca Bastagli, Frank Cowell, Howard Glennerster, Eleni Karagiannaki, Abigail McKnight and the members and secretariat of the Pensions Commission (Chapter 6); Jo Blanden, Lindsey Macmillan and the members and secretariat of the National Equality Panel (Chapter 7); Martin Evans, Ruth Hancock,

Holly Sutherland and Francesca Zantomio and the EUROMOD team (Chapter 8). I am also particularly grateful to Holly Holder for analysis of the European Social Survey used in Chapters 2 and 9. I hope I have done some justice to their work.

I am also very grateful to those whose figures are reproduced here with permission from other research, sometimes in a simplified form, including: Mike Brewer and colleagues (in Chapter 4); Stephen Jenkins (in Chapter 5); Jo Blanden, Miles Corak, Claire Crawford, Ingrid Esser and Lindsey Macmillan (in Chapter 7); David Phillips and colleagues at the Institute for Fiscal Studies, and Paola De Agostini and colleagues at the University of Essex (in Chapter 8). Figure 8.5 is Crown Copyright and reproduced under Class Licence C200600001 by kind permission of the Office of Public Sector Information (OPSI) and the Queen's Printer for Scotland. Other data used and analysed in the book was very kindly supplied by Alison Park and colleagues (from the British Social Attitudes survey), the Department for Work and Pensions (from the Family Resources Survey and for durations of receipt of benefits), and Elaine Chamberlain and Alan Newman at the Office for National Statistics (from the Wealth and Assets Survey).

I owe a great debt to Ben Richards, for analysis of data from the British Social Attitudes Survey, and in particular for checking nearly all of the numbers I include here and all of the text, and so saving me from a number of errors. The remaining ones are my responsibility alone. Cheryl Conner helped in many ways, including with the references and in preparing the text for publication – its completion would have been impossible without her support or that of Jane Dickson in managing CASE and all of the projects whose results are used here. More generally, all of my colleagues within CASE have shown extraordinary forbearance while fulfilling my other responsibilities has been delayed or neglected, in particular, Anne Power, for whom this has extended to home as well as office.

A number of people very kindly read all or parts of earlier drafts of the text and made many invaluable suggestions, including Ben Baumberg, Tania Burchardt, Lindsey Macmillan, Dawn Rushen, Alison Shaw, Kitty

Stewart, Holly Sutherland, Peter Taylor-Gooby, Nick Timmins and two anonymous referees for the Policy Press. I am sorry that there are places where space and time meant that I was unable to take up all of their suggestions, but their advice has greatly improved the book, as has the design work of Paulien Hosang, John Schwartz and their colleagues at Soapbox.

Throughout the book some of the points made are illustrated by stories of how they play out in the lives of the fictional Ackroyd and Osborne families. These were originally devised 25 years ago by Julian Le Grand and Don Jordan for two *World in Action* Granada TV documentaries in 1989 and 1991. I am very grateful to them both and to ITV for permission to explore and invent what has happened to these families and their children in the years since they first appeared.

There are three people, however, to whom I, and this book, owe the most. Tony Atkinson, Howard Glennerster and Julian Le Grand read and made many insightful comments on the entire draft text. I cannot thank them enough, not just for this, but for all of their inspiration, encouragement and support throughout my whole time working on issues of this kind at LSE.

1. Introduction

'Them and us'

A VISITOR TO Britain learning about our society and the public policy problems facing us from the newspapers and television could be forgiven for thinking that it is all very straightforward. A hard-pressed majority, whose living standards have been squeezed ever tighter and tighter since the start of the economic crisis in 2008, is paying higher and higher taxes to fund hand-outs – 'welfare' – to a minority living long term on benefits, people who have often never worked, and have no intention of doing so. That is, apart from the ones who really are working cash-in-hand on the side, while still claiming.

It's skivers against strivers; dishonest scroungers against honest taxpayers; families where three generations have never worked against hard-working families; people with their curtains still drawn mid-morning against alarm-clock Britain; 'Benefits Street' against the rest of the country; undeserving and deserving. It's them against us. *We* are always in work, pay our taxes and get nothing from the state. *They* are a welfare-dependent underclass, pay nothing to the taxman, and get everything from the state. If only we could get them to work through ever-more stringent conditions on getting benefits and through cutting back the value of what people who get them are allowed, we'd fix the public finances and get the economy moving at the same time.

This view of the country as separated into two distinct and unchanging groups is so pervasive it is often hardly noticed when it more subtly underpins policy debates. For instance, in June 2013, Chancellor George Osborne, discussing the Conservative-Liberal Coalition government's approach to 'welfare' in the Spending Review, argued that,

"*Two* groups need to be satisfied with our welfare system. Those who need it – who are old, who are vulnerable, who are disabled, or have lost their job and who *we* as a compassionate society want to support. And there's a *second* group. The people who pay for this welfare system: who go out to work, who pay their taxes and expect it to be fair on them too."[1] (emphasis added)

The following month, Work and Pensions Secretary Iain Duncan Smith similarly argued that the government was 'bringing in major changes to make the welfare state fair to both the people who use it and the taxpayers who pay for it'.[2] In the same month, BBC One broadcast a two-part documentary led by Nick Hewer and Margaret Mountford from *The Apprentice*. Called 'Nick and Margaret: We pay all your benefits', the programmes confronted a group of long-term benefit recipients with a contrasting group of 'taxpayers', each group presented as being distinct and opposing.

Built into such political statements and media coverage is a view of what welfare states and social policies in modern economies do, acting as an industrial-scale modern-day 'Robin Hood', taking from one group and giving to another. This, in itself, would be a simplistic view of what is actually going on, even if we lived in a memory-less goldfish bowl world where all that mattered was the instantaneous profit and loss account for the budgets of government and each household.

But we do not live in such an arid, unchanging world. Most of what the welfare state does is about coping with the complexities of lives that change and develop over time in often unpredictable ways. Some of this change is long term, as we move through life, from childhood and education to adulthood and paid work, from being single to being in a partnership and having children, and from work to retirement. But some of it is very short term, with most people who lose their jobs quickly returning to paid work after a short time, and with the incomes of those who stay in work often changing rapidly from week to week or month to month.

As a result, many more people will previously have contributed to the system at earlier stages of their lives than are paying one particular tax today. Many more will receive support from it later in their lives (sometimes sooner than they expected) than do so at one particular moment.

On the other side of the Atlantic, misunderstanding this was one of the factors that cost the Republican candidate, Mitt Romney, victory in the 2012 presidential election when he argued that there were, "47 per cent who will vote for the President no matter what ... who are dependent on government, who believe that they are victims, who believe that they are entitled to health care, to food, to housing, you name it."[3] On the basis of the proportion of Americans paying income tax at any one moment, Romney believed that the US was divided into two groups, one passively dependent on and entitled to support from the other 53 per cent of Americans. But many of the '47 per cent' were, for instance, retired from jobs where they previously had paid income tax and had made social insurance contributions over their whole careers at work, on the basis of which they were indeed 'entitled' to state pensions ('social security' in US terms) and healthcare. Misunderstanding this meant that Mr Romney was insulting a far greater proportion of voters than the just under half he identified.

Static or active?

Even when you look at who benefits from policies narrowly focused on those with low incomes or those without paid work, the difference between what a static snapshot picture shows and a dynamic video is crucial. But a related and recurring theme in the UK debate is that benefit policies have, until 'recently', only been concerned with their static effects. As Iain Duncan Smith put it in 2010, soon after taking office:

> "Too much of our current system is geared towards maintaining people on benefits rather than helping them flourish in

work; we need reforms that tackle the underlying problem of
welfare dependency."[4]

This was, in fact, hardly new. One of his Labour predecessors, Peter
Hain, had said much the same thing three years earlier:

> The core of our radical new approach will be to move people
> from being passive recipients of benefits to active jobseekers
> looking and preparing for work with access to training and job-
> focused activity.[5]

But this 'radical new' approach had also been flagged more than a decade
earlier by the then Prime Minister Tony Blair:

> "We are creating a system which is 'active' not 'passive',
> genuinely providing people with a 'hand up' not a 'hand out'.
> Previous governments were satisfied simply to dole out money."[6]

And you can actually find similar statements all the way back to the
proposals for post-war social insurance by William Beveridge in his
famous 1942 report, which laid some of the foundations for the post-
war welfare state:

> The insured persons should not feel that income for idleness,
> however caused, can come from a bottomless pit.[7]

In the summary of his report, Beveridge argued that receiving benefits
'will normally be subject to a condition of attendance at a work or
training centre after a certain period.'[8] In reality, policies towards
the unemployed have always had conditions attached to them, such
as 'actively seeking work'.[9] At the same time, Beveridge's vision was
based on the notion of a lifetime of shared risks – a world in which you
could not neatly divide the population into those who paid and those
who received.

Much of this book argues that seeing policies as static and benefit recipients as passive ignores the bulk of what social policies do and the complexity of the relationships between them. Most of those policies are directed at coping with or mitigating problems caused by the complex dynamics of people's lives, both the predictable ones associated with the life cycle and the less predictable ones facing people as they make their way in an uncertain world.

Many of the current reforms of the welfare state (and the controversies around them) are therefore not simply about point-in-time effects, such as who needs help today, and who should pay for it. For instance:

- How should tax credits and the new Universal Credit that is replacing them react as people's circumstances – such as their pay or hours – change from week to week or month to month?
- Should social housing tenants whose circumstances have improved be asked to move out a few years later, as they are no longer in need?
- What should happen to state pension ages as successive generations live longer?
- How do we help people accumulate wealth, and who does that help?
- Can we increase 'social mobility' and create 'equal opportunities' when people's family circumstances are so unequal?
- And what does the ageing of the population mean for the pressures on the welfare state and for public finances and the length of working lives over the coming decades?

To understand questions like these, we should look at the ways public and social policies operate – and the problems they are designed to address – across different time periods, from the very short term to the very long term. Our lives vary and circumstances change over different wave lengths. At one end of this spectrum is the *instantaneous* redistribution captured by the 'Robin Hood' analogy of taking from the rich and giving to the poor. Next come *short-term changes*, such as coping with loss of income from unemployment or illness, but also with a world where many people's circumstances change within the year, from week to week or month to month. Then there are issues operating over the *medium term*, such as funding people when they are students looking forward – often, but not always – to greater prosperity later.

At *longer wave lengths* come pensions and other structures that affect income in retirement, the ways we accumulate and then run down assets over the life cycle, or provide for social care in old age. The *longest wave* of variation is about intergenerational links – not just explicit transfers such as inheritance or lifetime transfers to children or grandchildren and the tax treatment of these, but also the web of other factors that link children's futures to the circumstances of their parents, and the range of policies that are designed or said to promote 'social mobility' and to create 'equality of opportunity'.

Two families

Each of the following seven chapters presents information on the environment within which the welfare state operates – looking at how people's lives vary and differ over different time periods, and how the welfare state affects those dynamics. But the kind of statistical data presented, drawing on a wide range of research, may not immediately convey the flavour of what this means for individuals and families. So, running through the book to introduce the analysis is a series of vignettes at the start of each of the chapters about the lives of members of two extended families – the Osborne family, from Alderley Edge in Cheshire, and the Ackroyd family, from Salford in Greater Manchester.

These two families first appeared in a *World in Action* TV documentary, 'Spongers', in 1989.[10] Presented as a spoof TV game show, it traced how (stereo-)typical working-class and middle-class families were affected by the welfare state of the time. Which were the true 'spongers' of the show's title, most 'dependent on government' in current formulations, if one looked over their whole lives?[11] As it happens, the longer-living, university-educated, opera-loving middle-class Osbornes turned out to be the winners, and the working-class Ackroyds the losers. A follow-up programme, 'Beat the Taxman', two years later looked at which family had done best out of the tax reforms of the Thatcher years.[12] Perhaps less surprisingly, the Osbornes won that one too.

What was special about these families was that, in the words of the game show host Nicholas Parsons, "we've invented them". And that is true of the stories at the start of each chapter describing what has happened to both families and to their children and grandchildren a quarter of a century later. As the stories illustrate different aspects of people's lives, different members of the families appear in particular chapters. To help keep track of them, pages 8–9 show the two family trees.

Fictions like these may help point to some of the practical issues that lie behind the analysis in the chapters they introduce. They also raise some of the questions that we need to understand. But small numbers of hypothetical cases can never be truly representative of the rich variety of families and circumstances in the actual population. The handful of 'typical' families we see at Budget time, for instance, only ever show what has happened for a small proportion of the population – and if they are not balanced across actual family types and income levels, they can be positively misleading. The overall position can only be captured through using high-quality survey information, where possible for the country as a whole, which is what the core of each chapter is based on. This is possible because of the investment that has been made in the UK over recent decades in a series of surveys and studies, some of which look across the country as a snapshot today, which we can compare with the past, but others of which have followed the same people's lives as they have developed over 40 years or more. Detailed notes of sources for such statistics and figures are collected at the end of the book.

Structure of the book

Chapter 2 looks at the immediate redistributive effects of social spending and the way it is paid for – the picture you get if you take a snapshot view. It starts by describing how two of the now grown-up children of our families, solicitor Henry Osborne and single mother

THE OSBORNE AND ACKROYD FAMILIES

The Osbornes

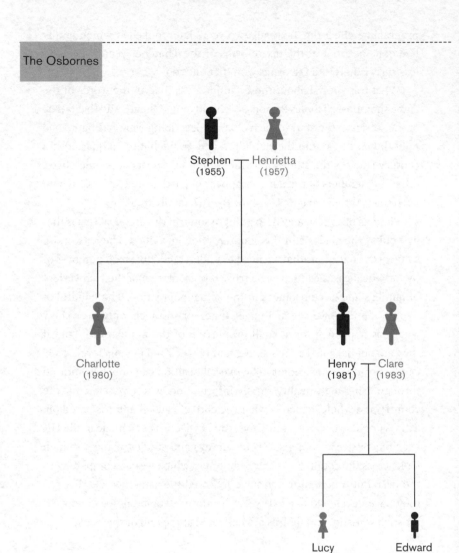

Stephen (1955) — Henrietta (1957)

Charlotte (1980)

Henry (1981) — Clare (1983)

Lucy (2008)

Edward (2013)

Note: Dates of birth in brackets

The Ackroyds

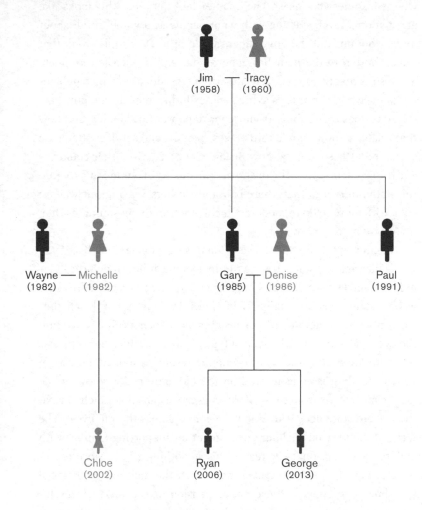

Jim
(1958) — Tracy
(1960)

Wayne — Michelle
(1982)   (1982)

Gary — Denise
(1985)   (1986)

Paul
(1991)

Chloe
(2002)

Ryan
(2006)

George
(2013)

Michelle Ackroyd, are affected in a single year by benefits and services from the welfare state, and the taxes that finance them. How much does each family receive and how much do they pay in? In other words, who gains and who loses? The chapter looks at what this looks like at a national level, starting with what people as a whole think about 'redistribution' and the government's role in it. Do people think that redistribution to the poor has gone too far and now costs too much, and if so, is that true? It starts by describing the situation which policies try to cope with, in this case inequalities in incomes. It explains how the state does redistribute from richer to poorer households, and how that relates to how people think taxes, benefits and services should be structured. It also looks at how Britain compares with other countries and the problems caused by the greater inequality of our incomes before the state intervenes than there is in most others, leaving our welfare state with more to do to moderate inequalities of living standards than elsewhere in the rich world.

Chapter 3 gives an initial discussion of what policies look like if you take a life cycle view, illustrating this by looking at how much the older Ackroyd and Osborne couples might have expected to receive from the welfare state over their complete lifetimes. The analysis of the chapter starts from Seebohm Rowntree's insights more than a century ago into the cycle of 'want' and 'plenty' in a typical labourer's life, and contrasts this with life cycle patterns of economic resources today. The way in which spending is concentrated on the old and on the young, while taxes come mostly from those of working age, means that much of what the welfare state does is to smooth incomes across the life cycle. The focus of the previous Labour government on supporting families with children and pensioners increased this smoothing effect. More recent policies have increased the extent to which the main effect of social spending is to support those above pension age, while services for younger people are cut back. The chapter analyses what this all means in terms of the total amounts that both rich and poor might expect to receive from education, healthcare, pensions and other social security over their whole lives. The scale of this may come as a surprise to some readers, with the implication that many more people have a larger stake in the system than they realise.

Chapter 4 looks at the often considerable short-term variations in some people's circumstances from week to week. For some, such as Henry Osborne's civil servant sister Charlotte, comparatively little changes over the year. But for Michelle Ackroyd's brother Gary and his wife Denise, like many other low-income families, the money coming in changes constantly across the year. This chapter discusses the extent of this for lower-income families more generally, and the ways in which income varies for many when they are in work. At the same time, there is in reality rapid turnover between unemployment and being in work, rather than it being common for those becoming unemployed to stay out of work long term. This complicated reality causes problems for systems such as the tax credits introduced by the previous Labour government after 1999, and for the Conservative-Liberal Coalition flagship Universal Credit system currently being introduced to replace it.

Stretching out the time window, Chapter 5 looks at what happens to people's incomes from year to year, starting with a description of how both Jim and Tracy Ackroyd's and Stephen and Henrietta Osborne's incomes changed through the 2000s, as their families grew up, and as they were affected by unemployment or sickness. The analysis starts by looking at what we now know from surveys that have followed people's lives from year to year over the last two decades, and at what this tells us about whether we are dealing with an unchanging 'underclass', or at the other end, with a world where everything changes randomly from year to year. How are we able to cope with the much more complicated reality of *some* continuity and *some* change that lies between these two extremes? Better understanding of this would help in how we think about a range of policies, illustrated here by looking at current issues within social housing and means-tested support for students.

The next two chapters are about the longer term. Chapter 6 looks at how different aspects of the tax system and welfare state have helped or hindered families like the older Osbornes and Ackroyds to build up their savings and wealth, and where this has left them towards the ends of their working lives. Wealth – people's savings and assets – has become much larger in relation to people's annual incomes, and it is distributed far more unequally. The chapter looks at what national wealth inequality now looks like, and at how it differs, both between different generations and within those generations. Is the key issue wealth inequality between generations, such as the 'baby boomers' and the rest, or is it inequality within each generation? It examines two kinds of policies concerned with how the state helps people accumulate resources over their lives: pensions policy, and the rationale for the recent wave of pension reforms in the UK; and the other hugely varied (and often contradictory) range of policies that affect or are affected by the way people accumulate wealth and other assets.

Chapter 7 then looks at financial and other links across the generations. Given their very different family backgrounds, what do the life chances look like of young George Ackroyd compared to those of young Edward Osborne, both born in July 2013? It describes what the national evidence shows on how differences in outcomes develop through education and on into people's careers, how differences in family resources can set up patterns of advantage and disadvantage that reinforce themselves through the lives of the following generation, and what this means for overall policy aims of increasing 'social mobility'. Can we really achieve 'equality of opportunity' when inequalities between people's starting points – the outcomes for their parents – are so great?

Chapter 8 then looks at the ways in which social policies both affect and are affected by changes in the wider economy and society over time, specifically by inflation, economic growth or recession and population ageing. It starts by looking at how austerity policies since 2010 of cuts and restrictions in benefits and of tax increases have affected the poorest of the hypothetical families, single-parent Michelle Ackroyd, and the richest, the affluent Stephen and Henrietta Osborne. How much has each lost as a share of their incomes through the different measures, and is this representative of what has happened at a national level? Over the longer term, as and when economic growth returns, how will sometimes invisible decisions about the ways in which benefits and taxes are adjusted for growth and inflation affect different income groups? And what will be the longer-term implications of an ageing population for the costs of providing a welfare state of the kind we currently have?

The final chapter summarises the picture shown by the research and analysis presented through the book, and brings together the implications of this way of thinking, about what social policies and the welfare state are for, and who they affect. Britain's welfare state is widely misunderstood, with many people believing in particular that the bulk of what it does consists of hand-outs to unemployed people, and that its beneficiaries are an unchanging group, separate and distinct from those who pay for it. Neither of these beliefs is true. But myths of this kind have consequences – not just for those at the sharp end of reforms designed to make significant savings from what is, in fact, only a small fraction of what is really spent on the welfare state, but also for the much wider group of us – indeed, the vast majority of us – who are or who will be affected by the welfare state in different ways across our changing lives, in good times and in bad ones.

ARE THE POOR TOO EXPENSIVE?

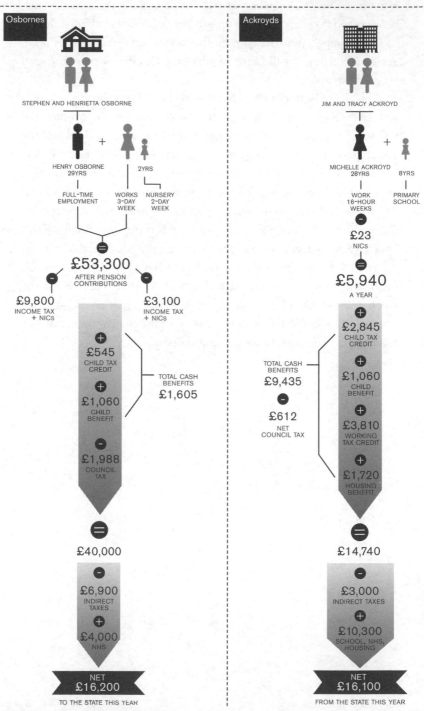

Note: Numbers here (and elsewhere) may not add up precisely due to rounding.

2. Are the poor too expensive?

Redistribution and the welfare state

In April 2010, 29-year-old Henry Osborne's life and career were going well. He had grown up in Alderley Edge, outside Manchester, where his parents, Stephen and Henrietta, had managed to buy a house in the 1980s before it became quite so fashionable. His father was a successful accountant and his mother a teacher, so they were comfortably off. He and his elder sister Charlotte had been sent to private boarding schools for the first part of their secondary education, but then to a state sixth form college before doing a gap year abroad and then getting a good law degree from the University of Bristol.[1]

Henry had landed a traineeship at the Manchester offices of one of the big national solicitors' firms, where a recent promotion had taken him to a salary of just under £40,000. That really was successful – only about a tenth of men of his age were paid that much, around £20 per hour.[2]

Henry met Clare at a party of his sister's after he had moved back to Manchester, when she was training as a teacher. One thing led to another and they married in 2005; their daughter, Lucy, was now aged two. Clare had started back at work three days a week a year before, with Lucy in a private day nursery for two of the days, and his mother, Henrietta, child-minding for one day (having cut back her own working hours to help out).

Henry and Clare didn't feel particularly well off – especially after paying towards a £130,000 mortgage (luckily Henry's parents had helped them with most of the rest of the purchase of their Stockport house, with part of an inheritance from his grandmother) and the £100 a week the nursery charged. And between them, they seemed to pay a lot of tax. Where it went wasn't that clear to Henry. What he did know from what he read about in the papers was that other people were doing well out of the system through the hand-outs that had increased under the Labour government, and he and Clare seemed to be the ones paying for it.

Part of Henry's father's accountancy had rubbed off on him, so one weekend he sat down and worked it out. Between them, he and Clare earned £57,200, or £53,300 after knocking off their pension contributions.[3] His Income Tax and National Insurance Contributions (NICs) added up to £9,800 and Clare's to £3,100.[4] Bizarrely, in Henry's view, they received an odd £545 per year in Child Tax Credit,[5] plus £1,060 in Child Benefit. But their Council Tax was £1,988 per year. Allowing for that, they took home £40,000 – losing £13,300 to the state, or about a quarter of their pre-tax incomes. That seemed a lot to be paying in every year to subsidise people who were out of work and lone parents in council flats they had managed to somehow get themselves into. Somehow it felt as if it had all got too expensive.

After paying the mortgage and the £100 nursery fees, Henry worked out that he and Clare were left with £539 a week for everything else – just £28,000 a year. That didn't seem to make them particularly rich – he'd read about people on benefits getting that sort of amount, which just didn't seem right, especially as they would not have to pay the train fares into work he had to, or for the car Clare needed to get to school and to drop Lucy off with his mother.

In fact, just at this moment in their lives, Henry could have made himself gloomier. People with their kind of disposable income were paying around £6,900 in indirect taxes of one kind or another, including the ones that the Office for National Statistics (ONS) reckons are passed on by firms to the people who buy their products such as business rates.[6] On the other hand, the value of the NHS to families like theirs might be worth around £4,000 on average.[7] Lucy was too young to be benefiting from state education, even from the free nursery hours that Labour had recently introduced for three- and four-year-olds. Throwing in indirect taxes net of the NHS, Henry could have shown that they were paying a net £16,200 into the system.

If asked, like most of us Henry and Clare would have described themselves as having 'middle incomes'.[8] In fact, even though they were early in their careers, as a family they were actually better off on official calculations than four-fifths of the population in terms of their incomes before allowing for housing costs (or three-quarters, after allowing for them).[9]

If Michelle Ackroyd had made a similar calculation, she would have come to a very different result. She was one of the single parents in social housing – in her case, a two-bedroom housing association flat in Salford, not so far from the council house her parents Jim and Tracy still lived in – that Henry was so exercised about. She was 28 now, and her daughter, Chloe, 8. After her partner Wayne had left, leaving her on her own, she had been on Income Support for several years but now had a 16-hour a week job in a supermarket that qualified her for the extra tax credits Labour had brought in.[10]

Michelle was earning £7.14 an hour – not a lot, but better than 30 per cent of women of her age. After a small amount of National Insurance (she earned too little to pay Income Tax) she took home just under £114 per week, or £5,940 a year. But benefits and tax credits more than doubled that – £20 in Child Benefit, £54.50 in Child Tax Credit, £73 in Working Tax Credit.[11] Since moving into work she now had to pay a little over half of the £71 per week rent that the housing association charged, but with £33 in Housing Benefit going directly to her landlord. The rent went in on the dot – her Manchester-based housing association put its tenants who paid on time onto its 'gold service' when there were maintenance problems, and offered a range of special offers. She also got Council Tax Benefit of £5.20 towards her Council Tax of just under £17 per week.

Putting all of that together, Michelle was entitled to £9,400 of cash benefits of one kind or another, but paid NICs and net Council Tax adding up to a little over £600, leaving her with a net income of £14,740. Calculated along Henry's lines, that would put her £8,800 up from her dealings with the state.

In fact, allowing for wider factors, Michelle's net gain was larger. True, she might be paying nearly £3,000 in indirect taxes one way or another,[12] but Chloe's primary school place cost Salford Council £6,050 a year,[13] her free school meals were worth £290 over the whole year, and NHS spending for the two of them would average out at around £3,000. It is a bit hard to be precise about the value of the subsidies that kept down her housing association rent, but they could add another £1,000 a year to the 'benefits in kind' she was receiving.[14]

Allowing for all of that, Michelle's net gain from the welfare state, after the taxes she paid, would have come to £16,100 – as it happens, almost exactly what Henry and Clare were paying in.[15]

SPRING CREEK CAMPUS

Looking at Labour's tax and benefit reforms, working single-parent families like Michelle's – along with pensioners – were among the biggest gainers. As a result, official calculations would put her above the poverty line. In fact, before allowing for her rent and Council Tax (but including benefits towards them), her net income of just under £300 per week meant that she was better off than a third of all households, both before and after allowing for her housing costs.[16]

Thanks to the tax credits she got in work, even though she now had to pay half the rent and most of the Council Tax, she was around £70 a week better off than she had been when she was on Income Support (less her bus fares to work). That made the difference between being £40 clear of the poverty line after all her bills, and being £30 below it. For her, and indeed for most people in a similar position, 'work paid'.

IN A SNAPSHOT, then, more affluent families like Henry and Clare's are putting more into the system than they get out, while the reverse is true for poorer ones such as Michelle's. In this particular case the system is effectively redistributing £16,000 per year from one that is a quarter of the way from the top of the income distribution to one that as a result ends up a third of the way from the bottom.

These are just two illustrative examples, however, and in particular circumstances (for instance, after Lucy's birth using the NHS but before her early years education starts). This chapter uses national survey data to look at whether this kind of redistribution is what most people want, and whether families like the Osbornes and the Ackroyds are typical. In particular, is there more redistribution going on than there used to be, and is that why people like Henry and Clare have ended up feeling so aggrieved?

The poor got too expensive

Soon after the 2010 General Election and Chancellor George Osborne's first Budget, I was involved in a seminar on housing policy held in very grand surroundings. Part of my presentation was about the way in which the new Coalition government's plans for benefits would hit some families with low incomes. Another participant, apparently as grand as the surroundings, nodded in agreement with the analysis, but added, "The trouble is, the poor got too expensive."

This kind of view – although not necessarily expressed so directly – underlies much current policy towards benefits and the welfare state more widely and discussion of it. The word 'welfare' itself is used to conjure up a picture that the source of Britain's Budget deficit – and with it the economic crisis itself – was an explosion of millions of Michelle Ackroyds, living on ever more generous benefits, driving up the tax rates of a separate hard-working and hard-pressed group of taxpaying Henry Osbornes. For some, in an ideal world, it might be nice to help the poor, but we just cannot afford it any more. For others, the help benefits – 'welfare' – give is the source of the problem, creating the 'dependency culture' without which they would already have improved their own lives (although, of course, in Michelle's case, she is actually in work).

Those views are underpinned by two beliefs: first, that what the welfare state mainly does is 'redistribution' – taking money from the richer (not necessarily much richer) and giving it to the poorer; and second, that a large and growing part of the social security budget is spent on hand-outs to those who do not work. Later chapters return to the other things the welfare state does, and to what spending on it now adds up to in Chapter 9, but this chapter concentrates on what the state does achieve by way of redistributing income, and how the scale of that has changed over time.

'Redistribution' has indeed become less popular since the 1980s, as Figure 2.1, drawn from the long-running British Social Attitudes (BSA) survey suggests. But the picture it paints is not quite as simple as that. First, although fewer people now agree with the statement, that the 'government should redistribute income from the better-off to those who are less well-off' than did 20 years ago, quite a lot more (42 per cent in 2013) agree with this sentiment than disagree with it (29 per cent). Second, the big changes in the balance between the two came in the late 1990s, with a further dip in support between 2004 and 2007, which has completely reversed since the start of the economic crisis. By 2013, as many respondents were agreeing as had done back in the mid-1990s, and nearly as many as when the series started in 1986.[17] The crisis and experience of austerity has been accompanied by rising support for redistribution.

More support 'redistribution' since the start of the economic crisis

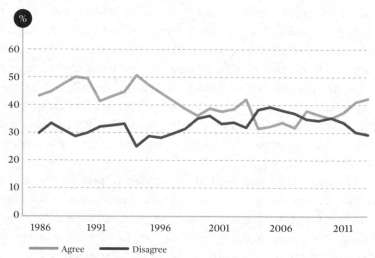

Figure 2.1 – 'Should government redistribute income from the better-off to those who are less well off?'

One reason for being cautious in interpreting this kind of picture, however, is that it is unclear when people are answering whether they are thinking of whether there should be any redistribution *at all* (or market incomes should be left as they are), or whether they think that there should be *more* redistribution than is already taking place. The changes over time are more consistent with the latter. Many thought the Thatcher and early Major governments were not doing enough. By contrast, they thought the Blair and Brown governments *were* doing enough – and 'New Labour' avoided using the language of redistribution in public debate from the mid-1990s, so it was less the focus of debate.[18] But by 2012 more thought again that the Coalition government should do more. As discussed below, they also favour, on grounds of fairness, ways that the government should tax and spend that end up being 'redistributive', even if that is not their explicit aim in itself.[19]

What people say they think about inequality and what government should do about it depends on exactly what question is asked. Figures 2.2 to 2.4 show what proportion of people agreed and disagreed with three other statements getting at this:

- 'The gap between those with high incomes and those with low incomes is too large.'
- 'It is government's responsibility to reduce differences in income between the rich and the poor' or 'to reduce differences between those with high and low incomes.'
- 'Government should spend more on welfare benefits for the poor, even if it leads to higher taxes.'

More than three-quarters consistently say that income gaps are too large

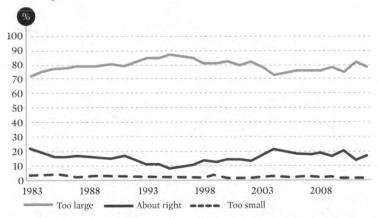

Figure 2.2 – 'Would you say the gap between those with high incomes and those with low incomes is too large, about right or too small?'

Consistently throughout the last three decades many more people have said that they think income differences are too large than have disagreed (see Figure 2.2). In fact, more than 70 per cent have agreed with this in every year – around 80 per cent for most of the period, including 79 per cent in 2013. For most of the time, fewer than 20 per cent thought income differences 'about right', and fewer than 3 per cent that they were 'too small'. There has been no move away from inequality being seen as a concern.

Many more people also agree than disagree that it is the government's responsibility to do something about it than not, at least when phrased as 'between the rich and the poor', where two-thirds or more have agreed when asked since the mid-1990s (see Figure 2.3). However, when the wording is changed slightly to reduce income differences 'between those with high incomes and those with low incomes', the majority is somewhat smaller – 49 per cent agreeing compared to 22 per cent disagreeing in 2010, for instance. In both cases agreement has varied over time, but with no strong trend since the mid-1980s.

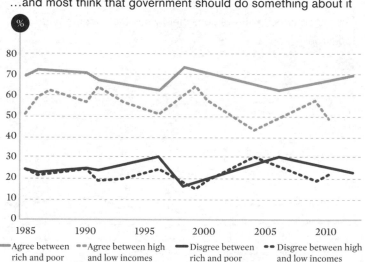

...and most think that government should do something about it

Figure 2.3 – 'Should it be the government's responsibility to reduce income differences?'

However, as shown in Figure 2.1 above, fewer people think that the 'something' to be done is redistribution than did in the early 1990s. And Figure 2.4 shows that the movement away from that being achieved through spending more on 'welfare benefits' has been more continuous. Sixty-one per cent agreed with this in 1989 and only 15 per cent disagreed. By 2013 only 36 per cent agreed, while 32 disagreed. This was, however, a sharp swing back in favour of spending on 'welfare benefits' through the recession and first years of the Coalition government from 2009, when only 27 per cent agreed and the larger group, 43 per cent, had disagreed.

But support for 'welfare benefits' is much lower than 20 years ago

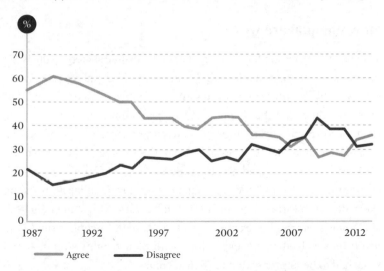

Figure 2.4 – 'Should government spend more money on welfare benefits for the poor, even if it leads to higher taxes?'

The longer-term change in public mood is therefore more about tactics and the role of the welfare state, specifically about benefits, than about ultimate concerns about inequality being too high, which have remained widespread. When asked directly in the 2009 BSA survey about *what* government should do to reduce the income gap, more than half wanted better education or training, reduced taxes for those on low incomes, and a higher minimum wage. Forty per cent wanted increased taxes for those on high incomes. A quarter or fewer wanted an upper limit on high incomes, creation of jobs for all, or higher benefits for those on low incomes.[20]

The chapters that follow challenge the memory-less 'goldfish' view that the effects of the welfare state are best understood by looking at what happens at a single moment, with no thought to what happened before today or what will happen tomorrow. But before that, this chapter looks at what is going on if we do take a snapshot of who gains and loses at one moment, and at whether that really does show an ever-growing scale of redistribution away from families like Henry and Clare's and of hand-outs to families like Michelle's.

How unequal are we?

To set all this in context, we look first at how unequal society really is. To do this we need high quality information from national representative surveys. This chapter concentrates on inequalities in income – the *flow* of money (like pay) that people receive each month or year. Later on, Chapter 6 presents information on inequalities in wealth – people's *stock* of assets (such as their savings or value of their home, if they own one).

Picturing income and wealth differences is difficult. The Dutch economist Jan Pen pointed out that we are more familiar with seeing every day in the street how people's heights vary, with some being tall and some short. So he described what a parade of people would look like if they walked past over an hour, with their heights stretched and squashed to be in proportion to their incomes.

Figure 2.5 shows a picture of that kind for Britain, based on the best guide to differences in how much money people have to live on each week, those given in the Department for Work and Pensions' (DWP) annual publication, *Households Below Average Income* (HBAI), in this case, for the financial year 2010–11.[21] This chapter focuses on 2010–11, because this is the year for which we have the most complete data of different kinds. The effects of changes in policy since the 2010 change of government are discussed later in Chapter 8.

Three things should be noted about the numbers. They show 'net' incomes after people have paid direct taxes such as Income Tax and NICs, and *include* incomes from social security benefits such as the state pension, tax credits and Jobseeker's Allowance. They therefore show the position *after* taking account of the main ways in which government affects the distribution of income, just as was calculated for the fictional families at the start of the chapter. The numbers also include Housing Benefit, which helps tenants with their rents, and Council Tax Benefit (as it was in 2010–11), but do not subtract things such as rent, Council Tax or mortgage payments – so the incomes are 'before housing costs'.

Finally, if we are interested in the living standards made possible by a given amount of net household income, we need to allow for the way in which the needs of a larger household will be greater than those of a smaller household. The way this is done in the figures is to rescale each household's income by a factor that varies with the number of people living in it. This gives the amount of income that would allow a couple with no children to have the same standard of living (called 'equivalent income'). Larger families need more income to reach a particular standard, and single people less. Each member of a household is then allocated the same amount of income – making the very strong assumption that they will all share the same standard of living.[22]

Figure 2.5 shows the income parade with the poorest people on the left and those with the highest incomes on the right. One per cent of people have incomes below the first bar, 2 per cent below the second bar, and so on, up to the right-most bar – 99 per cent have income below that, but 1 per cent above it. Obviously – and this was Jan Pen's point – there is far more variation in people's incomes than there is in their heights. The *average* income in 2010–11 calculated this way was £510 per week (£26,600 per year). But the first tenth of the parade had incomes below £216 per week. It is as if the smallest tenth of a parade of adults had heights below 2 feet 4 inches.[23] At the other end, a tenth of people had incomes above £846 per week – the equivalent of 9 feet 2 inches. The top 1 per cent in the parade had incomes of more than £2,090 per week – 22 feet 8 inches in Pen's analogy.[24] That may seem tall, but inequalities *within* the top 1 per cent mean that the very last people in the parade would tower well above that.

Another remarkable thing about the picture is that so many people have incomes below the 'average'. Halfway through the parade we get to the 'median' income of £419 per week. This means that half of the people had weekly incomes below £419, and half above it. But this was only 80 per cent of 'average' income – the average is pulled up by the large amounts going to people right at the top.[25] In fact, 65 per cent – nearly two-thirds – of all people had incomes that were below the 'average'. We are a long way from Garrison Keillor's Lake Wobegon, where 'all the children are "above average"'.

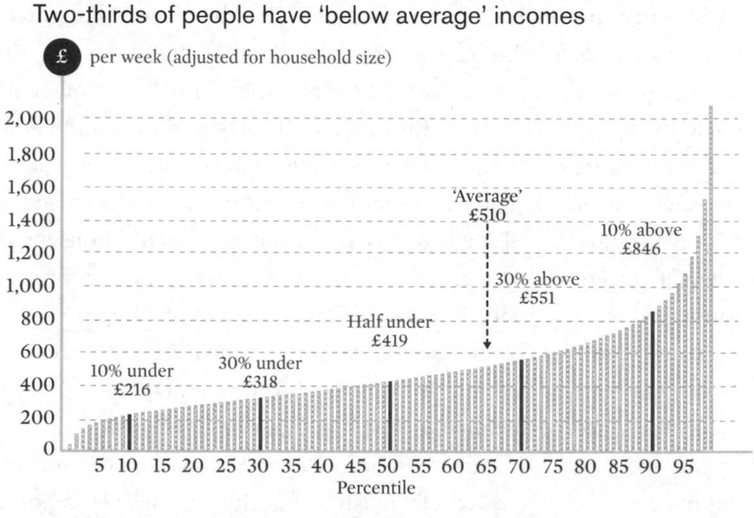

Two-thirds of people have 'below average' incomes

£ per week (adjusted for household size)

Figure 2.5 – Pen's parade of incomes in the UK, 2010–11

This kind of picture makes Britain one of the most unequal countries in the industrialised world. There are many different ways of comparing how unequal countries are. The different ways of doing this depend on what *kind* of inequality people are most worried about – between those at the bottom and those in the middle, between those near the top and those near the bottom, or between the very poorest and the very richest, for instance. One index number that is often used is the 'Gini coefficient'.

This index would be zero in a completely equal society, where everyone had the same income. It would be 100 (when measured as a percentage) if one plutocrat had all the money and everyone else nothing.[26]

The international comparison shown in Figure 2.6 puts the UK in 2010 as having the fifth most unequal income distribution (after allowing for benefits and income taxes) out of the 31 countries shown. It was behind only Portugal of the European countries included, and behind only Portugal and the US out of the richer ones.

By 2010 only four industrialised countries had more unequal incomes than the UK

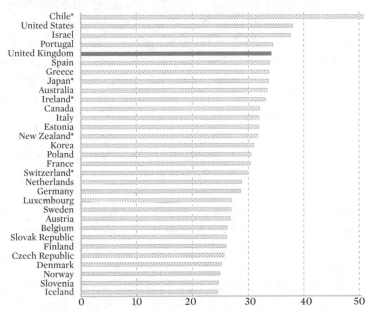

Figure 2.6 – Inequality in disposable incomes in industrialised countries, 2010 (Gini coefficients, %)

In passing, it should be noted that inequality in income is put in the shade by inequalities in wealth – the level of a household's assets (or debts). These are described later in Chapter 6, and their profound implications for the life chances of people with wealthier and less wealthy parents, and the huge challenges they present to attempts to create 'equality of opportunity', are discussed later in Chapter 7.

Without the welfare state we would be much more unequal

But this level of inequality comes *after* taking account of the way in which benefits and taxes equalise the distribution. If we were to look only at the incomes people get from the 'market' rather than from government – their earnings, private pensions, investment income – the picture is even more unequal. A different annual publication, produced by the Office for National Statistics (ONS), allows us to see how this happens, with the results shown in the three panels of Figure 2.7.[27] In this case the incomes shown are the total amounts received by each *household* (rather than each individual). The bar on the left shows the average income of the poorest tenth of households, the bar on the right the average income of the top tenth of households, and so on.[28]

The first panel shows that the top tenth of households had average market incomes of £105,000 per year (£2,025 per week), with £74,000 coming from earnings, £19,000 from self-employment, £5,800 from private pensions, and £3,900 from investment income (dividends and savings interest). This total was nearly *30 times* greater than the £3,600 average market income for the poorest tenth – £2,000 of this coming from earnings, £700 from self-employment, and £500 from private pensions.

But cash benefits, shown on top of market incomes in each bar of the first panel make, in arithmetical terms, a big difference to this inequality.[29] They add up to £6,000 for the bottom tenth, but only £1,900 for the top tenth (£1,100 of that coming from state pensions). This takes the average 'gross' income of the bottom tenth to £9,600, with the top group now having 11 times as much.

Before the state intervenes, the top tenth has incomes 30 times the poorest; after it they have cash incomes 14 times as much

(a) Market incomes and cash benefits

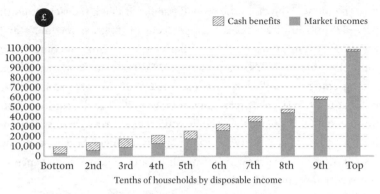

(b) Disposable incomes (after direct taxes)

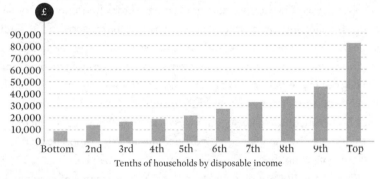

(c) Post-tax incomes (after indirect taxes) and benefits in kind

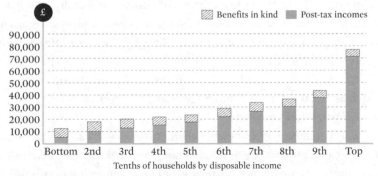

Figure 2.7 – Distribution of household incomes, 2010–11

29

Given that Income Tax and NICs are designed to be 'progressive' (taking a larger share of income from the rich than the poor), one might expect that incomes would be much more equal after allowing for them, to give the picture shown in the second panel.[30] Indeed, the richest tenth pays £25,600 in direct taxes – 24 per cent of its gross income – and the poorest tenth only £1,100 – 12 per cent of its gross income.[31] The top tenth of households end up with £82,000 of disposable income on average, but this is still nearly 10 times the £8,500 average income of the poorest tenth.[32] In these terms, *direct* taxes make the distribution a bit more equal (and shrink the absolute difference across the distribution by a lot), but it is cash benefits that really change the shape of the distribution because they are of much greater relative importance to those with low and middle incomes.

The final panel of Figure 2.7 shows the effects of two more parts of the ONS's analysis. The bottom part of each bar shows household incomes after also allowing for *indirect* taxes (such as VAT or tobacco and alcohol duties) to give 'post-tax' income. In contrast to direct taxes, these are strikingly *regressive* – taking up a bigger share of disposable incomes for the poor than the rich (partly because those with lower incomes are more likely to be spending more than their incomes – borrowing – and those with higher incomes to be spending less – saving). They reduce incomes at the bottom by the biggest proportion and take the ratio between top and bottom groups back up to more than fourteen to one.

Finally, the bottom panel adds in the ONS's estimates of how much is spent on 'in kind' (rather than cash) benefits for each household from the NHS, state education, housing subsidies, and so on – what is sometimes called the 'social wage'.[33] These add up to £7,400 for the poorest households, but nearly as much, £5,600, for the richest ones. If you add these in, to give what the ONS calls 'final incomes', these reached £12,400 for the bottom tenth and £78,000 for the top tenth, now only six times as much.

These numbers again need to be interpreted with care. Receiving a lot of healthcare from the NHS does not really make people 'better off' than those who do not need that care (although the recipients would be a lot worse off if they had to pay for it privately). But they do illustrate that the 'social wage' is proportionately far more important for those with low incomes than it is for those with high incomes. I come back to the implications of this in Chapter 8, in terms of the difference in impact between the government reducing its deficit through spending cuts or through tax rises.

So taxes and benefits are doing quite a lot to make the income distribution less unequal, but we still end up being one of the most unequal of the industrialised countries. The reason for this is illustrated by Figure 2.8, which shows – for the same countries as in Figure 2.6 – a comparison of how unequal their incomes would have been *without* the effects of cash benefits and taxes. This comparison shows quite how unequal the distribution of market incomes is in the UK. Only Ireland and Chile had more inequality before the state intervened.

Before taxes and benefits, UK incomes are among the most unequal in the rich world

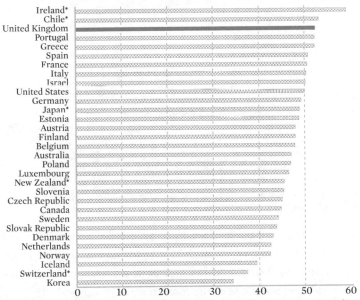

Figure 2.8 – *Inequality of market incomes in industrialised countries, 2010 (Gini coefficients, %)*

The difference between inequality in market incomes and in disposable incomes gives one measure of how much redistribution the direct tax and benefit systems achieve. In these terms the UK does quite a lot. The difference in inequality between the indexes shown in Figures 2.8 and 2.6 was greater in the UK than the average for the 31 countries shown, with only 11 of them doing more.[34] Taxes and benefits narrowed income inequality in the UK *more* than in archetypal egalitarian countries such as Sweden, Norway and Denmark. As Figure 2.9 comparing the UK and Sweden shows, inequality ends up much higher in the UK than in Sweden, because it *starts* so much higher, despite the UK's greater redistributive effort.

So that even with relatively large redistribution, the UK still ends up very unequal

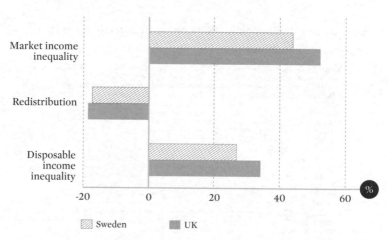

Figure 2.9 – Inequality before and after redistribution in the UK and Sweden, 2010 (Gini coefficients, %)

Our problem as a country is, if we want to achieve a relatively equal result, that the inequality in market incomes means that so much redistribution is needed. Despite our greater than average redistributive effort, we still end up as one of the most unequal countries in the rich world because there is so much inequality in the incomes people receive from the market compared with elsewhere. The British welfare state is left with more to do – leaving less room for its other, often more popular, aims.

Mechanics of redistribution

Figure 2.7, looking at the inequality of incomes when they are measured in different ways, showed how allowing for cash benefits makes incomes more equal. Allowing for direct taxes and for 'benefits in kind' also makes things more equal, but allowing for indirect taxes makes things less equal. Figure 2.10 presents the same numbers in another way. It shows, again for each tenth of households from poorest to richest, the average amounts they received from cash benefits, what was spent on services for them, and what they paid in direct and indirect taxes. It presents for a representative sample of the whole population the results of the kinds of calculations described for Henry and Clare and for Michelle at the start of the chapter.

Above the line comes what the state spent on education, an average of £2,800 per household (including free school meals). This varied rather little between poorer and richer households, but was a little more – over £3,000 – for the poorest three-tenths and a little less – under £2,000 – for the top tenth. The average cost of services from the NHS allocated by the ONS was larger, £4,100 per household (to which £25 of housing subsidies is added). This was also spread across the income range, but with a bit more at the bottom (£3,900 for the bottom tenth) than at the top (£3,400 for the top tenth).

The top two sections of each bar add in the state pension (averaging £2,600) and other cash benefits (averaging £3,100, some of these going to pensioners as well). These are more skewed to the bottom half – for instance, the second and third tenths each get more than £8,000 in cash benefits, but the top tenth just under £2,000.

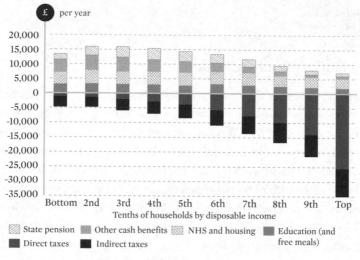

Even in a snapshot, benefits and services are spread across the income distribution

£ per year

Tenths of households by disposable income

State pension   Other cash benefits   NHS and housing   Education (and free meals)
Direct taxes   Indirect taxes

Figure 2.10 – Taxes and benefits by household income group, 2010–11

Putting it all together creates the humped shape above the line. Households in the second to fourth tenths, like Michelle's, receive what may seem a surprisingly large total of more than £15,000. The bottom tenth receives a little less – partly because it contains households that are less generously treated by the system (working-age people without children), and partly because it contains some households that do not receive everything they are entitled to. Those right at the top receive half as much – £7,000 – although this is still quite a substantial amount, showing immediately the fallacy in the idea that only the poorest are beneficiaries of the welfare state.

This has to be paid for, however. In that year, 2010–11, the taxes the ONS allocated to households averaged £12,700, almost the same as the £12,600 average benefits and services allocated to them.[35] But those taxes are much greater on average for those with higher incomes – nearly £35,000 for the top tenth, but under £5,000 for the bottom tenth – reflecting the eleven to one differences in their gross incomes shown in Figure 2.7(a).[36]

Putting the two together, in this snapshot the bottom six-tenths of the distribution received more from benefits and services than they paid in taxes. The top four-tenths paid for more than they received. For the bottom tenth the net gain was equivalent to £8,700 per year. For the top tenth, the net loss was equivalent to £27,800.

But this is what we want

Put in those terms, the top fifth, and with them Henry and Clare Osborne, might protest. As shown in Figure 2.1, more people now do say they want 'redistribution' than say they do not, but not by great margins in recent years, and yet this shows redistribution apparently going on at a grand scale.

What we see, however, is the result of the interaction of two principles that are, in fact, very widely supported:

• benefits and services should go equally to people according to their needs, and so spread across the income distribution; and
• taxes should be paid in proportion to people's incomes (or with those on higher incomes paying a higher proportion).

If you start with unequal incomes, the combination of flat-rate benefits and proportional taxes *automatically* ends up redistributing from rich to poor.

While the majority supporting redistribution *explicitly* has varied over time, people overwhelmingly support combinations of principles for how the welfare state and taxation should operate that are *implicitly* redistributive.[37] Indeed, people in Britain do so more strongly than elsewhere in Europe: in some countries principles of social insurance remain strong, with the idea that things such as pensions and unemployment benefits should be higher for those who made the biggest contributions in the past.

In a 2008 survey across European countries we asked people to choose between different principles for taxation:

- low and high earners should pay the *same share* of income in tax (a *proportional* system);
- higher earners should pay a *higher share* of income in tax (a *progressive* system);
- both should pay the *same amount* in tax (a *regressive* system).

They were also asked how state pensions and unemployment benefits should relate to their previous earnings – whether they should vary according to past *contributions* or likely *need*:

- previous high earners should get more because they had paid in more, that is, they should be *earnings-related*;
- they should get the same, through *flat-rate* entitlements;
- previous low earners should get more because their needs are greater, implying, for instance, that benefits should be *means-tested*.

Looking at the results across 11 older European Union (EU) member states, just under half – 49 per cent – favoured progressive taxation and another 45 per cent proportional taxes. Only 7 per cent chose the regressive option. At the same time, 49 per cent thought that pensions and unemployment benefits should be higher for those who previously had higher earnings, 36 per cent that they should be flat rate, and only 15 per cent that they should be means tested.[38]

Figure 2.11 shows how many supported different combinations of these options – nine in all. Those in the top right-hand corner are implicitly the most redistributive, with progressive taxes paying for means-tested benefits. But the other shaded combinations are also redistributive. For instance, if proportional taxes pay for flat-rate benefits, higher earners pay in more than low earners but get out the same – in the same way as the British system shown in Figure 2.10. More than two-thirds – 68 per cent – of people went for one of the redistributive combinations, and only 32 per cent for neutral (or even pro-rich) combinations.

But the UK respondents were even more strongly in favour of redistributive combinations, as the lower panel shows. Overall, slightly fewer, 47 per cent, went for progressive taxes than across all the countries and fewer for proportional ones. But still only 12 per cent chose the regressive tax option. Meanwhile, 59 per cent in the UK said that pensions and unemployment benefits should be flat rate, and only 21 per cent that they should be earnings-related. Overall, in the UK 78 per cent went for redistributive combinations, and only 22 per cent for neutral or pro-rich ones.

Nearly four-fifths of people in the UK favour redistributive combinations of taxes and benefits

(a) Average for 11 EU members

Structure of taxation	Structure of pensions and unemployment benefit		
	Earnings-related	Flat-rate	Means-tested
Progressive	22	18	9
Proportional	25	15	5
Regressive	2	3	1

(b) UK

Structure of taxation	Structure of pensions and unemployment benefit		
	Earnings-related	Flat-rate	Means-tested
Progressive	8	27	11
Proportional	10	25	6
Regressive	3	7	2

Figure 2.11 – Preferences for taxation and cash benefits, 2008 (%)

This presents a paradox. When asked whether 'government should take measures to reduce income differences' – an explicit question about redistribution – fewer people in the UK agreed in 2008 than in most other European countries.[39] But when asked about the principles that should underlie the two sides of the government budget, *more* people implicitly support redistribution in the UK than elsewhere.

The paradox of redistribution?

The way in which benefits and services, even when universal rather than targeted at the poorest, are redistributive lies behind the related 'paradox of redistribution' identified by Walter Korpi and Joakim Palme in the 1990s when they compared how much inequality was reduced in different countries.[40] They compared countries with heavily means-tested systems (such as the US) with others where social security was more universal, such as Sweden. Instead of finding that inequality reduction was greatest in the countries with targeted systems, they found the reverse. Their explanation was that targeted systems ended up with less political support, and so less was spent on them, while many of the poor fell through the gaps of complicated means-testing arrangements. The larger universal systems commanding greater support achieved more. They concluded that, 'the more we target benefits to the poor ... the less we are likely to reduce poverty and inequality'.

This was a striking conclusion, but more recent analysis and data suggest that times may have changed so far as part of their conclusion is concerned. First, Lane Kenworthy tracked 10 countries for which data are available from 1980 to 2005. He showed that in the 1980s the pattern was indeed as Korpi and Palme suggested. The countries with the most universal systems achieved the most redistribution. But in the 1990s and even more in the 2000s, the pattern changed. Indeed, by the end, there was very little apparent relationship either way between the degree of targeting or universalism and the amount of redistribution.[41] Targeting no longer seemed to act against inequality reduction – but on the other hand, it did not improve it either.

As part of the recent European research programme on 'Growing Inequalities' Impacts' (GINI), Ive Marx and Tim van Rie looked at this in more detail across 25 industrialised countries in the mid-2000s.[42] They confirmed that there is now little relationship between the extent to which a country concentrates benefits on the poor and the degree of redistribution achieved. Part of the explanation of this is that some of the more generous systems – such as Denmark's – have become more targeted, while some of the less generous systems – such as the US – have become more 'universal' in the sense that their systems have become more dominated by pensions and tax credits for those in work.

But what remains clear is that it is the countries with the largest social spending – welfare states – that still achieve most redistribution – it is the overall scale that matters most, more than how it is structured.

They conclude,

> ... adequate poverty relief requires more than well-targeted minimum income provisions.... It requires substantial social spending channelled through various programmes.... The reality remains that the countries with the most redistributive systems combine a relatively strong level of targeting with a relatively high level of effort spending.

In other words, size still matters. So if we want to reduce poverty and inequality, we will need to pay for it.

But *did* the poor get too expensive?

That there is redistribution – at a single point of time – from the rich to the poor may reflect the kind of outcome many people really want from taxes and services, but has the *scale* of redistribution become greater over time, explaining why people might think that it has all gone too far?

What people have in mind when they talk of 'the poor' varies, but the total proportion of the population counted as poor on the current official definition has been something under a fifth since the mid-1990s. So the ONS's estimates of how much the bottom fifth receives in benefits and services, less the amount they pay in taxes, gives an idea of how much 'the poor' are 'costing' the rest of us at any time. Figure 2.12 shows what the totals looked like not just in 2010–11 (as in Figure 2.10), but also back in 1979 and 1996–97.

By 2010–11, the average household in the poorest fifth received £7,000 in cash benefits and benefited from £7,800 in services. Michelle Ackroyd, receiving benefits of £9,400 per year and services of £10,000, was receiving rather more (enough to take her out of poverty, in fact). Again, this reinforces the importance of looking at the position across a representative sample of households, rather than just a few hypothetical examples, however helpful they are for understanding what is going on.

After inflation, the gain to the poorest fifth has doubled since 1979

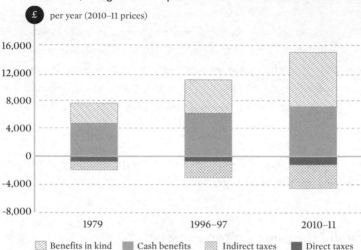

Figure 2.12 – The poor cost more? Benefits and taxes going to poorest fifth of all households, 1979, 1996–97 and 2010–11

Compared with what their equivalents received back in 1979, cash benefits for the poorest fifth had risen by 52 per cent and in kind services by 172 per cent. In that sense the poor were indeed costing *twice as much*, after allowing for inflation in 2010–11, as back in 1979. But they were also paying more tax – up from £2,000 in 1979 to £4,600 in 2010–11. So their net gain from redistribution slightly less than doubled, from £5,500 to £10,200.

So in what sense might that mean that they could in some way be seen as 'too expensive'? By the standards of 1979, cash benefits and services for people on low incomes were indeed much more expensive. But overall we are much better off now than we were in 1979. Over the period shown *average* market incomes had also almost doubled after allowing for inflation, from £16,900 to £32,100. If the burden of transfers to those with low incomes was becoming insupportable, you might think that would mean that the taxes that would have to be charged on households as a whole would be rising. As the bars for 'all households' show in Figure 2.13, the net gain to the poorest fifth from redistribution in 2010–11 was equivalent to 32 per cent of average market incomes – very slightly *down* on the 33 per cent equivalent in 1979, and the same as in 1996–97.[43]

In other words, the relative scale of transfers to the poor did *not* rise over the period. If the population was prepared to support a transfer at this sort of rate in 1979 and 1996–97, why should that be a problem in 2010–11? In contrast to the popular assumption, transfers to the poor were no more 'expensive' to us all than they had been in 1979.

There is one possible objection to this, however. Who 'the poor' are has changed a lot over that period. Back in 1979, many of those with the lowest incomes were pensioners. By 2010–11 pensioners were, for the first time, no more likely to be poor than the population as a whole.[44] So today's low-income population has a lot more non-pensioners in it than that of 1979. It might be, then, that the objection is to the transfers going to the – perhaps thought as less deserving – non-pensioners?

But the cost of transfers to the poor is the same share of average incomes as in 1979

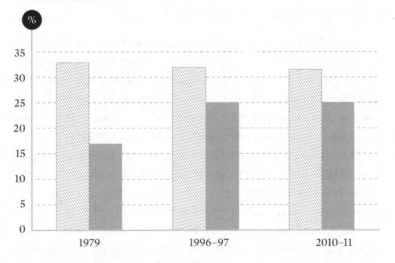

Figure 2.13 – Net gain to poorest fifth of all and of non-retired households as a percentage of average market income

Compared with all poor households in Figure 2.13, in 2010–11 the poorest *non-retired* households received less in cash benefits but rather more from services.[45] But they also paid more tax, so the overall net gain was much the same as for the poorest fifth overall – £10,100. This represented 25 per cent of the market incomes of non-retired households on average. Back in 1979 the net transfer to the poorest fifth was only 17 per cent of average non-retired market incomes, but this had risen to 25 per cent in 1996–97, reflecting higher unemployment and worklessness. After that it rose no further, despite Labour's higher spending on health and education, as Figure 2.13 shows.

So there is one sense in which the poor 'got more expensive', that is, if one concentrates on non-pensioners, and looks at what happened between 1979 and 1996–97, as unemployment grew. Having higher levels of unemployment and more households without work was indeed more expensive to us all, but that increasing cost predated 1997, rather than coming after it.

So who did get more expensive?

Why, then, should there be a perception that middle-income people have been getting a raw deal, if that has *not* come from rising redistribution towards the poor in recent years? The explanation might lie somewhere else entirely. Figure 2.14 suggests where this might be. This shows what shares of overall income (after benefits and direct taxes) went to each fifth of the income distribution in 1979, 1996–97 and 2010–11.[46]

What this shows is a slow decline in the share of income going to the middle fifth – to 'middle Britain', as it were. Back in 1979 they received 18 per cent of the total – just under the fifth all groups would get in a completely egalitarian society. But this fell to 17 per cent by 1996–97 and again to 16 per cent in 2010–11. If they felt they were losing ground compared to the total available income, they were right.

But this was not because the poor got more. The share of the poorest fifth *fell* from 10 per cent in 1979 to 8 per cent in 1996–97, and all Labour's 'redistribution by stealth' succeeded in doing was to prevent this share falling any further by 2010–11.

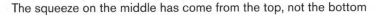

The squeeze on the middle has come from the top, not the bottom

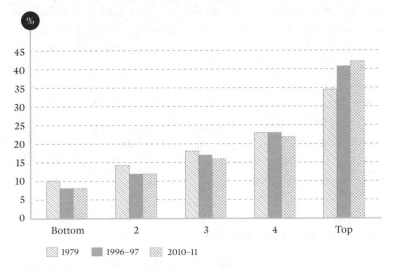

1979   1996–97   2010–11

Figure 2.14 – Shares of income going to each fifth of distribution, 1979 to 2010–11

Instead, the reason why the shares of all of the bottom four-fifths fell over this period was that the share of the top fifth grew – from 35 per cent in 1979 to 41 per cent in 1996–97 – and again, albeit more slowly, during the Labour years, to 42 per cent in 2010–11. In fact, virtually all of this increase in both the Conservative and Labour years went to the top 10 per cent – from 21 to 26 and then 27 per cent of the total – with little change for the next-to-top-tenth.

Going beyond that, most of the increase actually went to those in the top 10 per cent who were in the top 1 per cent. Information from the World Top Incomes database, established by Tony Atkinson, Emmanuel Saez and Thomas Piketty, shows that the after tax incomes of the top 1 per cent in the UK doubled from 4.7 of the national total in 1979 to 9.5 per cent in 1996 and 12.6 per cent on the eve of the economic crisis in 2007.[47] There was a change in definition between 1989 and 1990 (when independent taxation was brought in), but even excluding the change over that period, the overall increase in their share over that period – just under 7 percentage points – was enough to account for the gain of the whole top 10 per cent. In this sense, the slogan 'We are the 99 per cent' has some bite – it was the top 1 per cent whose share was increasing, while the shares of other groups lost ground or stood still.

What has happened to the shares of the very top since 2007 is less clear, especially as top taxpayers adjusted which years they officially received their incomes in to avoid the ones when the top rate of Income Tax was 50 per cent. By 2011, the reported share of the top 1 per cent was down to 9.6 per cent. This dip is likely to be temporary, as the tax 'forestalling' effect unwinds, but they still had double their 1979 share, and their gain still accounted for the majority of the extra share going to the top tenth since then.

Summary and conclusions

A large majority of the public think that it is the government's responsibility to narrow income inequalities. The gap between the larger number who say they support 'redistribution' to do this and those who oppose it is not as great as it was in the late 1980s, but has grown in the more recent years of recession and austerity.

The UK's welfare state and the taxes that pay for it do indeed redistribute between richer and poorer if we look at a snapshot of household accounts, as this chapter has explained. In the example at the start of the chapter, single mother Michelle Ackroyd received considerably more in benefits and services than she paid in taxes, while comparatively well-paid young parents Henry and Clare Osborne paid an equivalent amount extra in tax beyond what they received in benefits and services.

Looking across the whole population the redistribution happens because taxes add up to much the same *proportion* of the incomes of all groups. These pay for benefits and services that are widely spread (including to those with middle and higher incomes), but are proportionately more important for those with lower incomes. The redistribution that results is a form of by-product of what most people see as fair on both the tax side and on the benefit side, even though support for explicit 'redistribution' has been more equivocal. People widely support a tax system that is proportional or progressive, and benefits that are spread equally, according to needs. As a result, incomes after allowing for benefits, services and taxes are much less unequal than those that come from the market (pre-tax earnings and investment incomes).

But Britain's market incomes are so unequal (behind only Ireland and Chile among the industrialised countries) that even after allowing for cash benefits and income taxes, the UK remains one of the six most unequal countries in the industrialised world. Because the UK has so much inequality to start with, our welfare state has to work much harder than in other countries even to get to this position.

In the last decade, even before the economic crisis, the incomes of those in the middle were being squeezed. One popular explanation of this is the perception that 'the poor had got too expensive'. But, in fact, the net gain that the poorest were receiving in a snapshot of redistribution through the welfare state and household taxes was no higher as a share of overall market incomes in 2010 than it had been in 1996. The overall share of income going to the poorest fifth fell considerably as inequality grew between 1979 and 1996, and simply stabilised between then and 2010. It was the share of the *top* tenth that grew, squeezing everyone else. Within that, nearly all of those gains from 1979 to 2007 went to just the top 1 per cent, with their *gain* nearly equivalent to the whole of the income share that goes to the bottom 20 per cent.

If we are looking for a reason for pressure on those with middle incomes, it is not at the bottom end we should be looking. Rather, it is at the top. If anyone got too expensive, it has, in fact, been the rich.[48]

THE LONG VIEW

Stephen and Henrietta Osborne

Jim and Tracy Ackroyd

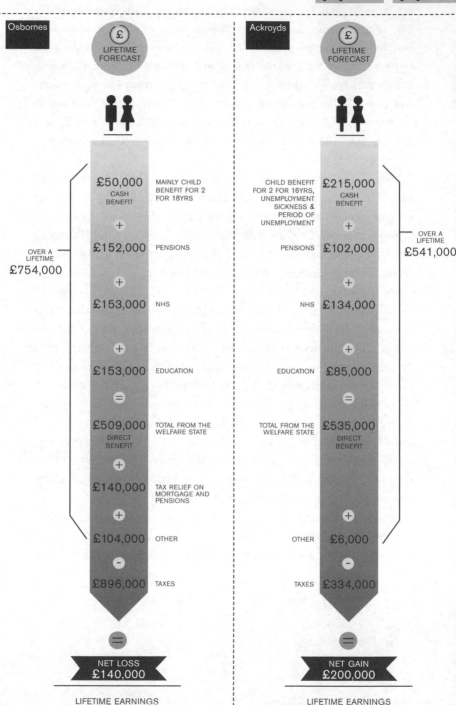

Osbornes

£ LIFETIME FORECAST

£50,000 CASH BENEFIT — MAINLY CHILD BENEFIT FOR 2 FOR 18YRS

+

£152,000 — PENSIONS

+

£153,000 — NHS

+

£153,000 — EDUCATION

=

£509,000 DIRECT BENEFIT — TOTAL FROM THE WELFARE STATE

+

£140,000 — TAX RELIEF ON MORTGAGE AND PENSIONS

+

£104,000 — OTHER

−

£896,000 — TAXES

=

NET LOSS £140,000

OVER A LIFETIME £754,000

LIFETIME EARNINGS
£2.7 MILLION

Ackroyds

£ LIFETIME FORECAST

CHILD BENEFIT FOR 2 FOR 16YRS, UNEMPLOYMENT SICKNESS & PERIOD OF UNEMPLOYMENT — £215,000 CASH BENEFIT

+

PENSIONS — £102,000

+

NHS — £134,000

+

EDUCATION — £85,000

=

TOTAL FROM THE WELFARE STATE — £535,000 DIRECT BENEFIT

+

— £6,000 OTHER

−

TAXES — £334,000

=

NET GAIN £200,000

OVER A LIFETIME £541,000

LIFETIME EARNINGS
£1 MILLION

3. The long view

Social policies and the life cycle

When Henry Osborne told his father, Stephen, over Sunday lunch the next week about his calculations of how much he and Clare were putting in, and how little they felt they were getting out, Stephen laughed and told him about the television documentary he and Henrietta had agreed to take part in, back in 1989. Although they had rather regretted being exposed like that afterwards, it had been a bit of an eye-opener.

As explained in Chapter 1, the idea of the programme had been to pit the two of them against a working-class couple – Jim and Tracy Ackroyd – to see who would get the most out of 'the welfare state' over their entire lives, and not just in a single year. To their surprise – and to Jim and Tracy's annoyance – it was the middle-class Osbornes who won the game.

After lunch Stephen dug out his notes from the programme and ran through the totals with Henry. To make it easier to compare with 2010 incomes, he multiplied all of the original numbers by the amount earnings had grown since they were originally calculated.[1]

Unsurprisingly, Jim and Tracy had been forecast to gain most from cash benefits – a total of £215,000 over their lives in today's money, compared with only £50,000 for Stephen and Henrietta – mainly from the Child Benefit they got for 18 years each for Henry and his sister (as they stayed on at school). Jim's periods of unemployment and sickness meant he was expected to get much more – although the Ackroyds only received 16 years of Child Benefit for each of their children, as it stops when children leave school.

But the researchers for the programme thought that Stephen and Henrietta would live longer than the Ackroyds and so collect more in state pensions. They also – and this was rather uncomfortable to think about – reckoned that they would eventually get a little more out of the NHS, reflecting the heart attacks

Stephen did indeed have in 2002 and 2003, and the first-rate heart by-pass operation he had had at the time. And they thought that they would get almost twice as much out of state education – £153,000 – as the Ackroyds, given that universities were free in those days, and both Henry and Charlotte were expected to go on to university education. In reality that would have been knocked down a bit by the £1,000 fees in place by the time they did actually go.

Adding all of that up, the programme's forecast was that the Osbornes would collect the equivalent of £509,000 in direct benefits from the welfare state, only a little less than the £535,000 forecast for the Ackroyds. This is the equivalent of a couple of houses in most of the country (although not in Alderley Edge), even these days, Stephen pointed out. And given that everyone is now expected to live longer than we thought back then, the numbers would probably be even bigger now. So Henry and Clare would eventually get back out quite a lot of what they paid in, even if Henry thought they were way out of pocket today, in their late twenties.

And the programme makers had added in a few other things – such as the tax relief Stephen and Henrietta got for their mortgage when they were buying it (now abolished), and for their pension contributions (still in place), adding up to £140,000 worth in all. And the value of subsidies for his commute to work on the train, and – this seemed very unfair to Stephen – subsidies for the theatre and opera they still enjoyed, which really ought, in his view, to be counted as paying for the country's cultural heritage, not as a benefit for them, as individuals.

All in all, the total had come out at £754,000 for Stephen and Henrietta, and only £541,000 for Jim and Tracy. It had been weeks before the office had stopped joshing him about being one of the country's biggest 'spongers'.

But as Henry had pointed out, that all had to be paid for somehow. What the television programme described as its 'boffins' reckoned that the lifetime taxes contributed to pay for the welfare state would add up to £896,000 for Stephen and Henrietta – nearly three times as much as Jim and Tracy's £334,000.

The bottom line was that the Ackroyds were net gainers over their whole lives by about £200,000, while Stephen and Henrietta were down by about £140,000. Looked at this way, maybe it wasn't so unfair, given that they were going to end up with nearly three times the lifetime earnings (£2.7 million in today's money, compared to £1 million for Jim and Tracy).

But more remarkably, even an upper-middle-class family like the Osbornes would get back five-sixths of what they had paid in. Even if you cut out the alleged rail and arts subsidies, it was still nearly three-quarters. If things kept going well for Henry and Clare, they would probably pay in more in tax than they would get out, but in the end, most of it would come back – and coping with a lot of the risks they would otherwise have to cover themselves would be more expensive if it was all turned over to private insurance, so they were saving from that as well.

THIS STORY SUGGESTS that things can look very different over people's whole lives than in a single year. But how typical were the Ackroyds and the Osbornes even 25 years ago? And how have things changed since then? This chapter moves away from the snapshot of the last to look at how the welfare state and the taxes that pay for it affect people over their life cycles.

Cycles of want and plenty

The idea that social problems – and hence the policies required to counter them – vary across the life cycle is hardly a new one. The Victorian social researcher and member of the chocolate manufacturing family, Seebohm Rowntree, used his ground-breaking survey of poverty in York in 1899 to identify the 'five alternating periods of want and comparative plenty' in the life of a labourer, shown in Figure 3.1. Through childhood, children were more likely to fall into poverty as more brothers and sisters arrived. As siblings started earning and then after leaving home with no children, times would improve. But then the labourer's own children would arrive, bringing with them greater want, until they, too, started earning, and, 'The man enjoys another period of prosperity only to sink back again into poverty when his children have left him, and he himself is too old for work.'[2]

The idea that people's circumstances change over their lives is not new

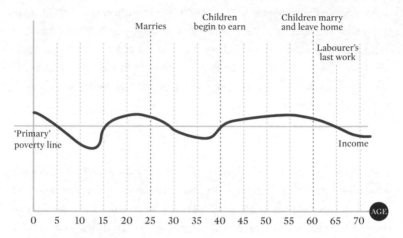

Figure 3.1 – Seebohm Rowntree's 'cycles of want and plenty' in a labourer's life, York, 1899

William Beveridge's 1942 report, *Social insurance and allied services*, took Rowntree's findings from his second survey of York in 1936 to identify the key risks against which people needed to be protected if what he described as one of the 'five giants on the road to reconstruction', Want, was to be defeated. He believed that this could be achieved through a social insurance system under which people paid contributions – in his model, on a flat-rate, essentially Poll Tax, basis – when in paid work. In return for these, people would then be entitled to benefit payments when income from work failed for one reason or another, particularly because of old age. Supplementing these would be, in one of the famous 'assumptions' he made in framing his report that went well beyond his brief to tidy up social insurance, a system of allowances for all families with two or more children (surviving in what is today Child Benefit).

Social insurance was designed to transfer resources across the life cycle

Figure 3.2 – Schematic effects of Beveridge's social insurance over the life cycle

These two measures were designed directly to smooth out Rowntree's life cycle of want and plenty, as shown schematically in Figure 3.2. Contributions in good times when at work would build up pension entitlement to bring income in old age up above the poverty line. Tax-funded family allowances would bring up the incomes of larger families, filling in the other two dips in Rowntree's life cycle.

… and to times when earnings were interrupted by unemployment or illness

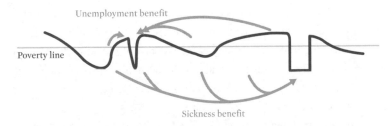

Figure 3.3 – Schematic effects of Beveridge's social insurance and short-term income changes

Accompanying this, social insurance would cover the other major risks Beveridge saw as leading to poverty – unemployment and sickness. These are illustrated schematically in Figure 3.3. Superimposed on the average life cycle pattern are individual variations, particularly interruptions in earnings when people are unemployed or sick. Again, the resultant fall in income could be moderated through benefits for which entitlement had been earned by social insurance contributions made when at work.

The post-war welfare state owed much to Beveridge's vision, even though the idea of basing social security on strict contribution-based entitlements has been modified almost out of all recognition.[3] Much of what social policy does is still motivated by such life cycle variations in resources and needs. While the current British debate is often conducted as if the only aim of social security systems was poverty relief, just as important an aim – stressed more prominently in continental European systems – is smoothing income across the life cycle. Indeed, as discussed further below, the *dominant* effect of social spending in the UK is to redistribute income across people's *own* life cycles, rather than on a lifetime basis, between people.

Incomes and the life cycle today

The world, and the structure of market incomes, has moved on in the century since Rowntree's sketch. Figure 3.4 shows a modern equivalent for the 21st century, drawn from analysis carried out by the ONS of the redistributive effects of taxes and benefits discussed in Chapter 2. The results are shown here by age,[4] rather than by income group, as used there. The line shows the average pattern of households' 'market' incomes (mainly earnings, but also things such as private pensions) *before* the effects of the state (but adjusted for household size, and so capturing the effects of having children).

The pattern of income by age differs from Rowntree's partly because families are much smaller than they were. Family sizes grow – now often through people's thirties, rather than earlier – but then children start leaving home, so there is rather little variation in average incomes between those in their late twenties and late fifties. However, the fundamental factors driving the pattern are not so different.[5] Average market incomes rise steadily on average between households in their twenties and those in their late forties, dominated by rising earnings, including those of two-earner couples.

In the year for which the ONS published results by age, 2005–06, they peaked at £35,000 for those in their late forties.[6] For older age groups wages tended to be lower and employment rates fell, particularly after retirement, and so market incomes fell rapidly for groups from age 60 onwards, cushioned only a little on average by non-state pensions (part of this reflects a 'cohort effect' – many of today's oldest pensioners retired on lower pensions than some of those nearing or recently entering retirement will enjoy). For households aged 70 or over, market incomes averaged £10,000 or less, under a third of the peak for younger ones.

With fewer children, market incomes dip less in middle age now

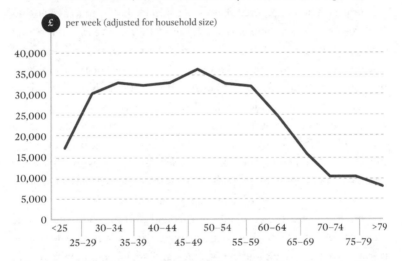

Figure 3.4 – Market income by age of household, 2005–06

These numbers are, of course, averages. The patterns for particular households will vary around these for all sorts of reasons, because they are better or worse off (as discussed below), and because real life does not usually change slowly (as Chapters 4 and 5 describe in detail). And individuals move in and out of different households through their lives, and while in them, resources may or may not be equally shared. Where they are not equally shared, gender differences in the incomes men and women receive in their own right are important –

and these move in different ways across the life cycle (see Figure 5.3 in Chapter 5 later).

An even bigger change over the last century was the arrival of the welfare state and of the taxes needed to pay for it. In Chapter 2 we looked at how social spending and direct taxes narrow inequalities between rich and poor of all ages. Figure 3.5 shows how there are also pronounced differences in their effects by age. It shows the overall effects of social spending (including from the NHS and education as well as from cash benefits) and of taxation in 2005–06. The upper bars show the average value of pensions, other cash benefits (including tax credits), and from health and education to households of different ages.

Total cash benefits were fairly even for households up to age 60, but then became more valuable, rising up to £8,000 per year as a result of state pension receipts. Benefits in kind had a first peak for households in their forties, particularly as a result of education for their children, and then rose again for older households, particularly as a result of healthcare. For households with a head aged over 80, average social benefits reached £16,000. Taxes, by contrast, peaked at an average of around £17,000 for those in their late forties, falling back for older households – reflecting the pattern of market incomes in Figure 3.4. Overall, 43 per cent of all social benefits went to households aged 60 or over, but only 19 per cent of taxes came from them.

Looking at just the cash side of this and putting both sides of the equation together, households aged from 25 to 64 were net losers on average from the combination of taxes and social spending (some of their net loss funding other forms of public spending, including health and education), but older households were net gainers, particularly the oldest ones.

This means that there was much less variation in disposable incomes than there was in the market incomes shown in Figure 3.4. Figure 3.6 shows 'disposable' incomes by age. These are after adding in cash (but not in kind) benefits, and after deducting direct taxes (Income Tax and NICs). As can be seen, disposable incomes were lower than market incomes for the working-age population, but higher for those over 60.

The combination of taxes and benefits smoothed out a large part of the variation between age groups. The highest disposable incomes – about £28,000 – were still for those in their late forties, but state pensions and other benefits raised average income for the older age groups to above £17,000, nearly two-thirds of the maximum rather than less than one-third.

Working-age households pay more in tax than they receive, but this reverses after retirement

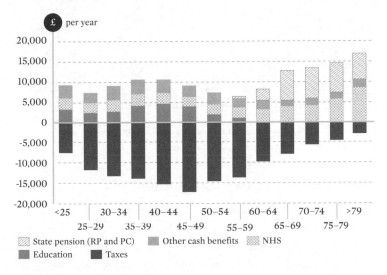

Figure 3.5 – Taxes and benefits by age of household, 2005–06

At this *average* level for entire age groups, Rowntree's more rapid cycles of want and plenty have disappeared – partly because of the welfare state and partly because families are now smaller. Instead, we have something with a fairly broad peak in disposable incomes for middle-aged households, and then a less precipitous descent for older ones.

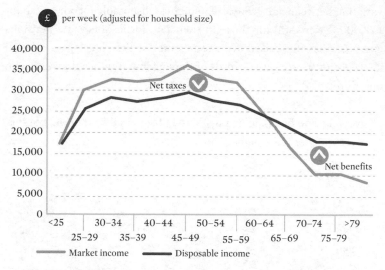

Figure 3.6 – Market and disposable incomes by age of household, 2005–06

Changes in life cycle redistribution[7]

These figures show the country as it was before the economic crisis, and only part of the way through the last government's term in office. They also show results for households taken as a single unit, with children counted within their parents' households. We can use a different source to show how incomes vary across people's whole life cycles, including as children (depending on how well-off their families are), and how this changed between 1997–98, as Tony Blair became Prime Minister, and 2010–11, as Labour lost office.

Labour's social security and anti-poverty policies focused primarily on pensioners and families with children – almost exclusively as far as cash transfers (benefits and tax credits) were concerned. Most of the increase in spending on benefits and Labour's new tax credits over and above inflation went to pensioners. Spending on all cash transfers rose from £114 billion in 1996–97 to £183 billion in 2010–11 (at 2009–10 prices).[8] Of the total increase of £69 billion, £38 billion went to higher benefits for pensioners, so pensioner spending rose to £95 billion, more than half the total. Another £24 billion of the increase went to benefits and tax credits related to families having children. Even with unemployment rising in the recession after the 2008 financial crisis, other benefits and tax credits for working-age families only rose by £7 billion over the 14 years (all of that as the economic crisis hit). While cash transfers for pensioners and related to children both represented a greater share of national income in 2010–11 than they had in 1996–97, other working-age transfers *fell* as a share of national income, contradicting the popular image of a government that increased 'hand-outs' to the unemployed.

One result of these policies was that the risk of being in poverty became much closer for people in different age groups. Figure 3.7 shows how poverty rates for pensioners, children and their parents fell, while those for working-age people without children rose. By the end of the period, for the first time, being a pensioner no longer meant being at greater risk of poverty than others.[9]

By 2010, poverty risks had converged for different age groups

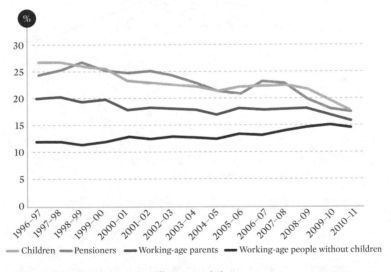

Figure 3.7 – Poverty rates for different population groups

But a less well-known effect of Labour's policies was to considerably smooth out the extent to which *typical* incomes varied across the life cycle. Figure 3.8 shows how incomes (after taxes and cash benefits) varied between age groups – using the median (middle) income for each – in 1997–98 and in 2010–11.[10] This now covers the whole life cycle, with childhood shown as well, as in Rowntree's sketch. The 1997–98 pattern had two distinct peaks in incomes: for young adult households, before many had children, and later, when higher earnings coincided with a growing proportion of 'empty-nesters' before retirement. Incomes for children (based on that of the household they live in) were lower, along with those of their parents, contributing to the middle-aged sag between the peaks. Incomes of older people were generally lower.

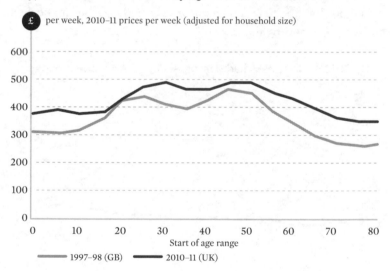

Typical incomes varied less by age in 2010 than in 1997

£ per week, 2010–11 prices per week (adjusted for household size)

Figure 3.8 – Net incomes by age, 1997–98 (GB) and 2010–11 (UK)

Over the 13 years to 2010–11, however, the biggest increases were for children up to the age of 16 (and their parents) and for those aged over 60. Incomes for those in their early twenties were barely any higher after allowing for inflation than they had been in 1997–98, when they had been a relatively prosperous group. Middle-aged families with children also benefited. As a result, the line in 2010–11 is much flatter by age than before.

The extent to which incomes have become flattened by age is shown more starkly in Figure 3.9. This shows the percentage difference in median (middle) incomes for each age group from the overall median. The extent to which the incomes of children and of those over 65 fell below the rest of the population reduced considerably. Overall, purely age-related income differences fell by more than a third. Labour may not have set out to achieve this, but it was a striking effect of its policies.

For middle incomes, age-related variations fell by a third

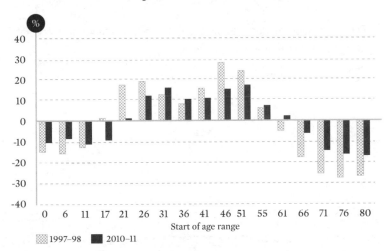

Figure 3.9 – Difference in median net income for each age group from overall median, 1997–98 and 2010–11

Combined with the poverty avoidance aims of the social security system, the results of life cycle smoothing are much more pronounced at the bottom of the income distribution than at the top, as can be seen in Figure 3.10. This shows the 10th and 90th percentiles of disposable incomes within each age group, as well as their median values, in 2010–11 (10 per cent have lower incomes than the 10th percentile and 10 per cent have more than the 90th). The bottom line is almost flat – less than a tenth of each age group have incomes below about £200 per week (adjusted for household size to the equivalent for a couple with no children). If someone stayed near the bottom like this all through their life – which we will see in Chapters 4 and 5 is very unlikely – they would face a flat, if bleak, pattern of incomes across their lives.

Age-related variations are biggest for the richest in each age group. While the cut-off for the best-off tenth of children and young adults is under £800 per week, a tenth of people in their early thirties have incomes over £1,000. This leaves them better off than their older equivalents, although there is a second peak of nearly £1,000 for those in their early fifties (as children leave home and family sizes fall).

The floor given by benefits means that the lowest incomes are flat by age, but the highest ones vary more

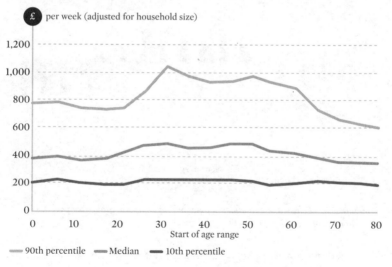

Figure 3.10 – Range of net incomes by age, 2010–11

Henry and Clare Osborne, whose position was described at the start of the last chapter, had a net income (adjusted for family size) of around £670 per week in 2010–11, putting them between the median and 90th percentile for their 26- to 30-year-old age group, in fact, just within the top quarter of it. Michelle Ackroyd, with an income of £270 on the same basis, was in the bottom fifth of the same age group.

Changing effects of policy

All of this relates to the recent past, but the policies of the Coalition government in office since May 2010 are changing this picture – both through the pattern of cuts being made to public spending and some of its structural reforms, the balance of spending between age groups is changing. Under the previous Labour government benefits and tax credits for families with children and pensioners were increased, but not other benefits for those of working age. Under the Coalition government, benefits and services for pensioners have been generally protected, but others have been cut. Chapter 8 describes the changes in more detail, and their effects on different income groups, but they also have sharply different effects by age group.

For *children* (and their parents), spending on state schools has been protected (with some extra resources to schools through the 'pupil premium' for children with low-income parents). But Child Benefit was cut in real terms (and withdrawn altogether from some higher-income families), tax credits for parents were cut back, Education Maintenance Allowances (EMAs) (for lower-income children staying on after 16) were abolished, as were Child Trust Funds for children born since 2011.[11] And with large cuts to council budgets, youth and early years provision were cut back in many areas.

Some of those of *working age* will benefit from greater tax-free Income Tax allowances, but most of the changes are cuts. The biggest cuts are those coming from linking most benefits and tax credits first to the consumer price index (CPI), and then increasing them for three years from 2013 by only 1 per cent each year, well below the inflation rate. Limits were put on Housing Benefit for private tenants and the 'Bedroom Tax' introduced for social tenants deemed to be under-occupying their property (but only for those of working age). Council

Tax Benefit was cut back in April 2013 (again only for working-age households) and large savings are being made through reforms to disability benefits. For English students going to university from the autumn of 2012, fees were greatly increased, with the effect that repayments will now stretch longer through graduates' subsequent careers (see Chapter 5). In future, those currently of working age will have to wait longer for their pensions (although they are also expected to live longer on average).

For *pensioners*, most services, pensions and benefits have been protected. The NHS budget – of most importance to older people – is protected in real terms (although it has not increased in line with greater demands on it as the population ages). State pensions are now protected by a 'triple lock' – rising each year by the highest of inflation, earnings growth, or 2.5 per cent. Reforms legislated by the last government will tilt the state pension system more towards those who had lower lifetime earnings, and these are being accelerated for those retiring from 2016 (see Chapter 6). Special payments, such as the Winter Fuel Payment which goes to all those over state pension age, have also been protected. In the other direction, care services for older people are under pressure from cuts to council budgets, and the special additional Income Tax allowance, the Age Allowance, was abolished in the 2012 Budget – a move immediately dubbed the 'granny tax'.

Figure 3.11 summarises the effects of this schematically in terms of the range of incomes by age. The biggest downward effects are on low and middle-income people of working age, and on low-income children. By contrast, the net effects on low and middle-income pensioners are mildly positive. If the Labour years had a marked effect in smoothing out incomes over the whole life cycle, the Coalition years are reversing this for younger people, but leaving in place many of the gains for older people. The overall effect is to move towards a welfare state that looks much more like that of the US, with substantial spending through 'social security' (state pensions) and Medicare (healthcare for older people), but less generous and more stigmatised 'welfare' for those of working age.[12]

Since 2010 cuts to benefits for working-age people and children have tilted the system towards pensioners

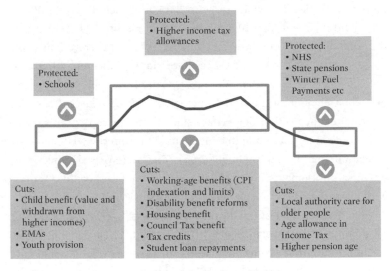

Protected:
• Higher income tax allowances

Protected:
• NHS
• State pensions
• Winter Fuel Payments etc

Protected:
• Schools

Cuts:
• Child benefit (value and withdrawn from higher incomes)
• EMAs
• Youth provision

Cuts:
• Working-age benefits (CPI indexation and limits)
• Disability benefit reforms
• Housing benefit
• Council Tax benefit
• Tax credits
• Student loan repayments

Cuts:
• Local authority care for older people
• Age allowance in Income Tax
• Higher pension age

Figure 3.11 – Overall balance of cuts and reforms after 2010 by age

What does it all add up to?

If we take people as a whole, then, they pay more into the system in their working lives than they get out from it, but after retirement, the reverse is true. If the system remained static as it was in 2005, the picture presented in Figure 3.5 suggests that a household that formed at age 20 and stayed intact until age 59 would have received £117,000 in cash benefits on average and £218,000 in benefits in kind from the NHS and state education (at 2005–06 prices).[13] These are already startlingly large numbers – totalling more than one-and-a-half times the average value of a house, for instance. But they would have paid much more, £536,000, in taxes – more than two houses' worth. Importantly, however, they would already have got back nearly two-thirds – 63 per cent – of what they had paid in. But at that point they would be £202,000 out of pocket.

If they carried on as an 'average' household until they were 84, and the world stayed stuck in 2005 (as shown in Figure 3.5), their lifetime cash benefits would grow to £315,000 (including £159,000 in state pensions) and their lifetime benefits in kind to £342,000. Again, the total of £656,000 is worth comment. What an *average* household could eventually get out of the welfare state of the mid-2000s was the equivalent of more than 25 years' worth of the average disposable household income of the time – the value of three houses. Reflecting their dominance within the welfare state, three-quarters of this would have come in pensions and in benefits in kind from the NHS and state education (mainly for their children). The system is dominated by universal entitlements, not by the stigmatised 'welfare' benefits for those with low incomes; as a result, most people's stakes in it are very large.

For a household surviving and remaining 'average' to this age, total lifetime taxes would amount to £692,000. Their gains just from social benefits after 60, over and above the taxes they paid, would have made up nearly all of the ground they had lost before then. The precise mechanics of the 'social insurance' system Beveridge hoped to establish 70 years ago, with people paying in contributions and receiving benefits in some way related to them, may now be an accounting fiction.[14] But as a general pattern, what people do is to pay into the system during their working lives in return both for receiving services then (or as children), and for pensions and services in retirement.

It is, of course, more complicated than this. First, there are other parts of government spending to pay for and to benefit from, including services not included here, such as early years provision, personal care for older people or housing subsidies, as well as things that are outside the welfare state (although the welfare state now dominates public spending, as described in Chapter 9). There are also taxes of other kinds from those allocated to households by the ONS in exercises of this kind. Some people live long into retirement, but others do not. People with higher lifetime incomes, such as Stephen and Henrietta Osborne, pay more tax, and those with lower ones, such as Jim and Tracy Ackroyd, are more likely to receive more support from means-tested benefits and tax credits. Those who are lucky enough to enjoy good health make fewer demands on the NHS, while those who stay in education longest get the most from state education.

To untangle what this all adds up to for different kinds of people would mean not just following them across their whole lives, but also getting them to live in a world that stayed the same forever (as in the film, *Groundhog Day*). Neither is possible, which is why stories of the kind described at the start of this chapter are useful, if only to jolt preconceptions of whom the welfare state is for. But single examples depend on the precise assumptions made. The Osbornes 'won' Granada TV's game show 25 years ago as a result of their greater use of state education – particularly then heavily subsidised universities – and some expensive medical care, which their middle-class 'sharp elbows' helped them receive. They also lived and collected pensions longer (which would still be true today), and the programme makers threw in their subsidised opera and rail travel for good measure. Even so, they paid in more in lifetime tax than they got out, while the reverse was true of the working-class Ackroyds.

But hypothetical examples like these may be misleading as a guide to the population as a whole. To try to allow for all the complications in people's lives, 20 years ago we constructed a whole series of people's lives – 4,000 of them – to see what the variation in lifetime services and taxes looked like for a more representative group of the population.[15] Figure 3.12 presents some of what this model of hypothetical life histories showed. The numbers are adjusted to 2010 prices (using earnings growth since 1985)[16] for comparability with other figures in this chapter, but are based on the 1991 tax and social security systems and on people's lives – life expectancy, health, education, marriage and divorce patterns, earnings and so on – as they were in the 1980s, so they give the picture of a generation ago. They show lifetime totals for each individual, rather than for each household, and the bars in the figure are arranged in order of average annual lifetime incomes, with the lifetime poorest tenth on the left and the lifetime richest on the right.

In a range of model life histories, rich and poor got the same out of the welfare state but the rich paid more in

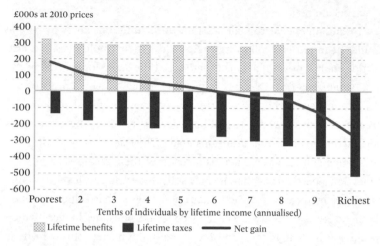

Figure 3.12 – Lifetime social benefits and taxes by income group (1991 tax and social security systems)

The most remarkable thing in Figure 3.12 is the way in which the total services and benefits for the rich and the poor are so similar. On average those in each lifetime income group would receive from cradle to grave almost exactly the same – around £280,000 *per person* at 2010 prices. This is of a similar magnitude to the average £656,000 *per household* remaining intact to age 84 derived above from spending in the mid-2000s, but the more recent numbers reflect factors such as the faster growth in healthcare spending than earnings and greater longevity than in the mid-1980s.

According to the modelling exercise, randomly picked richer people would normally end up with much the same as randomly picked poorer people in terms of what they get *out* of the system in total – the potential benefits of longer pension receipt and more use of sixth forms and universities for the middle classes were offset by higher benefits for those with lower incomes. In that sense, the Ackroyds and Osbornes were not so atypical in their use of the main parts of the welfare state.

The difference comes in how those benefits and services were paid for. Average lifetime taxes were only £140,000 for those in the poorest tenth, but over £500,000 for those in the top tenth. As a result, the average lifetime gain modelled for the poorest tenth was £180,000, but the average loss for the lifetime richest was £250,000.[17]

Another implication of this is that even the lifetime poorest pay *themselves* for a little under half of the benefits they receive – they are significant 'taxpayers' too – but the lifetime richest tenth would pay not just for their own benefits but also as much again towards the cost of those going to others. On a lifetime basis the system *is* redistributive from rich to poor, with net gains for the bottom half of the model population and net losses for the top half on average, although the scale of this is much less than seen in the single moment snapshot pictures shown earlier in Chapter 2. But even within the richest tenth there are a few who make a net gain over their whole lives for one reason or another, such as heavy use of healthcare or very long lives and pension receipt: needs vary, and in unpredictable ways.

The system is also redistributive by gender, even assuming that couples share their incomes equally for the parts of their lives that they are together. In terms of today's incomes, the average lifetime transfer from men to women within the model population was around £100,000, reflecting both women's lower lifetime incomes and greater longevity.[18]

But the larger part of what is going on is people paying for their *own* benefits. Apart from the poorest group, within all the other groups more than half of what comes out represents what people themselves pay in at other points in their lives – 'self-financed' benefits. Overall nearly *three-quarters* of what the welfare state was doing in the late 1980s and early 1990s could be seen as 'savings bank' redistribution across the life cycle, and not much over a quarter was 'Robin Hood' redistribution between different people.[19]

The implications of this are crucial in terms of how much we all have a stake in it: without the NHS, state education, and pensions, all households would have to pay private medical insurance, school fees, and much higher private pension contributions. For some, with perfect knowledge of their own and their children's futures, the private alternative might be cheaper for themselves than the tax-funded system. But for most, not only does the great majority of what they pay in come back (or more), but it also offers something more, providing insurance against the unexpected that our lives might throw at us. In the absence of a tax-funded welfare state, there would, of course, have to be much wider use of private insurance and savings. But for many that would be much more expensive – as witnessed by high charges for private pension saving for those with low and middle incomes[20] – and for many uncertain and long-term risks, private markets may fail altogether.[21]

Of course, the world has moved on since the 1990s and with it, the importance of different parts of the welfare state. If someone went through the laborious process of creating 4,000 more modern lives, they would find something different from Figure 3.12, but it is unlikely that the overall pattern would be so different.

First, the welfare state – and indeed public spending as a whole – is increasingly dominated by the universal, life cycle-related services of school education, the NHS, and state pensions. Spending on the NHS has risen sharply as a share of national income – for instance, from 5.3 to 8.3 per cent of GDP between 1995–96 and 2009–10 – while education spending rose from 4.7 to 6.2 per cent.[22] Over the same period cash benefits going to pensioners rose from 5.4 to 6.5 per cent of national income.[23] Spending on other benefits and cash transfers rose less rapidly – indeed, those unrelated to children fell. These will have boosted the importance of life cycle rather than 'Robin Hood' redistribution.

But within those totals structural changes have pushed in the other direction. When we modelled pension entitlements in the early 1990s, SERPS pensions were still in place, and we allowed for its effects over people's whole lives – bringing greater benefits to those with higher earnings. The same exercise today would be based on reformed systems where people's pension rights are returning to being much the same flat-rate entitlement for all. While the number of years' difference in life expectancy remains as wide between different social classes, they have increased for all classes by much the same amount. This means a bigger proportionate gain in eventual pension receipts for those with lower lifetime incomes than those with higher lifetime incomes.

With much higher fees, repaid on the basis of later earnings, higher education is less pro-rich than it was. Non-pension social security has generally become more means tested, although less focused on the very poorest as a result of expanding tax credits for families with low earnings – people such as Michelle Ackroyd. On the other side of the equation, incomes and earnings have become more unequal since the 1980s, with the effect that while the tax system overall has remained stubbornly proportional (rather than progressive or regressive),[24] a larger share of overall taxes will be coming from the lifetime rich. These less pro-rich or more pro-poor structures would tend to boost 'Robin Hood' redistribution to some extent.[25] Looking at direct taxes and social security benefits (but not wider public services) using a model for earnings through people's working careers, Mike Brewer and colleagues at the Institute for Fiscal Studies (IFS) conclude that, 'Changes to the tax and benefit system over the last two decades have strengthened its ability to reduce inequalities in lifetime income.'[26]

Overall these factors are most likely to have cancelled out – looked at on a lifetime basis, the bulk of what the system does remains dominated by its 'savings bank' function, with redistribution between lifetime rich and lifetime poor having an important but smaller effect.

The stakes have got bigger

The kinds of 'lifetime' calculations illustrated in Figure 3.12 are based on a world that is static in another sense, however. They assume that the structure of the welfare state remains unchanged across people's lives. But that is clearly not the case. A woman born in 1930 would have had her childhood in the pre-war welfare state, reached adulthood as the Attlee government's expansion of it got under way, and retired in the 1990s into a pension system built on a mixture of Barbara Castle's 1980 system as reformed by the Thatcher government, but would have received most of her healthcare and pensions under Blair, Brown and Cameron – and may still be going strong as new reforms and cuts take effect in her mid-eighties.

Successive age cohorts – those born in particular years – have fared differently from one another, depending on the generosity of the system for their age group as they went through each part of it, and its generosity to other generations as they paid towards it in their working lives. Figure 3.13 attempts to show how the totals have evolved for each five-year generation, based on actual spending over the 20th century and projections from the systems in place in the early 2000s using official forecasts of life expectancy then.

What each generation pays in and gets out of the system represents many more years of income than in the past

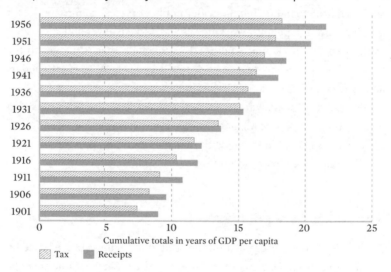

Figure 3.13 – Projected lifetime receipts from health, education and social security, and taxes paid towards them by year of birth, 1901–1960, GB

To give a scorecard of what each generation got out of the system, the amounts they received from public spending on education, social security, and healthcare were converted into percentages of average national income per person in that year, and then totalled across their complete lives. Thus, each member of the generation born between

1901 and 1906 received average total receipts equivalent to about nine years' worth of national income per person.[27] Even projecting spending and taxes – heroically – through to 2051, however, the generations born after 1961 would still have more to come, so the projections for them are incomplete and are not included here.

The immediate thing that leaps out is that the scale of what we are talking about *doubled* in relation to incomes between those born at the start of the 1900s and those born after 1950. Those born in the early 1950s (like the author) look set to benefit from public spending on health, education and social security equivalent to well over 20 years' worth of national income per capita on average over their lives. Since those calculations were done, improved life expectancy, more generous plans for state pensions, and increased resources for the NHS will have pushed this up further for that generation and its successors.

The other side of the coin is who pays for all of this. Figure 3.13 also shows, using the same accounting system, how much each generation has paid or will pay in towards it through taxes. A large part of this is paying towards the pensions and healthcare of their parents' generation. For the earliest generations, this meant there was less to put in – only seven or eight years' of national income, compared with the nine or ten they got out. Those born in the 1920s to the 1940s look to have got out something roughly equivalent to what they paid in. Those born in the 1950s emerge as winners again. But in no case is there a vast difference between what went in and what came out. There is no generation that managed to go through getting all the good parts of social provision without putting in much for earlier ones. At the same time, however, on this basis, what each generation has put in has dropped a little short of what it has taken out. If equity between generations was taken as meaning that these sums should balance, we have some adjustments to make. The implications of these issues are discussed further in Chapters 6 and 8.

What will happen to later generations depends on whether this intergenerational game keeps running. Those born in 1901 benefited from its scale growing as they moved into retirement, and those born in the

1950s from likely life expectancies out-running increases in state pension age (see Chapter 6), and so what look likely to be more years receiving pensions. But generally each generation pays in for its parents and then expects equivalent treatment from its children, so it roughly balances out.

By implication, if it all was suddenly brought to a juddering halt, and we decided to move away from this 'pay as you go' system, shrinking its scale substantially, a generation could find itself greatly out of pocket. This generation might have 'paid in' for parents' pensions and healthcare on top of children's education in the expectation that they would get something equivalent out in turn. If that did not happen, and they were now expected, for instance, also to save for their own healthcare privately, they would have a major grievance – facing a 'double burden'. Indeed, this generation would have such a large grievance that it is hard to imagine it being politically possible, outside a collapse of the whole economy. Like it or not, this means that we are locked into a system whose overall shape can probably only be slowly changed over decades, whatever a government's ambitions.

Summary and conclusions

The incomes people get from the 'market' – mainly from earnings – vary greatly across their life cycles. The living standards they can afford from market incomes vary even more, after allowing for periods when they have larger families. The welfare state – back to Lloyd George's old age pensions a century ago and even more strongly after the Second World War – has always had a major aim of smoothing out some of these variations. In fact, allowing for services such as healthcare and education as well as benefits such as pensions, the *large majority* of what the welfare state does is 'life cycle smoothing'. This is because it is dominated by universal entitlements (such as pensions, education and healthcare), not by stigmatised 'welfare benefits' for the poor.

The result of this is that incomes after allowing for the benefits people receive and the taxes they pay are much flatter across the life cycle than those from the market. The reforms of the Blair/Brown governments intensified this effect, looking at families with middle incomes, not just those with low ones. Overall, age-related income differences fell by a third between 1997 and 2010. This was because Labour's extra spending went on pensions and on benefits and tax credits for families with children, not on other working-age benefits. The Coalition government's reforms and cuts since 2010 have generally protected pensioners, but children and their parents are losing ground, so that part of life cycle smoothing is currently in retreat.

Over their lives all families pay into the system through taxes as well as receiving benefits and services. Even those who turn out to be in the poorest tenth over their lifetimes would – on one set of modelling results – pay for half of what they get back. Those with higher lifetime incomes pay for more, but still get back most of what they pay in. For instance, in the stories at the start of the chapter, the low-income Ackroyds paid for more than two-thirds of what they got back over their lifetime. The lifetime high-income Osbornes paid in more than they got out – but still got back five-sixths of what they paid in.

The scale of all this grew over the 20th century and is now very large – up to 25 years' worth of net annual income going in and out when you add it up over a whole lifetime on average. To put it in perspective, by the time a typical family reaches its late fifties, it could have received cash benefits equivalent to half the value of a house, and services from health and education equivalent to a whole house. But it would have paid in more than two houses' worth of taxes. If it survived into its mid-eighties, the lifetime taxes would have reached the equivalent of three houses, but this would be balanced by one-and-a-half houses' worth of benefits and state pensions and the same again in healthcare and education.

One implication of this is that nearly all families have a major stake in the system, both through what they are likely to get out of it in the end, but also from the way it insulates people from risks, including those of living longer than anticipated. This stake is particularly high for those who have so far been paying taxes covering the pensions and healthcare of their parent's generation, but who are currently out of pocket.

IT'S COMPLICATED

Charlotte Osborne

Gary and Denise Ackroyd

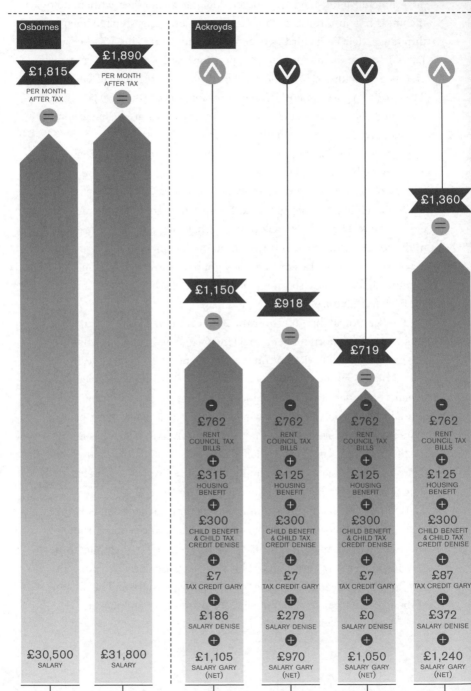

Osbornes

£1,815
PER MONTH AFTER TAX
=

£1,890
PER MONTH AFTER TAX
=

£30,500
SALARY

£31,800
SALARY

APRIL –
JULY

OCTOBER –
MARCH

Ackroyds

£1,150
=

£918
=

£719
=

£1,360
=

APRIL

−
£762
RENT
COUNCIL TAX
BILLS
+
£315
HOUSING
BENEFIT
+
£300
CHILD BENEFIT
& CHILD TAX
CREDIT DENISE
+
£7
TAX CREDIT GARY
+
£186
SALARY DENISE
+
£1,105
SALARY GARY
(NET)

MAY

−
£762
RENT
COUNCIL TAX
BILLS
+
£125
HOUSING
BENEFIT
+
£300
CHILD BENEFIT
& CHILD TAX
CREDIT DENISE
+
£7
TAX CREDIT GARY
+
£279
SALARY DENISE
+
£970
SALARY GARY
(NET)

AUGUST

−
£762
RENT
COUNCIL TAX
BILLS
+
£125
HOUSING
BENEFIT
+
£300
CHILD BENEFIT
& CHILD TAX
CREDIT DENISE
+
£7
TAX CREDIT GARY
+
£0
SALARY DENISE
+
£1,050
SALARY GARY
(NET)

SEPTEMBER

−
£762
RENT
COUNCIL TAX
BILLS
+
£125
HOUSING
BENEFIT
+
£300
CHILD BENEFIT
& CHILD TAX
CREDIT DENISE
+
£87
TAX CREDIT GARY
+
£372
SALARY DENISE
+
£1,240
SALARY GARY
(NET)

4. It's complicated

High frequency living

Charlotte Osborne is just a year older than her brother Henry. After a spell back in Manchester having finished university she got a job in the civil service in London and moved down to share a flat with two friends while she tried to save up more of a deposit (to add to an inheritance from her grandmother) to buy somewhere of her own.

By October 2010 Charlotte was on a salary of £31,800. After pension contributions, Income Tax and National Insurance, she was taking home £1,890 per month.[1] If you had asked her, she would have described herself as a careful money manager, and her financial organisation reflected that. The money coming in did not change much over the financial year. She had received a 1 per cent pay increase that August, and had just had an increment of £1,000 in October. The pay as you earn system meant that the right amount of Income Tax and National Insurance was worked out by the department she worked for and deducted each month from her pay. Back in April that year, she had taken home £1,815, so the step up to £1,890 in October was nice, but hardly affected her planning. The only blips in her income were the yearly dividends and interest she received on the money she had from her inheritance (parts of which were now transferred over into a tax-free Individual Savings Account, ISA) – but she was ploughing that back into her savings anyway, so it didn't affect her spending money.

Charlotte paid her £650 share of the rent by direct debit each month, and Council Tax, gas and electricity bills went out by direct debit at much the same rates over the year, while her regular savings, gym membership, charity contributions and other amounts went out by standing order. It all left her with around £200 a week for other spending, saving up for holidays, and so on.

Denise Ackroyd, who had married Michelle's brother Gary a few years before, was also a careful money manager – and she had to be. It would have been hard enough if their income from Gary's job as a van driver and her term-time hours doing school lunches (since their son Ryan had gone into Reception year) and all the benefits and tax credits had come in steadily. Denise had compared notes with Michelle, who had the advantage of a housing association rent at £71, compared to Gary and Denise's privately rented flat at £149 per week. Working it all through in a normal week, Denise and Gary would end up with about £264 after their housing costs, £50 more than Michelle (see Chapter 2), but with one more mouth to feed. Allowing for that, they were worse off – in fact, the official calculations would have put them in the bottom quarter of the national income distribution, albeit above the poverty line.[2]

So things would have been tight even if they were steady. But they were anything but steady. First, Gary's hours varied – in a good month they might be 40 hours a week, but in a bad one, only 30, and sometimes less. Then, Denise only got paid in term-time – it was convenient hours and worth having, but there was less coming in each fortnight over half-terms and nothing in the school holidays. The Child Benefit she got was a steady £81.20 every four weeks, and so was her Child Tax Credit – another £109 a fortnight (although that could change when she told the tax credit people at HMRC about any changes).

But other benefits and tax credits were all over the place. At the start of the year, Gary had a Working Tax Credit of just £7 a month added in with his pay. When Denise queried this with the HMRC helpline, they explained that this was the right amount given the amount of pay they had last reported to them. That was when she filled in the form in July 2009, telling them how much Gary had earned in 2008–09, two years earlier, which had been quite a good year. When she filled in the next form, HMRC would make sure it was adjusted to what they ought to be getting. So they had eventually sent off the form, telling them how much Gary had been on in 2009–10, a much less good year, and in July they heard that not only ought he to be getting more than £60 a month in his tax credit, but they would make up the missing amount over the rest of the year, so it would jump up to £87.

Council Tax was much the same every month, £115 for 10 months, with February and March off, which was handy as that was when the fuel bills were at their worst, but Gary earned too much for them to get any Council Tax Benefit. And Housing Benefit kept changing. It was almost as if 1 April came as a surprise to the council every year. First they would get a letter saying that the amount they were getting in April was going up because they had changed all the benefit rates. Then a couple of weeks later they would get another letter saying it would be a bit more allowing for their rent just having gone up. And then there would be another one when they told them about the tax credits having changed. And it was even worse later on in the year when they cut it back by two-thirds of what Denise was getting from the school.

And something that made it more complicated was that some things happened every month – like Gary's pay and tax credit and the rent – but others happened every four weeks, like Denise's tax credit and Child Benefit, or every fortnight, like her pay. She tried to budget on a fortnightly basis, but that was sometimes messed up when two fortnights went by without the end of a month in them, making it harder to plan.

In April things had been fairly steady – Gary brought in £1,112 including his tax credit, Denise got £186 for two weeks, and the Child Benefit and her tax credit came in as normal, up a bit on March. They were still getting Housing Benefit at £315 for the month at that point. After paying rent and Council Tax they had £1,150 left for the month.

But in May, with shorter hours, Gary's pay after tax and National Insurance was down to £970, his tax credit was still only £7, Denise lost money over half-term, and their Housing Benefit had been cut to £125. They were down to £918 for the month. August was worse with the school closed, and Gary's hours down again, and they ended up with only £719. But they were almost twice as well off in September – Denise's work started up again, Gary was getting 40 hours a week, and his tax credit had jumped up to £87. This time they were left with £1,360.

If Denise could have taken the whole year's income and divided it up into 12 equal chunks, and then put those aside for each month through the year, it would be manageable. But on a tight margin she couldn't do that – a fortnight or four weeks at a time was the most she could plan ahead. And that meant there were some months when they had to go without or find some way of tiding themselves over, borrowing from her or Gary's parents if she couldn't avoid it.

IF YOU PLOTTED Charlotte's income across the year, it would be fairly dull – a flat line with a couple of small steps, and a couple of blips when her investment income came in. But if you plotted Denise and Gary's, it would look more like the hospital heart monitor of someone in trouble, with big jumps and falls from week to week. Not all of those fluctuations came from their hours varying – some of them came from the tax credit and benefit systems that were supposed to help people cope with bad times, but often did so with a lag that was very hard to understand or explain.

This chapter looks at how common that kind of variation is, and at how this affects the way tax credits are run and the Coalition government's plans for the amalgamated payment, Universal Credit.

Life is bumpy – family incomes across the year

Chapter 3 described the fairly familiar way that incomes change across the life cycle as people age, but the ways in which they can fluctuate within a year may be less familiar. For a civil servant or someone working for a large company – or most university academics, in fact – income flows are usually fairly steady and relatively easy to plan for. As for Charlotte Osborne, there might be a small rise in pay for inflation once a year (or not, as in recent years), and in some jobs there could be an annual step up or increment up a pay scale, or less frequently, a promotion. Some employers might pay some kind of annual bonus, meaning a blip up in income that month. And people might have some odd amounts of income from somewhere else or have received a gift. The 'pay as you earn' Income Tax system is designed to adjust through the year, so that by the end of it most people will have paid the right amount of tax, without any sudden changes or need for big bills at the end of the year, while NICs are charged on what is earned that week or month.

From this kind of perspective, designing a benefit or tax credit system is not so hard. You might want to pay more to people with lower incomes through some kind of means test, or to treat people in one kind of situation differently from another. But once you know what people's circumstances are, you can work out what the payments should be, pay them out weekly or monthly, and let them get on with it.

Similarly, when we describe what the income distribution is like or how the state affects it, as in Chapter 2, we talk as if that snapshot captures people's full circumstances. Often – as in that chapter – we take what people say their weekly or monthly income is at the particular moment the survey was carried out and multiply it by 52 or 12 to give an annual equivalent. The surveys often ask what people's 'usual' or 'normal' income is to try to avoid distortions from a particularly good or bad period, and might average out irregular payments such as from investments over a longer period, but they will still record a snapshot of what is 'normal' at that particular moment.

We also have surveys – with results presented in Chapter 5 – that go back to people once a year, which mean that we can compare one snapshot with another taken a year later. But we know very little about how quickly or slowly people's situations change in between those kinds of observation, how they change within the year. Is Charlotte or Denise and Gary more typical?

Collecting that kind of information is a very intensive exercise. If you ask most people at the end of the year exactly how much came in and when during a particular month or week half-way through it, their memory of it may not be very precise. But going back to the thousands of people interviewed for the big national surveys once a month or once a fortnight would be prohibitively expensive.

Instead, to shed some light on this, a few years ago we commissioned a survey that aimed to collect information on income week by week over a whole year for 60 couples with children or single parents.[3] This was a very intensive exercise, with telephone calls to run through what had come in since the last one every fortnight. We expected to lose some of the sample each time, as it all got too much, or people didn't have the time, so we started with 180 for the first interviews. In the event 129 stuck it out for six months, 110 for all 27 interviews over the whole year, and there was complete enough information on 93 of them for full analysis of the whole year, week by week.

We recruited the sample from families who had been receiving what was then the tax credit for relatively low-paid people with children in the winter of 2002–03, and then followed them through the financial year 2003–04. So this is a particular group of people – like Gary and Denise – with earnings between about £5,000 and £20,000 and with children. We were able – anonymously – to check what they had told us by the end of the year about their incomes and what they got in tax credits against what HMRC had paid out to them, and what they eventually reported to HMRC as their income for the whole year. It all checked out well. Although a small group, their mix of circumstances matched that of all those on low earnings receiving tax credits at the time, and the chopping and changing they reported in their tax credits also matched national patterns fairly well, with the representation we needed of different kinds of family.[4]

Some people do have incomes that stay the same from week to week

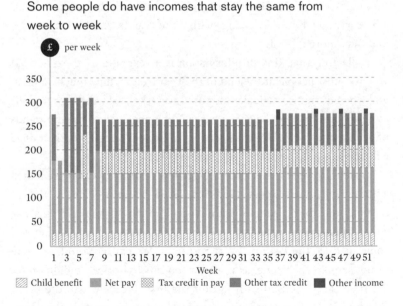

Figure 4.1 – Example case with regular weekly income: one-earner couple with two children and mortgage, 2003–04

Figure 4.1 gives a first example of the kind of information we collected. In this case it is for a couple where one of them was in steady weekly paid work, they had two children and were buying a house with a mortgage. Apart from a few wobbles at the start of the year as the tax credit system was reformed in April, what they got in was remarkably constant from week to week, with just a small pay rise in week 37, and everything else – Child Benefit, Child Tax Credit, and Working Tax Credit – all paid weekly too. If you had asked at any time from June to March what their income was, you would have got much the same answer – £260 per week up to Christmas and £270 afterwards. Although they were not nearly as well off as Charlotte Osborne, their life was equally easy to plan.

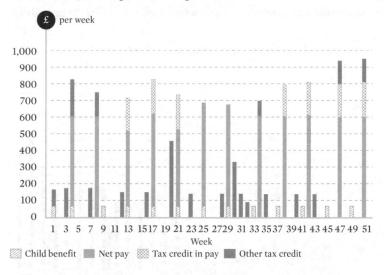

Figure 4.2 – Example case with unchanging circumstances but varying income: lone parent with one child and mortgage, 2003–04

But only a minority of the people we talked to were like this, with regular incomes every week, fortnight, four weeks or calendar month. Others looked more like the lone parent shown in Figure 4.2. There was no particular change in her circumstances over the year, but her net pay every month varied from £450 at the end of July to £600 in some others. Her Child Benefit came in pretty steadily, but her tax credits varied – and her four-weekly Child Tax Credit sometimes came in at the same time as her pay, but sometimes in another week.

Some people had much more dramatic changes than this, as illustrated in Figure 4.3. This is for another lone parent with one child, but in this case, the child became 16 a third of the way through the year. At the start of the year she was receiving just Income Support and Child Benefit (although she had been receiving in-work tax credits when originally recruited for the survey). But with her child reaching 16, she was no longer able to stay on Income Support, and had to switch to Jobseeker's Allowance, with conditions attached in terms of looking for work, whereas before she only had to attend regular interviews to talk about work. Over the last 10 years these rules have been tightened, and the conditions about looking for work now start applying around when children go to primary school.

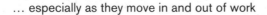

... especially as they move in and out of work

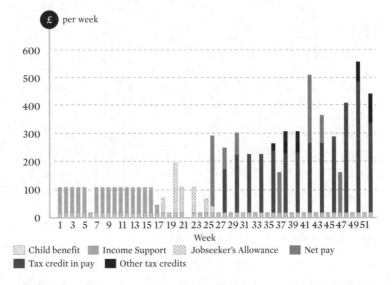

Figure 4.3 – Example case with changing circumstances: lone-parent tenant with one child, 2003–04

It took a few weeks for her Jobseeker's Allowance to settle down, and 10 weeks before she got her first tax credit. But then she found paid work again, starting on around £200 per fortnight, but increasing to £400 by the end of the year. Clearly her income was completely different at the end of the year than it had been at the start, so what she would have reported as her 'usual' income would have been very different in May, August, October or March. More often, however, the variability we were told about did not have any clear trend up or down over the year.[5]

Are fluctuating incomes very common?

There were all sorts of reasons – not necessarily ones we had expected – why the incomes people received each week could vary across the year:

- People might be in the same job, but paid varying amounts each time as hours changed or when there were bonuses.
- People changed jobs – sometimes with a short period out of work, sometimes not. When they changed jobs, they might go from weekly to monthly pay.
- Couples were often paid in different ways – such as one partner paid monthly and another weekly. Some kinds of income came in on a weekly pattern, some monthly.
- Some people – such as Denise Ackroyd – were only paid during school term, some paid for childcare during term time, which also led to tax credit entitlements varying.
- The kind of benefit people received could change with their circumstances, including the birth of a child, or a child reaching 16, as shown in Figure 4.3.
- Tax credit payments varied quite a lot for about half of the families – not just at the start of the year as the new system came in, but also later on, as they reported what their income had actually been in the previous year (as initial payments had been based on the year before that), and also as people told HMRC about changes during the year.

- Other kinds of income could vary a lot – particularly erratic child support payments from absent fathers, and things such as investment income, or children's income (from paper rounds and so on).
- A few people's circumstances varied more dramatically, as couples split up, or as lone parents acquired new partners.[6]

To summarise what we found, we divided the cases up, depending on how incomes varied between 13 four-week periods across the year.[7] Figure 4.4 shows what net incomes looked like on this basis for four 'highly stable' cases (A1–A4), where incomes stayed within 10 per cent of their average across the whole year.

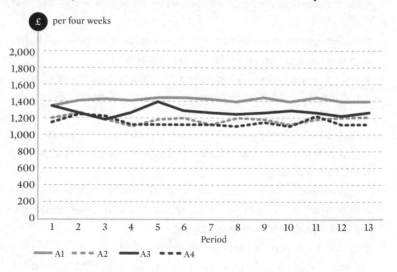

A minority of the families had stable incomes over the year

Figure 4.4 – Highly stable cases: incomes in four-week periods, 2003–04

Only seven of the 93 families looked like this, however. Eight had what we classed as 'highly erratic' incomes of the kind shown in Figure 4.5, with income in four or more periods above or below their annual average by more than 25 per cent, and with no clear trend, rising or falling over the year. For instance, case H1 was a two-child couple with one earner who changed jobs. This led to a period without income in the middle of the year, but eventually somewhat higher pay. Their tax credits were not assessed until July, when they received a £2,000 lump sum for arrears, with further adjustments in August and September, before eventually settling down at around £100 per week. The variation in income was partly driven by the job change and pay variation, but partly by the delay in their initial claim (or assessment) for tax credits.

… but as many had very large swings in their incomes

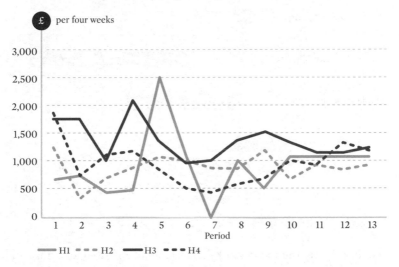

Figure 4.5 – Highly erratic cases: incomes in four-week periods, 2003–04

Figure 4.6 shows how the families divided between six categories, with the couples and lone parents shaded separately. Only seven of them – all couples – had the steady, highly stable, patterns of the kind shown in Figure 4.4. Another 21 – eight lone parents and 13 couples – had what we described as 'stable' or 'broadly stable' incomes.[8] The largest group were families that had incomes that stayed within 15 per cent of their average for 10 or more of the periods, but had 'blips' outside this for the others. A few cases – like the lone parent in Figure 4.3 – had incomes that fairly consistently rose or fell across the year. But more than a quarter – 26 of the 93 – had incomes that were more varied than any of these, including eight that had the 'highly erratic' pattern followed by the cases in Figure 4.5 (and probably by Gary and Denise Ackroyd).

Two-thirds of the study families had major income changes over the year

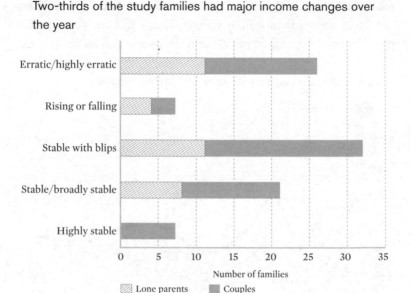

Figure 4.6 – Income trajectories followed by 93 families, 2003–04

Looking at why the incomes of the 26 families followed an erratic or highly erratic trajectory during the year, we could see four particular kinds of change (with some families affected by more than one):

- *Demographic:* four had a change in the number of children or in partnership status.
- *Labour market:* 12 had pay stopping or starting for one or more of the adults during the year, or changed to a new pay pattern (for example, from weekly to monthly).
- *Benefits:* four had one or more social security benefits stop or start during the year (excluding Child Benefit).
- *Tax credits:* five had one or more kind of tax credit stop or start for at

least two periods (excluding the first three months of the year, as the new system started up).

Only nine of these erratic or highly erratic cases were unaffected by such changes. By contrast, none of the 'highly stable' cases was affected by changes of any of these kinds.[9]

While this was a small sample of families, what we found has several implications. First, the design of benefits and tax credits needs to cope with what commonly seem to be complicated patterns of incomes across the year for many families. As discussed below, when this does not work well, problems can arise.

Second, benefits and tax credits generally stabilise incomes across the year, as one would hope they would. For instance, Jobseeker's Allowance should come in when someone loses their job entirely, while other means-tested benefits and tax credits should rise when income dips. For our sample, the variability of incomes over the year after allowing for benefits was considerably lower than that of net market incomes.[10] Tax credits also had a stabilising effect overall, but a slightly smaller one, despite the amounts involved being much larger. However, there were some cases where the way tax credits were paid *added* to instability of income (at the same time as increasing its level, of course). Again, we discuss below how that can happen.

Third, rapid income changes will have the greatest effect on people if they can only budget over a short period, and do not have the reserves to smooth things out over longer ones. At the end of the year over which we had followed them, we asked our respondents how long ahead they planned for 'basic expenses'. For the 82 that completed this final interview, 37 planned over about a month, and two over a longer period.[11] But 21 planned only over about a week, and eight of them only for two to three days at a time. For nearly half of them, their planning therefore did not even allow room for smoothing things out within a single month, and virtually none of them were planning over longer periods. As we discuss below in the context of the Coalition government's plans to pay the future Universal Credit in monthly instalments only, this kind of pattern does not seem atypical. If people are used to budgeting weekly or fortnightly to manage on a very tight budget, coping with monthly payments may prove hard for some.

But aren't people on benefits stuck on them?

These sorts of result suggest that among those in low-paid work there is much short-term variation in their circumstances. And these results are from 10 years ago. In the last few years, there has been a huge growth in the number of people on 'zero hours contracts', where they are committed to an employer, but the number of hours they get to work varies up and down, depending on what the employer needs from week to week. According to the ONS, by 2013 more than half a million people reported that they were on such contracts, three times the number reporting this in 2010 (although people may be more likely to report this status following recent publicity).[12] And using results from a survey of businesses, the ONS estimated that in early 2014 as many as 1.4 million employee contracts did not specify a minimum number of hours.[13] At the same time, most of the growth in employment since the low point of the recession has been in 'self-employment'. In many cases this involves highly variable, even casual, work, with very variable hours. If we repeated our survey today, we would probably find even more variation than there was a decade ago. This has contributed to the growth of what Guy Standing has labelled as a new 'precariat' – workers in insecure work with limited protection.[14]

The precariousness of people's jobs is not just about variable hours; it is also about whether they are in work at all. While we recruited the group described above from people who had been in work at the end of 2002, some of them were actually out of work by the time we started tracking their incomes, while others lost and regained jobs during the year. Some of them were, indeed, in what has become known as the 'low pay, no pay' cycle, where people move in and out of a series of low-paid jobs. Tracy Shildrick and colleagues have described the reality of lives in this cycle as, 'Like Sisyphus ... life stories of repeated labour with little progress, of recurrent engagement with hard work but constant returns to unemployment'.[15]

The existence of the 'low pay, no pay' cycle makes running benefits and tax credits more complicated. But it also suggests that the caricature of those on out-of-work benefits mainly consisting of an unchanging mass of people who are permanently out of work, dependent on benefits, cannot be right. In fact, there is a very high rate of turnover between being in work and being out of work, and most people who become unemployed get work again fairly quickly.

In a typical three-month quarter in recent years, about one million people will have stopped working and about one million will have gained jobs.[16] In periods of recession or recovery, these numbers change – for instance, 100,000 extra losing work and 50,000 fewer gaining it in a recession – so the total number out of work rises or falls. But the turnover remains fast.

Up to the crisis, most unemployed people had been out of work for less than six months

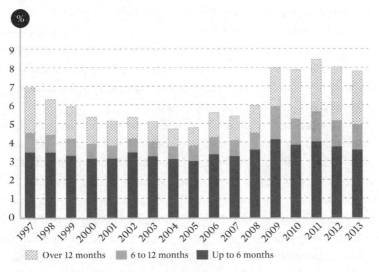

Figure 4.7 – Unemployment rate in the UK by duration

A first indication of this can be seen in Figure 4.7, which gives the proportion of the 'economically active' adult workforce that has been unemployed (so far) in the third quarter of different years since 1997.[17] Through the period up to the start of the crisis in 2008, most people who were unemployed at any one moment had been so for less than six months. Indeed, by 2004, fewer than 1 per cent of the whole labour force had been unemployed for more than a year, and only 1.6 per cent for more than six months. In times of growth, most people who become unemployed do so for short periods. Across the period from 1997 to 2009, the average amount of time that someone would remain unemployed after they lost their job remained between five and six months.[18] It was only after the recession started that long-term unemployment started to rise, so that by 2013 more than a third of currently unemployed people had been out of work for more than a year.

The figures above relate to 'uncompleted spells' – how long someone has been unemployed so far. But what we are really interested in to understand turnover in the labour market is how long they will remain unemployed in the end. We get some clues on this from data on how long people's claims for benefits last – although, of course, ending a spell on Jobseeker's Allowance does not necessarily mean someone has found a job, and if they do, it may not last. But with those provisos, DWP data in Figure 4.8 show a very different picture from the caricature of people who spend long periods on unemployment benefits (Chapter 5 looks at related data for incapacity benefits).

Most Jobseeker's Allowance claims are, in fact, very short. Of those who started a claim in April 2007 – just before the start of the economic crisis – fewer than half, 45 per cent, lasted more than two months. Five-sixths, 84 per cent, lasted no more than six months, and only 6 per cent lasted as long as a year. Staying on Jobseeker's Allowance for long periods is very rare: only 0.7 per cent of those who started in April 2007 were still on it after two years, and only 0.3 per cent after three years. With the recession, these numbers have worsened, but even for those starting in April 2009 or 2011, four-fifths of spells lasted no more than six months, and only one-tenth as long as a year. Part of the drop-off at particular anniversaries – such as at six months or two years – reflects new benefit conditions and changes in the treatment of people who reach those milestones, and in some cases, people are shuffled between benefits and training schemes, but what the figures show is how fast the turnover is, even at other durations.

Fewer than half of those starting a claim for Jobseeker's Allowance stay on it for longer than two months

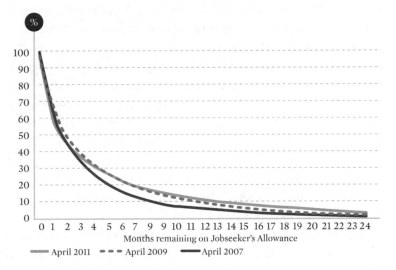

Figure 4.8 – Proportion of claimants remaining on Jobseeker's Allowance, spells starting in April 2007, 2009 and 2011

Because short-term recipients move off so fast, they account for a smaller proportion of claimants *at any one time*, but even so, back in May 2007 two-thirds of those receiving Jobseeker's Allowance had been on it for less than six months, and 82 per cent for less than a year. There are cases that stay on for longer, but they are unusual – at that date 2 per cent of claimants had been on Jobseeker's Allowance for five years or more. With the recession, the length people have stayed on benefit has lengthened, but still, in May 2013, half of current Jobseeker's Allowance claimants had been on it for less than six months, and 69 per cent for less than a year, while the proportion on it for more than five years had reached 3 per cent.[19] Prolonged receipt of Jobseeker's Allowance is very rare. Indeed, when the Centre for Social Justice recently ranked British cities by the number of people who had been receiving Jobseeker's Allowance for 10 years or more, the top place in the table was taken by Birmingham, where this was true of just 60 people.[20] Liverpool was second, with 50 people. Clearly the situation was deeply unsatisfactory for those 60 people for whatever reason, but, as Figure 4.8 shows, cases like those are wholly unrepresentative of what happens to the overwhelming majority of people who lose work and claim Jobseeker's Allowance.

In fact, far from being a British phenomenon, long-term unemployment is much less common in the UK than in most of the rest of the EU. Between 2004 and 2008, the proportion of the economically active population who had been out of work for more than 12 months remained below 1.5 per cent, while across the EU as a whole it was around 4 per cent for most of the period, dipping to 2.6 per cent at the end. With the recession, the UK rate rose to above 2.5 per cent by 2010–2012, but well below the rate of above 5 per cent across the whole of the EU in 2013.[21]

All this stopping and starting unemployment – and possibly claiming benefits – is a long way from the idea that those who are out of work now mostly have never worked, and possibly never wanted to. The reason why the long-term unemployment rate jumped between 2008 and 2010 was not that people suddenly became 'dependent'; it was because the economy shrank in the wake of the financial crisis.

But all this just relates to those classed as 'unemployed'. There are others of working age who are not in paid employment, but who are classed as not being employed because of disability or caring for their family, as well as those who are in education. There are also people who are unemployed, but who do not claim benefits (or who are not entitled to them). But only 2 per cent of those aged 18–59 had been receiving the main out-of-work benefits (excluding those on long-term disability benefits) of different kinds for more than three years out of the four years up to 2008 (some of whom will have had periods in work, or at least off benefits). This had jumped to 3.3 per cent by 2012, with the onset of the recession, but again does not bear out a picture of most people on benefits being there permanently.[22] If those who are receiving long-term disability and incapacity benefits are included, the proportion of the working-age population receiving out-of-work benefits for most of a four-year period rises to 8 per cent, but that is including many who have effectively already retired for health or disability reasons.

Again, the picture reflects substantial turnover. Looking at households (of working age), between 16 and 17 per cent were 'workless' for any reason (not just unemployment) at any particular moment between the late 1990s and late 2000s. But in any three-month quarter about a sixth of these would stop being workless, being replaced by others. Overall, about 3 per cent of all households became workless and 3 per cent stopped being workless each quarter.[23]

But if most people are unemployed or workless for only short periods, how is it that we hear of two-generation families that have never worked – or that there are even "some estates, where often three generations of the same family have never worked", as Iain Duncan Smith put it in 2009? Or even four generations, according to one of his colleagues.[24] The simple answer is that such cases are very rare. Indeed Robert Macdonald, Tracy Shildrick and Andy Furlong refer to their fruitless eight-month search for actual families where three generations had never worked in very high unemployment areas of Glasgow and Teesside as 'hunting the Yeti'.[25]

Nationally, Lindsey Macmillan and Paul Gregg looked at the information we do have from three different surveys where both parents and children have been tracked over time.[26] First, even one generation 'never working' is rare – with fewer than 1 per cent of sons never having worked by age 29, for instance, in two of the three surveys. So two or three generations 'never having worked' is even rarer. But they did find that 4 per cent of households with more than one generation of working age had both generations out of work *at once*, about three-quarters of whom had both been out of work for more than a year. So downturns in the labour market can hit two generations at once. Equally, the chances of people being out of work if their parents were out of work for part of their childhood are greater. But neither of these is the same as the picture of large numbers of families permanently outside the labour market, or of this being a good description of the large majority of people receiving benefits. People's lives – even those who are out of work at one moment – are much more fluid than that.

A brief history of in-work support, from Family Income Supplement to tax credits

A basic idea of the Beveridge model of social insurance, illustrated in Figure 3.3 in the last chapter, was that people's time could be divided into two sorts of period, in work and out of work. When in work, earnings would – if combined with family allowances, but no further benefits – keep people above the breadline. When out of work, flat-rate unemployment or sickness benefits would come in as a partial substitute, leaving people not as well off as in work, but no longer in need. Those benefits would depend on being out of work – and on 'actively seeking' it, as well as having paid contributions – but would not be means tested.

This neat split has eroded for a series of reasons. First, even from the start, many people who were out of work needed to have additional means-tested top-ups through what started as 'National Assistance' and eventually became Income Support to reach an acceptable 'national minimum'. Insurance benefits were never set high enough to avoid this, especially when high costs for things such as extra rent in expensive parts of the country were allowed for.[27] If equivalent help was not available for the extra costs of those who were in work, this narrowed the gap between incomes of those in and out of work. As rents have risen in relation to incomes, this has become a far greater issue. When Beveridge was making his proposals for post-war social insurance, he built in the idea that average rents would take up less than a quarter of the total amount of benefit that an unemployed family with two children would need.[28] Even at this level, variations between high and low-cost areas left him in two minds as to whether a standard allowance could cope with what he called the 'problem of rent'. Today we are grappling with rents that can be as high as the total amount we allow for all other living costs – in relative terms, the 'problem of rent' has become three to four times as big.

A first reaction was the spread of local schemes that helped low-income tenants with their rents and low-income households more generally with their rates (the predecessor but one of Council Tax). These were systematised into national model schemes of 'rent rebates' (for council tenants), 'rent allowances' (for private tenants) and 'rate rebates' in the early 1970s. Separate support for rents of those who were out of work continued, however, until two phases of reform in the 1980s brought in Housing Benefit, paid to those in and out of work in a system run by local councils covering both private and social tenants.

A second reaction was the introduction, again in the early 1970s, of an extra means-tested payment – Family Income Supplement, later to become Family Credit – for low-paid families with children. In the context of this chapter, an important feature of these was that the amounts paid were based on an assessment of what income *had been* in a recent period, which then led to benefits being paid out at a *fixed* amount for the next period. This pattern was carried over when Gordon Brown as Chancellor replaced Family Credit with the much more generous Working Families' Tax Credit (WFTC) in the autumn of 1999. Income would be assessed – using pay slips from the last few weeks or months – and then people would receive a fixed payment for the following six months.

This was changed in the reforms of April 2003 that turned WFTC (and what had been the separate child allowances in Income Support) into the Child Tax Credit and Working Tax Credit that Gary and Denise Ackroyd were receiving in 2010. There were four features of this new system:

- So far as means-tested help for children was concerned, Child Tax Credit would be a 'seamless' system for low-income families whether in or out of work and as they moved between them.

- To reduce stigma and increase the chances people would claim them (a priority at the time) – and so realise that they were better off in work than out of work – the new tax credits would be run along the same lines as the tax system as a kind of 'negative tax' by HMRC.
- Like Income Tax collected through pay as you earn, the amounts people received would *adjust* though the year, rather than being fixed. So if pay fell or something else changed, that could result in higher tax credits at once, rather than waiting until the next assessment period.
- As a corollary of this, again by analogy with Income Tax, the amounts people were eventually paid would depend on what their income added up to over the whole year. If they turned out not to have been paid enough during the year itself, they would get extra after the end of it. If they turned out to have been paid too much – for instance, because they had earned more than originally expected – they would have to give back the 'over-payment' (usually through reduced tax credits during the following year).

In designing this system, the government was aware that a similar scheme in Australia had ended up very unpopular because of the number of reclaims for over-payments it generated at the end of the year.[29] It therefore said that increases of income up to £2,500 above that originally allowed for (based on reported income in an earlier year) would be ignored. But it turned out that changes in incomes from year to year were frequently much larger than this, and other circumstances changed too. As a result, in the first year of the new system, a third of claimants were *over*-paid, despite the 'tolerance' for increased incomes – a third of these by more than £1,000. At the same time, 12 per cent of cases were *under*-paid, with a quarter of these by more than £1,000.[30] Reducing later payments to claw-back the over-payments was unpopular, so the tolerance for increased income from the initial assessment was increased hugely to £25,000 from 2006 (but cut back to £5,000 in 2012). As a result, people were protected through higher tax credits if income fell – something that was important to many people in the recession after

2008 – but most did not lose tax credits if income rose during the year. This asymmetry increased the cost of the system. It also meant that, if you could work it out, those with varying incomes over time got more than those with steadier ones.

The need to adjust tax credits in order to hit the right amount at the end of the year came from two sources. First, the credits initially paid in April in one year will in many cases (unless the claimant has reported a pay rise) be based on the income reported the *previous* summer for the year that ended in March that year. In other words, it will already be about 18 months out of date on average. A partial adjustment can be made in the summer – as for Gary and Denise – but even that will still be based on the previous year's income. Second, as we found in our own survey and as illustrated in the story at the start of the chapter, people's lives are complicated, and their circumstances change for many reasons. This has made running tax credits on an annual basis fraught with difficulty, for both government and recipients.

Universal Credit – solving the problems of tax credits?

The Coalition government's flagship benefits reform is in some ways designed exactly to cope with the issues that caused problems for tax credits. Partly because the existing system is so complex, explaining the transition to a new one raises many complicated issues – but it is also a reflection of the complexity of people's real lives.

The core idea of Universal Credit is to replace six separate means-tested benefits with a single system for those with low incomes in or out of work – generalising the 'seamless system' idea introduced by the last government in 2003 for payments related to children through Child Tax Credit. At present, people in work may simultaneously be receiving Working and Child Tax Credits, Housing Benefit and Council Tax support. The means tests for the tax credits are worked out by HMRC while the support for rent and Council Tax are worked out by their local council. Out of work, couples can be receiving means-tested Jobseeker's Allowance, some lone parents Income Support, and some disabled people Employment and

Support Allowance (ESA), again at the same time as Child Tax Credit, Housing Benefit and Council Tax support. Universal Credit is intended to replace all of these, with the surprising – given the aims of one part of government (the DWP) – omission of Council Tax support (which belongs to another part, Communities and Local Government).

If caught in the 'poverty trap', people can lose more than 90 per cent of a pay increase

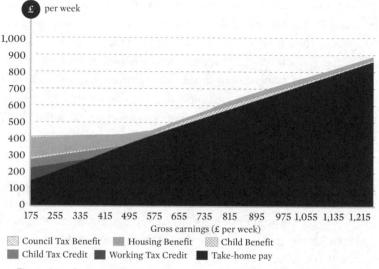

Figure 4.9 – Components of income for a couple with one child, 2010–11

The means tests that determine how much people get are calculated in different ways, relating to income over different periods. One obvious problem is that this means people have to give the same information to several different agencies, which then react at varying speeds, creating some of the complication in the flows of income coming in to people like Gary and Denise. Amalgamating them into one system may cut out duplication of effort both for those claiming benefits and tax credits and for those running them. Part of the latter advantage is undermined, however, by the decision to leave Council Tax support out of the amalgamation – councils will still have to collect information on people's incomes for this, even though they will lose responsibility for Housing Benefit.[31]

Second, the ways in which the different benefits and tax credits are reduced as income rises can overlap, and can overlap with tax and NICs. In some cases, if someone's income was £10 per week higher, they could lose more than £9 of this from higher taxes and lower tax credits and benefits. Many people would lose more than £7, once everything had been worked out.

Figure 4.9 shows how this would have worked in 2010–11 for a couple like Gary and Denise (although with only one of them earning in this case):

- At the bottom is their take-home pay, after allowing for Income Tax and National Insurance. This goes up by £69 for each extra £100 of gross pay for most of the earnings range up to about £840 per week.
- Next are their tax credits, reduced at this time by £39 for each extra £100 of gross pay.
- Then comes their Child Benefit, which then – and up until 2013 – was unaffected by their other income.
- On top of that is their Housing Benefit, cut back rapidly as other income rises,[32] but with those earning up to £560 per week still getting some.
- For earnings up to £290 per week, the couple would also have received small amounts – hardly visible here – of what was then Council Tax Benefit.

Figure 4.10 shows, for the same kind of family, what that meant in total in terms of what is officially called their 'effective marginal deduction rate' – how much of any extra £1 of earnings did they lose? We are used to hearing the arguments about whether people on very high incomes should face Income Tax of 45 per cent or 50 per cent on their top slices of income, but the rates shown in the figure are far higher for those with low earnings. In fact, the rate was 75 per cent or more for all of the earnings range shown, up to nearly £560 per week, that is, around median earnings. Those on very low earnings were facing rates of over 95 per cent. Where calculated entitlements dropped below a minimum amount, the loss on one extra pound of income – which is what this DWP chart shows – can be quite high, accounting for the spikes in marginal deductions where this happens for Housing Benefit, around £560 in this case, for instance.

Adding everything in, marginal tax rates are much higher for those on low to middle incomes than those on higher incomes

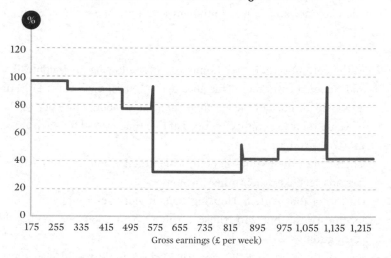

Figure 4.10 – Combined tax and benefit withdrawal rates for a couple with one child, 2010–11

As well as all of this, those on out-of-work benefits, such as Income Support, who had earnings above small 'disregarded' amounts, would lose 100 per cent of any additional amount. They would see no gain at all in net income until they met the 'hours rules' built into the Working Tax Credit – 16 hours per week for a lone parent or 30 hours for a couple. At that point, getting over the threshold would mean quite a large jump in net income, and a clear difference from income out of work.

People do not necessarily react directly to the potential theoretical disincentives to work more where schedules of the kind shown in Figure

4.10 apply to them – after all, they are hard to work out, even when you do not allow for the changes in situation from week to week that are a reality for many people's lives. But they do feed two perceptions. First, that it is *unfair* that someone who is working many more hours than another is barely any better off. And second, it is hard to change (usually incorrect) *perceptions* that people are better off out of work than in work when it is so hard to work out and explain.

The planned Universal Credit offers the biggest gains to lone parents working less than 16 hours per week

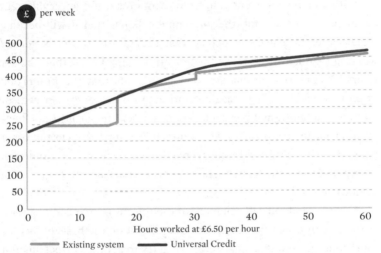

Figure 4.11 – Net income by hours worked under current system and Universal Credit, lone parent with two children

The idea of Universal Credit, then, is to change all of this by wrapping many of these benefits together in a system run by DWP, with a single rate of withdrawal ('taper') as income rises of 65 per cent and no hours rules. For those below Income Tax and National Insurance thresholds, that would set the marginal rate they faced at 65 per cent *plus* any reduction in Council Tax support (often meaning an extra 7 per cent, but now in a few areas an extra 10 per cent).[33] For those paying Income Tax and NICs, the combined rate would come out at 76 per cent plus any effects of Council Tax support reduction (which could take the total to well over 80 per cent).

Also, compared to the current situation, where the gain from working up to 15 hours for a lone parent or 29 hours for a couple can be small, even working, say, 10 hours per week would lead to a gain in net income. This is illustrated in Figure 4.11, showing what the relationship between net income and hours worked is intended to look like under Universal Credit compared with previous arrangements for a lone parent with two children (in the simplest case where there were no housing costs or support to allow for).

With a more consistent gain from extra hours, and fewer different components to allow for, the government hopes that it will become much easier to explain to people that they are in reality better off working than not working, and better off working longer than shorter hours. Overall, one recent assessment suggests that the proportion of all households facing marginal withdrawal rates of 80 per cent or more would fall from 2 per cent to 0.01 per cent (*excluding* the effects of other means tests, such as for Council Tax support). On the other hand, there is a cost to this: the proportion facing marginal withdrawal rates between 60 and 80 per cent would *rise* from 8.6 to 11.9 per cent of all households.[34]

A third – and radical – element of the reform is intended to get rid of the way in which tax credits are initially set on the basis of income some time ago and then adjusted later to try to get the correct amount paid out on the basis of total income over the year. The DWP is planning to piggy-back on the 'real-time information system' through which employers now report their employees' earnings month by month to HMRC for tax purposes. This will, it hopes, mean that exactly the right amount can be paid out each month on the basis of those reports without any later catch-up payments or claw-backs.

The way this is intended to work is that the DWP will collect and hold all the information they need about people's circumstances – who is in a couple with whom, how many children they have, what their rent is, and so on. Once a month employers' computers will send information about how much someone had earned into HMRC, which will then pass this to the DWP. The DWP's computers will then marry this together with the reported earnings of people's partners and what it knows of their other circumstances, calculate exactly the right amount of Universal Credit, and pay that out.

With this 'real-time' system, if people have a bad month, Universal Credit goes up immediately. If they have a good month, it will go down, but not by as much as take-home pay has risen. This could be very useful to people whose earnings change from month to month – like Gary Ackroyd. It could potentially be very useful to the growing numbers of people on 'zero hours contracts', who might have nearly full-time work one week but none or little the next. It could mean smoother and easier transitions as people move from being out of work altogether, to getting a few hours and then on to more. With a simpler system more people may claim what they are entitled to – the DWP has allowed for its spending to be £2.3 billion per year higher because of this – but fewer people should be over-paid, saving the government £2.1 billion per year, it thinks.[35] Over time administration costs would also fall as duplication in income assessments was reduced and later adjustments avoided.

So what could possibly go wrong?

When it announced this reform, the government planned for it to start to come in for new claims from October 2013, following pilots starting in April 2013. By April 2014 all new out-of-work claimants would be on the new system, and after that, all new in-work claimants would join it rather than applying for tax credits. By October 2017 all existing claimants would also have been 'migrated' to the new system and the transition to Universal Credit would be complete.

But progress up to the end of 2013 was much slower than planned. Pilots started in only one area in April 2013, and had reached only 10 'pathfinder' areas by October 2013. The computerised system was being piloted for only the simplest cases – single unemployed people with no dependants. If they had a change in circumstances, that was being dealt with through parallel systems. But this is testing only the most limited aspects of what will be required of the DWP's information systems for Universal Credit to work. Only 5,250 people had started on the pilot system by the end of January 2014.[36] As the Public Accounts Committee pointed out in November 2013, in the long run Universal Credit is intended to cover 10 million people in 7.5 million households who have between them 1.6 million changes in circumstances *every month*.[37] Even without the unhappy experiences and delays in the piloting process, and previous examples of large public sector computing projects going badly wrong, this is a very daunting administrative challenge. With them the government's ambitions for the speed of its introduction look, at the time of writing, hugely optimistic.

But some of the potential problems with Universal Credit go beyond whether the IT systems will eventually be able to cope with these challenges and those of moving people from 38 different current 'legacy' IT systems.[38]

To start with, the system puts people's eggs all in a single basket. If one of the several benefits and tax credits people are receiving at the moment goes wrong, at least the others should keep coming in. If, for whatever reason, a Universal Credit payment is missed, that could be all, or the majority, of someone's income. And the amounts involved can be very large in relation to what people have been used to budgeting around. This is for two reasons. First, the DWP wants to move away from the situation where many social tenants never see their Housing Benefit (it goes direct to their landlords, who then collect what rent is left over, in some cases nothing). Instead, it will come as cash to the claimant, who will then pay the rent in the same way that other people would. Second, payments will be made monthly, on the grounds that this matches how people in work live (although only half of those earning £10,000 or less are, in fact, paid monthly).[39] For a couple with one child who are out of work and have a rent of £150 per week, this could mean a single monthly cash payment of more than £1,400 (at 2014–15 rates).

Even if it all works perfectly, adjusting to monthly payments may be daunting for many. The people in our survey that tracked incomes over a year were not unusual. A survey of 5,000 benefit recipients in 2001 found that two-thirds of them said they budgeted daily or weekly, a tenth fortnightly, and only a sixth monthly (or four-weekly).[40] A recent small-scale survey investigating specifically how Universal Credit might work in practice found that more than half were budgeting daily or weekly.[41] In these circumstances, coping with a single very large lump going into a bank account once a month with nothing in between may prove hard. Some – maybe most – will adjust through quick payment of essential bills and careful allocation of what is left between each of the weeks of the month. But if people are facing demands on what are, in fact, very limited resources compared to others around them, the pressures to over-spend at the start of a month may prove overwhelming for some, leaving them later in the month at the mercy of pay-day lenders and so even less money in the long run, unless they can get short-term help from someone else.

This may be exacerbated by the way in which the single payment will now go into a single account for couples. The gender implications of this may be very large.[42] Until now, some of the payments will have gone to one partner or another, such as Child Tax Credit usually going to the mother. This may have been important in couples where income is not, in fact, shared equally between them. If one partner spends a large part of the single monthly payment early in the month, the other may be left picking up the pieces. At the very least, many couples will have to renegotiate and adjust ways they have evolved for who pays which bill or takes responsibility for what – what is seen as 'his money' and what is 'hers'. This could all be especially difficult where couples are forming – often a gradual process rather than one where people move from looking after their own money to full joint budgeting overnight. It may be worse where couples split, and it takes time for the Universal Credit system to do the same with the payments to them.

There are other barriers to a smooth transition to the new system. Once it is in place, some will benefit from the new structure, but others will lose.[43] First, it is being introduced at the time of a series of other cuts to benefits and tax credits, discussed in more detail in Chapter 8. It is much easier to introduce a simpler system from which some gain and some lose as previous wrinkles are ironed out, if in general people are getting more. At present, exactly the opposite is happening – any losses from the structural reforms embodied in Universal Credit will come on top of those from benefit caps, limits on private sector Housing Benefit, the 'Bedroom Tax', reduced Council Tax support, and so on. Many of those affected will have no margin to cope with the precise way the new system works, or with any glitches in its introduction, or will already be facing hardship.

The administrative gains pencilled in for the new system also presuppose that claims for it will be made online. But many of its recipients are not used to claiming online, and will need support – possibly on a continuing basis – to do so successfully, again with huge consequences for them if things go wrong. And many people have an income that does not come from an employer plugged into the new real-time information system. A total of 600,000 of the households expected to be receiving Universal Credit have one or more earner with income from self-employment that will still have to be dealt with through a separate system.[44] Think, for instance, of someone with income from several different cleaning jobs.

Finally, the current system is based on different treatment of those 'in work' – meeting the hours requirements – and those 'out of work', working fewer hours or none. The latter group is subject to increasingly tight conditions on looking for work. Without this distinction, the government will have to change the way in which it defines who has this 'conditionality' of what they have to do to find work applied to them. With no rule on minimum hours to qualify, some people might find it more convenient to cut their hours from the current minimum required – suiting their own choices, but increasing the cost to the state, as they would be earning less. In response, the government has said that conditions of looking for work will now apply to those working short hours – in fact, the conditions will continue to apply until they are earning the equivalent of the minimum wage for a certain number of hours per week. This will mean a large new group of people will be expected to look for longer hours of work, with new policing of their efforts to do so. With shorter working hours more common since the economic crisis started, finding those extra hours may be very difficult – as will policing whether part-time workers are 'trying hard enough' to get them.

Worse than this, the system could develop in a way that subsidises the casualisation of labour, as employers realise they no longer need to take the risk of offering people steady hours when demands change from day to day. They may decide that the state is offering to cover most of that risk for people, rather than that being built into normal employment conditions.

Another change of principle in the treatment of people who have been in work is that tax credit entitlements have not been affected by whether people have savings above a certain amount (although interest income is, for instance, taken into account). But with Universal Credit, the rules currently applying to out-of-work benefits will now be extended to those in low-paid work, ruling some out of entitlement altogether until they have run their savings down below a threshold (see Chapter 6).

Summary and conclusions

People's circumstances, even over quite short periods, do not stay static in a way that is easy for them, still less bureaucratic systems, to cope with. If there really was an unchanging 'underclass' of benefit recipients funded by an unchanging – if resentful – class of taxpayers, it would at least be easy to work out who should get what and who should pay what. But with around a million people losing work and around a million gaining it every three months, the situation is not like that. For instance, of those starting a claim for Jobseeker's Allowance in April 2007, fewer than half claimed for more than two months, and only 6 per cent for as long as a year. The time spent to leave the benefit lengthened with the recession, but still only a tenth of those starting a claim do so for as long as a year. As a corollary of this kind of turnover, the caricature families where two, let alone three, generations have 'never worked' are very rare, and wholly unrepresentative of those who become unemployed and get benefits, usually for a short time.

Even once in work, many people's incomes change substantially from week to week or month to month, and more so if the different kinds of income going to many couples are looked at together. And the rest of life goes on, with partnerships forming and dissolving, people moving home, children being born and leaving home. Many of the ways in which the labour market has been changing – before as well as since the onset of the economic crisis – have increased the variability and insecurity of people's lives, for instance, with increasing numbers on 'zero hours contracts' that do not guarantee a minimum number of hours. An increasing number of people face the kind of juggling, sometimes between several jobs, described at the start of the chapter for Denise and Gary Ackroyd, rather than the steady income flows of a civil servant such as Charlotte Osborne.

As this chapter has described, this complexity has led to messy interactions between a whole series of separate tax and transfer systems designed in different ways to give the greatest help to those who need it most, while keeping down the overall cost. Where those systems adjust to people's changing circumstances only slowly, but then with a jolt, the end result can make things even messier.

The biggest current reform to the way the state interacts with people of working age is the Coalition government's plan for a single Universal Credit payment to replace six existing means-tested benefits and tax credits by 2017, with exactly the right amounts paid out each month on the basis of 'real-time information'. On paper, this aims precisely to cope with these complexities and pay out exactly the right amount each time. But to do this involves a heroic administrative effort to install systems that can cope with, for instance, 1.6 million changes in circumstances every month. Early evidence from attempts to pilot the system for even the simplest cases has not, at the time of writing, been promising.

But even if all the administrative glitches can be ironed out, some of the elements embodied in the new system will require major changes in how people with limited incomes budget and manage their money:

- People will be expected to make online claims.
- They will need to cope with a single payment each month, where many, if not most, of its recipients currently balance their budgets over much shorter periods.
- Couples will have to renegotiate who pays which bill, as the money coming in goes into a single account – which will be all the more difficult for those forming new partnerships or splitting up.
- All of this is already difficult, but the stakes involved in a new unified system mean getting things right will be very high.

The growing complexity of people's lives is one of the reasons why trying to simplify the ways in which the state makes things more complicated looks attractive. But that very complexity makes the current efforts to do so over the next few years fraught with difficulty, and may derail them entirely. Neither in the design of tax credits by the last government nor in the attempts of the current one to introduce Universal Credit does enough attention seem to have been paid to this. Caricaturing people on low incomes as being an unchanging and static underclass may make good propaganda, but it is a very poor basis for designing policy.

GOOD YEARS, BAD YEARS

Osbornes

2001

NATIONAL INCOME DISTRIBUTION	HOUSING SITUATION	INCOME
INCOME IN THE TOP 1%		£2,570 NET INCOME PER WEEK (IN 2010 TERMS)

2002

NATIONAL INCOME DISTRIBUTION	HOUSING SITUATION	INCOME
INCOME IN THE TOP 2%	MOVED BACK	£2,050 NET INCOME PER WEEK

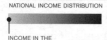

2003

NATIONAL INCOME DISTRIBUTION	HOUSING SITUATION	INCOME
INCOME IN THE TOP 2%	HEART SURGERY	£1,800 NET INCOME PER WEEK

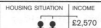

2005

NATIONAL INCOME DISTRIBUTION	HOUSING SITUATION	INCOME
INCOME IN THE TOP 2%		£1,550 NET INCOME PER WEEK

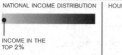
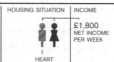

2006

NATIONAL INCOME DISTRIBUTION	HOUSING SITUATION	INCOME
INCOME IN THE TOP 2%		£1,710 NET INCOME PER WEEK

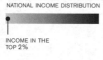

2008

NATIONAL INCOME DISTRIBUTION	HOUSING SITUATION	INCOME
INCOME IN THE TOP 2%		£1,900 NET INCOME PER WEEK

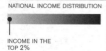

2010

NATIONAL INCOME DISTRIBUTION	HOUSING SITUATION	INCOME
REMAINED IN THE TOP 2% OF INCOME DISTRIBUTION		£1,800 NET INCOME PER WEEK

Ackroyds

2001

NATIONAL INCOME DISTRIBUTION	HOUSING SITUATION	INCOME
JUST ABOVE POOREST 5TH OF THE POPULATION		£510 NET INCOME PER WEEK (IN 2010 TERMS)

2003

NATIONAL INCOME DISTRIBUTION	HOUSING SITUATION	INCOME
MIDDLE 5TH OF THE NATIONAL INCOME DISTRIBUTION		£490 PER WEEK / £90 PER WEEK

2004

NATIONAL INCOME DISTRIBUTION	HOUSING SITUATION	INCOME
SECOND 5TH OF THE NATIONAL INCOME DISTRIBUTION	MOVED BACK + CHLOE	£490 PER WEEK / £100 PER WEEK / £140 PER WEEK CHILD TAX CREDIT & INCOME SUPPORT

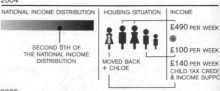

2005

NATIONAL INCOME DISTRIBUTION	HOUSING SITUATION	INCOME
ABOVE THE MIDDLE OF THE NATIONAL INCOME DISTRIBUTION		£490 PER WEEK / £250 PER WEEK

2006

NATIONAL INCOME DISTRIBUTION	HOUSING SITUATION	INCOME
OFFICIALLY 'POOR', INCOME JUST ABOVE THE BOTTOM TENTH		£300 PER WEEK NET PAY AND BENEFITS

2008

NATIONAL INCOME DISTRIBUTION	HOUSING SITUATION	INCOME
MIDDLE 5TH OF THE NATIONAL INCOME DISTRIBUTION		£503 PER WEEK

2010

NATIONAL INCOME DISTRIBUTION	HOUSING SITUATION	INCOME
TOP HALF OF THE NATIONAL INCOME DISTRIBUTION (BETTER OFF THAN NEARLY 60% OF THE POPULATION)		£473 PER WEEK

5. Good years, bad years

Reacting to change

Jim Ackroyd's original work as a fork-lift truck driver was much steadier, with regular hours, than his son Gary's was to be as a van driver. But over their lives Jim and Tracy's circumstances still changed a lot from year to year. This happened not just because of the period of unemployment he had in the mid-2000s, but also because of the changing size of their family as the children grew up, left home, and, in Michelle's case, came back for a while when she and her partner Wayne split up.

Looking over the 10 years up to 2010, things had been tight at the start in 2001. Jim was still earning two-thirds of average male earnings in the factory, and Tracy was working part time in a shop (earning the equivalent of £125 per week in terms of 2010 earnings, as with the other income figures below). But they still had all three children living at home – Michelle then 19, Gary just finishing school at 16, and their youngest, Paul, aged 10, just finishing primary school.[1] With Child Benefit for the two younger ones and a little bit from the new WFTC, their net income that year was around £510 per week (again in 2010 terms). But allowing for five of them to share that, the national income distribution figures would have put them only just above the poorest fifth of the population.[2]

But over the next two years, things got easier. Michelle moved out, and for the first time Gary and Paul had separate bedrooms in their three-bedroom council house. Gary started earning a little alongside some time in college for the next two years. By 2003, if you included the £90 per week Gary was now earning, so three of them were in work, the family's total income would have put them just into the middle fifth of the national income distribution.[3]

This did not last long. Michelle split up with Wayne and for a while in 2004 she and two-year-old Chloe moved back in with Jim and Tracy, and the boys had to share a bedroom again. Michelle was on Income Support and maximum Child Tax Credit, and Gary was now bringing in £100 per week. With that income, their overall position – if it wasn't for crowding with the two boys back in one bedroom and Michelle and Chloe in the other – wasn't too much worse than the year before.[4]

By the next year Michelle got her own housing association flat, partly because of their over-crowding, and Gary now had a (usually) full-time job, bringing in £250 per week after tax. Together, the family's income was enough to put them just above the middle of the income distribution for the first time – £740 per week for the four of them still at home.[5]

In 2006 Gary met Denise and he moved out. And then the company Jim worked for went bust and he was laid off. Despite his strenuous efforts – and some short-term jobs – he was still out of work a year later in 2007. To start with, Jim got Jobseeker's Allowance on the basis of his uninterrupted National Insurance record since the 1980s. Tracy kept working, but one effect of that was that even with Jim out of work, they only received assistance of £26 towards their rent and £11 towards Council Tax. Altogether, their income now for the three of them came to around £300 per week, before paying rent and Council Tax. For the first time in their lives they would officially be counted as poor, with their income just above the bottom tenth.[6]

By 2007 Jim's insurance-based benefits had run out and he had to claim the means-tested version. With the stress of it all, Tracy also stopped working for a short period. For a while they were on means-tested Jobseeker's Allowance and full Housing and Council Tax Benefit. But by now Paul was 16 and staying on at school for the sixth form after doing well in his GCSEs, and he got an Education Maintenance Allowance. Overall, this left them in pretty much the same place as they had been the year before.[7]

After that, life got easier. Later in 2007, despite the looming financial crisis, Jim got a new job, slightly better paid than the old one, and Tracy got back into work, so they were both at work again in 2008. Paul did well in his A-levels, and by 2010 he was the first member of the family to go to university. That left Jim and Tracy, now aged 52 and 50, at home as empty-nesters. Their earnings weren't much different compared to national averages than they ever had been, but with only the two of them to worry about now, their income of £473 per week put them back in the top half of the income distribution – in fact, better off than nearly 60 per cent of the population. For the moment, they were better off than they had ever been.

Stephen and Henrietta Osborne had an eventful decade too. Back in 1990 Stephen, now aged 46, had left the big accountancy firm he had started in and set up as a self-employed consultant, helping with company restructuring. It was long hours, international travel, and a lot of stress, but it went very well. By 2001 his gross earnings from it had reached £140,000 (at 2010–11 levels). He was left with £112,000 after tax, allowing for his (tax-efficient) savings. The part-time teaching Henrietta had done since the children were in secondary school brought in another £10,000, and the income she got from the (rather conservatively invested) inheritance she had received in 1990, a further £12,000. All in all, they had an after tax income of more than £2,500 per week, and with both the children off – most of the time – at university, they were already empty-nesters. It felt comfortable – and indeed their income was comfortably within the top 1 per cent.

But in 2002, while Charlotte was back with them after university, Stephen had his first heart attack, and then in 2003, a more serious one, followed by heart surgery. This meant several months away from work those years, and in 2003 Henrietta also took time off work to help after the operation. Overall, their net income dropped to £2,050 per week over 2002 (with three of them in the household) and about £1,800 in 2003 (between the two of them), with part coming from Stephen's insurance while he was off work. Despite the drop in income, they were still in the top 2 per cent of the income distribution (as can be seen from Figure 2.5 in Chapter 2).[8]

But after this, Stephen decided he had to reduce his stress levels so he took a more regular job back with a local accountancy firm. That meant a drop in pay – to £70,000 gross, or £50,000 after tax, not so different from what he had been on back in the late 1980s (but without such long hours). But he started to draw down income from the very successful property trust he had been investing in since the early 1990s, bringing in another £8,000 a year (net of its rather favourable tax treatment). Their income was down to £1,550 a week in 2005, slowly building back up again to £1,900 in 2008.

In the last two years of the decade, Henrietta cut back her teaching so she had a day a week to help Henry and Clare with their first granddaughter, Lucy. At the same time, the stock market fell, and her investment income, which had built up to £18,000 in the boom by 2008, dipped to £12,000 in 2009, partly recovering to £16,000 in 2010. Although the underlying value of Stephen's property portfolio had fallen a bit, property prices had doubled in the 10 years before, so there was plenty of room for Stephen to draw down much the same income from it. By 2010, with Stephen now earning £61,000 after tax and Henrietta £7,000, their total income was still more than £90,000, or nearly £1,800 per week. Despite the change in lifestyle Stephen's health problems had led to, and his less hectic working life, and despite the variations in the real value of their incomes over the decade, they remained within the top 2 per cent of the income distribution, as they had been since 2002.

THIS CHAPTER LOOKS at what these kinds of year-to-year variations look like across the whole population. Does the national survey evidence suggest that the swings in position experienced by the Ackroyds over the 10 years described are common or unusual, and do people at or near the top like the Osbornes tend to stay there?

Chapter 4 looked at the way in which people's circumstances can change rapidly from week to week or month to month within a single year. This chapter looks at the evidence on how people's circumstances change over the medium term – over a number of years – and what the implications can be for thinking about policy, illustrated by two examples: who should live in social housing, and how we help some lower-income students pay for their higher education.

The message of the research reviewed is something that often seems hard for those debating policy to grasp: there is both continuity *and* change in people's circumstances from year to year. We do not live in a country where there is an annual lottery to determine at random who is rich and who is poor for the coming year regardless of where they started last year. But nor do people generally stay stuck in the same place. Those who start poor are more *likely* to stay poor the next year than those who do not, and those who start rich more *likely* to stay rich. But many in each group – and those in between – move up or down the income ladder from year to year.

Tangled spaghetti

The fact that we can carry out this research is thanks to a survey, the British Household Panel Survey (BHPS), which started in the early 1990s and has gone back to interview the same people each year since.[9] Over time, some people refused to take part any more, some died, and some could not be traced after they had moved. In the second year, 88 per cent of those originally interviewed took part again, and by the third year, 79 per cent of them. But after that, the drop-out rate fell, and by the 13th wave of interviews in 2004, 65 per cent of the original participants were still in the survey, and 55 per cent had been interviewed in all the waves.[10] As we know what the people who dropped out were like, the findings from those who remain can be adjusted to be representative of all those who started.

Stephen Jenkins and colleagues pioneered analysis of what respondents told the survey about their changing incomes, and this is now built into the DWP's annual analysis of trends in low incomes, with patterns now visible for up to 17 years since 1991.[11]

Jenkins has likened trying to understand the patterns that underlie the picture revealed by the BHPS to 'untangling cooked spaghetti'. Quite how tangled that spaghetti is when you analyse it can be seen in Figure 5.1, looking at the incomes of a restricted group of the sample – women with A-levels or better qualifications born in 1966 and so aged 25 at the start of the survey. The incomes shown are defined in the same way as those used to look at income distribution in Chapter 2 – household income after direct taxes, adjusted for household size. The vertical scale is logarithmic, so movements up and down correspond to similar *percentage* rises and falls.

Even similar people do not live their economic lives in parallel

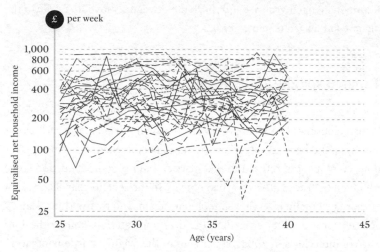

Figure 5.1– Income-age trajectories for women born in 1966 from 1991 to 2007

Right at the top of Figure 5.1, the richest woman – with an initial income of around £900 per week (at January 2008 prices) – has a rather dull time of it until she is 32, after which her income drops and she joins the tangle of the other trajectories shown. But apart from that observation Figure 5.1 (and its equivalent for men, not shown here) shows considerable variation from year to year. There is a general tendency for income to rise, particularly after the late 1990s, and people do not often move right across the income range. But what Figure 5.1 and other analysis show is certainly not one of economic lives lived in parallel, with people's relative positions fixed rigidly in place from year to year.

To try to make sense of these complicated patterns, John Rigg and Tom Sefton took the data from the first 10 waves of the BHPS and divided the patterns they saw for all members of the survey into six 'trajectory types'. How often they saw each type is shown in Figure 5.2, by comparison with how 10,000 randomly generated trajectories would be classified. The types were:

- *Flat:* within a band around the individual's mean income for the 10 years (or waves).[12]
- *Flat with blips:* flat, apart from two periods outside that band.
- *Rising:* a significant move up the income distribution over the 10 waves.
- *Falling:* a significant fall down the distribution over the 10 waves.
- *Fluctuating:* at least three substantive movements up and down the distribution over the 10-year period.
- *Other:* all other patterns.

While incomes change a lot, they do not do so at random

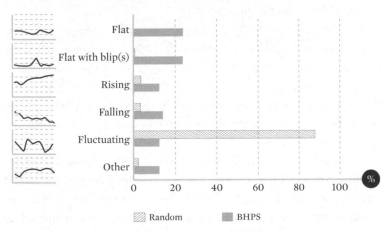

Figure 5.2 – Income trajectories in the first 10 years of BHPS compared to random patterns

An example trajectory in each group is shown in the icon to the left of the bars in the figure. In these terms, Jim and Tracy Ackroyd's incomes between 2001 and 2010 would be counted as 'fluctuating', with a rise up the distribution from the 21st percentile in 2001 to the 55th in 2005, then a fall to a low point of the 11th and 12th percentiles in 2006 and 2007, before rising again to the 59th percentile at the end of the period. Stephen and Henrietta Osborne's income would be counted as 'flat': they spent their time either in the top 1 per cent of the distribution (at the start) or in the next 1 per cent after Stephen's heart attacks in 2002 and 2003. Their income for most of the period was around a quarter less than it had been in the peak year of 2001, but they were so far up the income ladder at that point that even with that lower income, they remained very close to the top.

Although there is a great deal of movement, using these criteria, half of the sample had income trajectories over the 10 years classified as 'flat' or 'flat with blips', that is, they spent the 10 years with at most two exceptions within a fairly narrow band in the income distribution. Another quarter had incomes that rose or fell significantly over the period. But the remaining quarter had trajectories that fluctuated up and down substantially over time or were more erratic and not caught by any of these classifications.

By contrast, if we really did live in a lottery country, the patterns would look very different. Essentially nobody's income would be expected to be 'flat' on this basis – the odds would be lower than that of rolling 10 sixes in a row with a fair die. Overall, only 9 per cent rather than the actual 75 per cent would fall in the first four classifications. Nearly nine out of ten randomly generated income paths would fall into the 'fluctuating' category.

The implication of all this is that there is a lot of income variability, as illustrated in Figure 5.1, but it is not random. For many, it is as if income variations are held within limits – what Stephen Jenkins has called a 'rubber band model' of income. People's incomes tend to fluctuate around a long-term average or trend, but usually come back towards it – unless some kind of shock snaps the rubber band, job gain or loss, or household formation or dissolution, for instance.[13]

Why do incomes change?

Demography

Looking at their 10-year results in more detail, Rigg and Sefton found that children, young single adults, single parents and adults in families with older children were most likely to have upward trajectories, while both younger and older couples without children were more likely to be downwardly mobile. Pensioners were the most likely to have flat trajectories. In a pattern that Seebohm Rowntree would have recognised a century before, the events most associated with rising incomes were partnership formation and children leaving home; those most associated with falling incomes were having children and retirement. Partnership breakdown was most associated with fluctuating incomes – except for fathers with children, for whom it was associated with *rising* incomes, as they moved to smaller households but kept more of their income.[14]

As with the speed with which people's labour market positions can change across the year described earlier in Chapter 4, changes in family circumstances are more common than often assumed. Looking just at the changes over one year at the start of the BHPS, between 1991 and 1992, a sixth of all those aged 15 or over experienced some form of change in household structure, such as leaving home, siblings leaving home, partnership formation, birth or departure of a child, separation or joining with another household, or death of a partner.[15] Looking over the period from 1991 to 2006, in each year:

- 1.3 per cent of those who started as single and had never married became married, and 5.9 per cent started cohabiting;
- 13 per cent of those who were cohabiting got married, but 7 per cent of those cohabiting split up;
- 98 per cent of those who were married remained married, but 7 per cent of those who were divorced and 14 per cent of those who were separated were married or cohabiting the following year.[16]

Looking more narrowly at families with children in the period from 2001 to 2005, 97 per cent of those who started as couples with children remained in couples the next year, but 3 per cent were lone-parent families the next year. Of those who were lone parents in one year, 9 per cent were in couples the next year.[17]

People also move house and change housing tenure. For instance, of those officially classed as the 'household reference person' (usually the higher earning adult in the household) in England in 2005–06, 8 per cent had moved within the year. Moving was most common for private tenants, with a third moving – 23 per cent moving within private renting, but 9 per cent moving out of the sector (most to owner-occupation). Five per cent of social tenants moved within social housing, and 2 per cent moved out of social housing. However, only 4 per cent of owner-occupiers moved, three-quarters of those staying within owner-occupation.[18]

Earnings

Over a period of years, as well as changes in job, some people benefit from career progression and rising wages relative to others as they become older and more experienced. But this is a more limited phenomenon than those lucky enough to benefit from it might suppose. Figure 5.3 shows the pattern revealed by Richard Disney and colleagues' analysis of data from the Labour Force Survey from 1994 to 2006. It shows average hourly wages in real terms by age for four categories of worker, all in the private sector – men and women with high levels of education as well as those with low levels of education.[19]

For men with high levels of education there is indeed career progression, with a steep rise from their early twenties to their early forties. But after that, wages flatten out, and after their early fifties, wages start to decline. But for women, even with high qualifications, the increase stops in their mid-thirties, after which average wages are lower. Within the public sector (not shown), wages for highly educated men rise all the way through their careers, while for highly educated women, wages level out (but do not decline) after their mid-thirties. By contrast, for those with low levels of education in the private sector, the rise in wages for men up to their late thirties is much slower, after which they gradually fall, while for women there is virtually no wage progression at all, with average hourly wages remaining much the same at all ages.

Superimposed on these average patterns of wages by age are, of course, individual variations of the kind discussed in Chapter 4 within the year, and job changes and periods of unemployment. But also, general economic growth – until recent years, at least – has meant that real wages have been increasing in general from year to year, the effects of which are excluded from Figure 5.3.

Rising career earnings are much more important for highly qualified men than for others

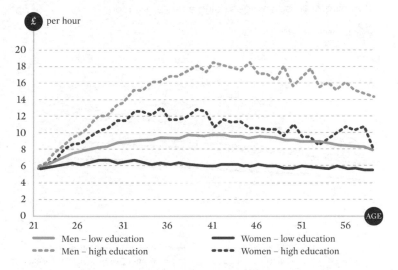

Figure 5.3 – Age-earnings profiles by gender, private sector employees with high and low education, UK (gross hourly wages in 2000 terms)

As part of his analysis 'untangling the spaghetti' of individual income trajectories of the kind shown in Figure 5.1, Stephen Jenkins used BHPS data from 1991 to 2007 to analyse what happened on average to hourly wages for men and women born before 1955, with three levels of qualifications. The results from this are shown in Figure 5.4. When overall growth in wages is allowed for on top of changes in *relative* wages as people age, nearly all of the groups actually experienced rising real wages as they aged from 25 to 50, apart from men with no qualifications after they were 45.

This is a reminder that the lower relative wages shown for some groups of older men and women in analysis such as that in Figure 5.3 do not always mean that their real wages have been falling as they got older – in good times, overall growth can offset the age effects. On the other hand, with at best stagnant average wages in real terms since around 2003, there will not have been the boost from economic growth to offset age effects of this kind.

But in the 1990s and early 2000s, overall economic growth meant that all groups saw wages rising as they got older

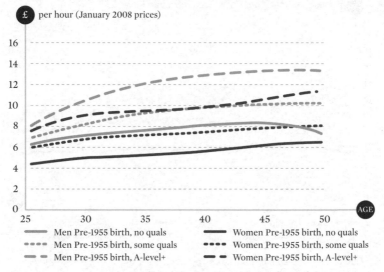

Figure 5.4 – Average hourly wage-age trajectories for men and women born before 1955 by qualifications

Disability

From popular discussion, it might be thought that when people develop conditions that lead to them becoming disabled, they enter a one-way street. But this is actually far from the case. For instance, Tania Burchardt found from analysing BHPS data in the 1990s that each year, 3 per cent of those in work newly reported that they had become 'limited in daily activities' in some way. Half of these reported that they were still limited a year later – but half did not. Where people did develop limiting conditions while in work, a sixth lost their job within the first year, compared with 7 per cent of those not developing such conditions. After this, disabled people regained work at only a sixth of the rate of non-disabled people (and at a quarter of the rate of non-disabled people, after allowing for the smaller proportion of disabled people who say they want to work).[20]

For some conditions, particularly those affecting mental health, change can be very rapid, a fact that is the source of considerable difficulty and distress for some people who are assessed for their 'fitness to work' in considering entitlement to disability benefits, if the assessment happens to be carried out on a 'good day'. The 'cliff edge' nature of benefit conditionality does not reflect how swiftly people's conditions can change.[21] Overall, half of claimants of incapacity benefits report that they have fluctuating conditions.[22]

Fewer than half of those starting on Incapacity Benefit in the mid-2000s stayed on it for more than a year

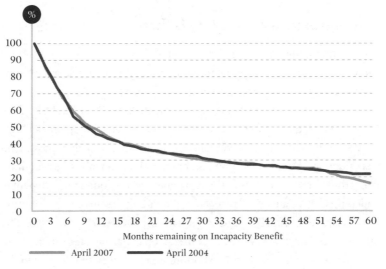

Figure 5.5 – Proportion of claimants remaining on Incapacity Benefit or Severe Disablement Allowance, spells starting in April 2004 and April 2007

One result of this is that receiving incapacity benefits can be much shorter term than some suppose, as can be seen from the DWP statistics in Figure 5.5, relating to claims of what used to be Incapacity Benefit (or Severe Disablement Allowance) starting in April 2004 (that is, before the economic crisis) or April 2007 (coinciding with the economic crisis). These figures are not entirely straightforward to interpret, as some of those starting to receive incapacity benefits were previously on sickness benefits paid by their firms, but did not recover within six months. This biases the sample towards those who recover more slowly. On the other hand, other entrants to Incapacity Benefit were previously receiving unemployment benefits and might be claiming for shorter periods of sickness.

While the turnover is much less rapid than for Jobseeker's Allowance (see Figure 4.8 in Chapter 4), it is still considerable. For those starting at either date, 2004 or 2007, fewer than half were still receiving benefits 12 months later. Two-thirds had ended their claim within 24 months, and three-quarters within four years.[23]

How much income mobility is there?

The combination of changes in people's family circumstances, their career paths, and their health conditions mean that many people change positions within the income distribution from year to year – and even more so over a longer period. Figure 5.6, again drawn from analysis of the BHPS following the same people from 1991 to 2006 by Stephen Jenkins, shows quite how much movement there is – but also that those who start poor are more likely to remain poor, and those who start rich more likely to stay rich. The bars of the two panels correspond to where people ended up in 1992 and 2006 respectively, dividing the income distribution into twentieths, with the people ending up poorest at the bottom. The different shadings show where those people had started up in 1991, showing those who *started* in the bottom tenth (darker shading) or in the top tenth (lighter shading).

Half of those who started in the poorest tenth in 1991 were also in it in 1992 (the two bottom bars of the first panel). But half had moved out of it. That was not usually very far, however, with nearly half of these just moving to the next tenth, and only a few moving from the modern equivalent of rags to riches in a single year.

Over longer periods people move further across the income distribution, but those starting poor remain more likely to end with low incomes

Original position in 1991:　█ Bottom 10%　▨ Top 10%

(a) Position in 1992 (Wave 2)

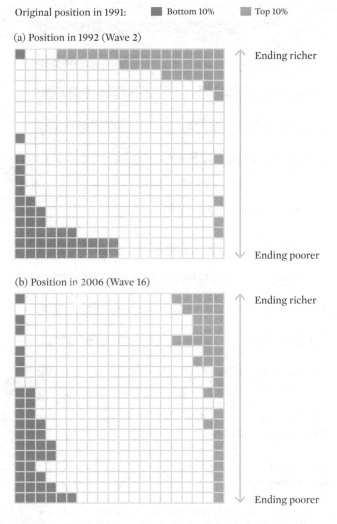

(b) Position in 2006 (Wave 16)

Figure 5.6 – Positions in income distributions of 1992 and 2006 of those who started in top and bottom tenths of distribution in 1991

Few people stay in the same income group every year, but many starting poor are poor in most years

(a) 1991 to 1999 by fifths of income in 1991

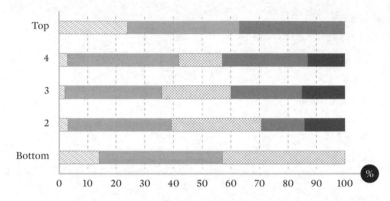

(b) 1991 to 2008 by fifths of income in 1991

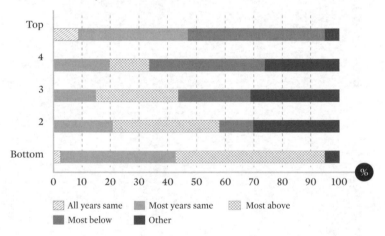

Figure 5.7 – Where people starting in different fifths of the income distribution spend their time over following years

There is somewhat less mobility, initially at least, at the top. Two-thirds of those ending in the richest tenth (the top two bars) in 1992 had started within it the previous year. Indeed, two-thirds of those in the richest 5 per cent in 1992 had also been in the richest 5 per cent in 1991.[24] None the less, there were some with high incomes who fell down the distribution, and even a few (but not many) whose reversal of fortune meant that they ended up in the bottom half.

The second panel breaks down movements over a much longer period – showing where people in different parts of the 2006 distribution had started from in 1991. Now there is much more change. Only a quarter of those ending up in the poorest tenth (the bottom two bars) had their origins in the bottom tenth in 1991. Most people who started in the bottom tenth were spread across the bottom half of the distribution, although a few had even reached the very top. Similarly, less than a quarter of those ending up in the richest tenth had started in it 15 years earlier. Those who started with the highest tenth of incomes were also spread out across the distribution, although still overwhelmingly within the top half of it. In this respect, Stephen and Henrietta Osborne are a little atypical in the way their incomes stayed right at the top through the 1990s and 2000s as described at the start of the chapter, while in reality only 15 per cent of those starting with the highest twentieth of incomes as long ago as 1991 were still there in 2006. Despite all the movement, however, someone who started in the poorest tenth was about five times as likely to end up in the poorest fifth 15 years later as someone who started in the top tenth. Someone who started in the top tenth was similarly around five times as likely to end up in the top fifth as someone who started in the bottom tenth. Someone who started in the bottom tenth was more than three times as likely to end up in the bottom half as someone who started in the top tenth.

Figure 5.7 gives another way of showing how much people change their positions over time, in this case taken from analysis by the DWP, first for the nine years from 1991 to 1999, and then for the 18 years from 1991 to 2008. Each of the bars shows the pattern that followed for those starting in successive fifths of the original distribution back in 1991. Twenty-four per cent of those starting in the top fifth stayed within it for all of the first nine years, although only 9 per cent of them managed to stay there for all of the 18 years. Forty-seven per cent of them spent at least the majority of all 18 years in the top fifth. More than half of those starting in the bottom fifth spent at least the majority of the first nine years there, and 43 per cent of them at least the majority of all 18 years. By contrast, there was much more movement up and down for those starting in one of the other fifths – and indeed, *none* of those spent all 18 years in the same fifth as they started in.

Looking over time, since 1991 the level of mobility from year to year – measured in a number of ways – has stayed much the same.[25]

This means that if we looked at income added up over a number of years, it would look somewhat less unequal than it does when measured at a single moment. At the same time, even averaging income over a large number of years would not eliminate inequality – people have good and bad years, but that does not mean they would all end up looking the same if they could smooth their incomes out over time.

Do poor people stay poor?

For policy purposes the extent to which people who are poor at one moment are likely to stay poor matters greatly. If they stayed remorselessly poor, that would of course be worse for them. It might also be confirmation of there being a cut-off 'underclass', permanently excluded from the rest of society – and perhaps from its sympathies. This could be a result of injustice, society's failures, or of a 'dependency culture'. On the other hand, if most poverty comes only in short spells, perhaps people could cope with it through their own savings, or some form of insurance – and to the extent they could not, the rest of society might be more sympathetic to those facing the same risks as themselves.

From what we have seen already, the truth looks likely to be a much more complicated situation between these two extremes, and Figure 5.8 shows why it is more complicated. It shows, for people who start a 'spell' of being poor in one year, for how many years in a row they would continue to be seen as being poor. Nearly half (45 per cent) would have left poverty by the end of the first year. After two years only 35 per cent remain poor. So most spells, or episodes of poverty, are fairly short. Jim and Tracy Ackroyd, poor in two successive snapshots in the mid-2000s but then out of poverty, would be in the 65 per cent whose poverty spells last no longer than this. But 10 per cent of those starting a spell in poverty remain poor for long spells of eight or more years. And, of course, some of those who escape from poverty in one year may drop back into it in another.

Only a third of those moving into poverty remain poor for more than two years, but a tenth remain poor for eight years or more

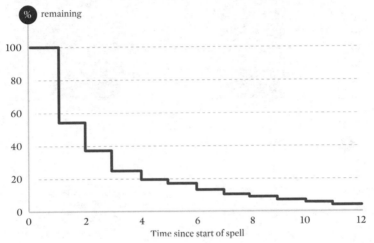

Figure 5.8 – Length of spell of poverty starting in one year

The result of this pattern of varying rates of escape from poverty – and of people dropping back into it – is that many more people have some experience of poverty at points over a number of years than are poor at any one time. Long-term persistent poverty is much more rare, although likely to a much more serious problem for those who suffer it. Figure 5.9 summarises what the patterns look like over two nine-year periods, one starting in 1991, and the other in 1998. In this case it shows a welcome decline in how many people are affected by the most persistent poverty comparing the two periods, and particularly for children.

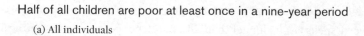

Half of all children are poor at least once in a nine-year period

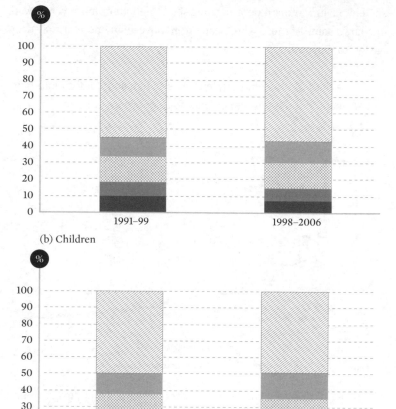

Figure 5.9 – Patterns of poverty persistence over nine-year periods

The top panel (a) shows that more than half of all individuals were never poor (using a relative definition) in either of the nine-year periods. On the other hand, more than two-fifths were affected by poverty at some point over either of the nine years – and the lower panel (b) shows that this was true of *half* of the children. In each case, this is around twice as many who were poor at any one time.[26] For an increasing proportion of those who did experience poverty, this was a one-off experience. By the second nine-year period, 30 per cent of all people, including 36 per cent of children, experienced poverty in more than one year. For most of these this took the form of two or more repeated spells, covering a total of two to six of the nine years. For a smaller group it was a single spell of two to six years. But in the first period a tenth of all individuals and children were poor in at least seven of the nine years. Looking at the period from 1998 to 2006, however, this 'long-term persistent poverty' rate was down to around 7 per cent, and slightly less for children.

On official measures persistent child poverty nearly halved between the early 1990s and mid-2000s

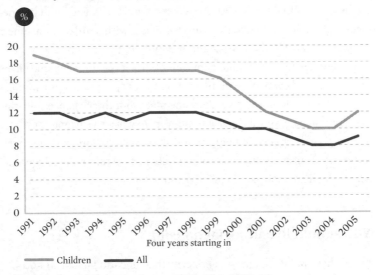

Figure 5.10 – Persistent low income 1991–94 to 2005–08

This fall in persistent poverty over the last two decades up to the crisis is confirmed by DWP figures using the official definition of 'persistent low income', used, for instance, as one of the key indicators in monitoring progress in reducing child poverty. This looks at whether people are found to be poor (using the threshold of 60 per cent of median contemporary income) in three or more years of a four-year period. The trends in this in four-year periods from 1991–94 to 2005–08 are shown in Figure 5.10.

Through the 1990s around 12 per cent of all people and a sixth of all children were persistently poor on this kind of definition. But these rates fell, particularly for children, after 1998. Overall poverty rates were falling – quite quickly for children (see Figure 3.7 in Chapter 3 earlier) – and this was not just a matter of fewer short-term spells. By 2003–07, only 8 per cent of all individuals were affected by persistent low income, and only 10 per cent of children – half the rate at the start of the 1990s. However, coinciding with the economic crisis, the total numbers in 2005–08 had risen, back to where they had been earlier in that decade (coinciding with a levelling out in the overall child poverty rate between 2005–06 and 2008–09) (see Figure 3.7). Falling pensioner poverty also contributed to the overall change, with a fifth of pensioners persistently poor in the 1990s, falling to only 14 per cent by 2005–08.

In summary, there is quite a lot of mobility in people's incomes from year to year, and even more mobility if we look at people across a number of years. People do not stay stuck in one place. But their chances of being poor are much greater if they were poor in an earlier year, and they have a much greater chance of being rich if they were rich in an earlier year. These two facts are at the heart of a number of current policy dilemmas, two of which are looked at in more detail below.

Who should live in social housing?

One of these policy dilemmas concerns the allocation of social housing. Today, social housing – rented out at below market rents by councils and not-for-profit housing associations – is in many people's minds synonymous with housing people with low incomes. But it was not always like that – back in 1979, more than 30 per cent of people with incomes in the *top* half of the income distribution lived in social housing. By 2004, it was fewer than 10 per cent.[27] Between those years, the supply of social housing available to let to new tenants each year dwindled – fewer new houses were built; property was sold off through the 'Right to Buy', so that when occupants moved or died it was not available as social housing; and fewer tenants moved out of social housing or died. The reaction was increasingly to allocate what became available to those in the greatest need rather than, for instance, those who had been waiting the longest.

The large majority of social tenants do indeed now have incomes in the bottom half of the income distribution, although not all are poor – 27 per cent were poor in 2011–12 before allowing for housing costs, 43 per cent after allowing for them.[28] Fewer are *persistently* poor – 22 per cent of those living in social housing were poor (before housing costs) for three or more years of the four years from 2005–08, for instance, although that was more than twice the rate for the population as a whole.[29]

There are two contrasting reactions to this situation. One is to argue that, given the acute shortage of social housing and long queues trying to get into it, we should make sure the housing is lived in *only* by those who are currently poor. If people's circumstances change, as we have shown, and they entered social housing because they were in need, why should they continue to get the benefits of a below-market rent when they are no longer in need?

One proposal following from this is that social housing should only be let on a short-term basis, as a kind of temporary refuge. Every few years, people should be reassessed, and if they are no longer in need, their tenancy should come to an end, and they should move. Indeed, the current Coalition government has allowed social landlords to offer short-term tenancies to new tenants, and some have begun to do this.[30]

It does not need much thought, however, to see the disastrous disincentive this kind of situation might set up: 'get a job, lose your home'. This would more than negate one of the advantages of social housing compared to paying private rents, that the 'poverty trap' (where the income people take home increases by only a very small proportion of any increase in earnings, as illustrated in Figure 4.9) extends much less far. If someone is out of work and having their rent covered along with the standard amounts for the rest of their living costs, their Housing Benefit is a larger sum, the higher the rent they pay. If benefits are withdrawn as a fixed share in the pound (the means-testing 'taper'), it takes more income in work to get clear of means testing, and from the disincentives that involves.

Of course, people don't necessarily act on financial incentives, of the kind implied by the proposal, but the feeling of injustice that someone had 'done the right thing' by working and then lost their home as a result would be acute. So would be the suspicions surrounding those who survived a test of whether they were still 'needy enough' – either that they had not tried hard enough to get work, or that they had managed to hide the work they did have from the inspectors.

Because so much social housing was originally built as estates, rather than 'pepper-potted' around towns and cities, this kind of idea – that if people become better off, they should move out – also reinforces geographical polarisation between income groups, something which has already worsened since the early 1990s.[31] It may mean removing people who might have a lot to contribute to community life and most involvement in the world of work. At a personal level, it obviously disrupts people's ties to their neighbours, and where there are children, a move may also disrupt their schooling.[32]

A somewhat gentler alternative would be to allow people with higher incomes to stay, but only if they pay a higher rent – power to do this has recently been given to social landlords,[33] and Chancellor George Osborne suggested in January 2014 that this is one of the two immediate ways in which the 'welfare' budget might be cut after the 2015 General Election.[34] This is, in effect, what the Housing Benefit system does, until people's income is high enough for it to reduce the benefit to zero. Making social rents themselves means tested as well would have to extend this in some way – either carrying on with the means test once, for instance, Housing Benefit stops, or imposing a means test at some higher level of income. This could mean extending the main parts of the poverty trap further into the middle of the national income distribution.

Alternatively it could involve inventing a new means test higher up (at £60,000 in the government's proposals) – in reality, affecting very few people, but at the cost of greater complexity, and of the need for landlords to assess and check up on their tenants' changing incomes, with little net gain.

An alternative reaction to the situation would be to turn the logic round: if people do not use the 'breathing space' that a social housing allocation gives them to get into work, maybe they should lose their tenancy – 'get a job or you'll lose your home'.[35] This could act as a powerful incentive to try to get into work at all costs, but given the weak labour market position of many social tenants, many would not. Looking over the 10-year period from 1994 to 2004, for instance, just under half of social tenants who had been unemployed in 1994 were employed in 2004. Fifteen per cent of them were again unemployed 10 years later, and 26 per cent economically inactive for other reasons (such as long-term sickness or disability); others were over pension age.[36] In between, as we saw in both the last chapter and this, there will have been a lot of turnover in and out of work. The precise timing of when a tenancy was renewed and someone had to show that they were in work would matter a lot. But whenever it was, there would be some who would be out of work. And if they lost their tenancy, then what? Would they lose all support for their housing costs despite being out of work, or would their move to private rented housing cost more in Housing Benefit? And would it be easier or harder to get work during or after a forced move?

What these suggestions are trying to grapple with is that people's lives change. Where that involves them becoming better off, this is something to celebrate and encourage, rather than to penalise. But it may open up opportunities to support people to build their lives in other ways, and possibly to change – rather than end – their relationship with a social landlord.[37]

First, the stability of social tenancies and the lower strain put on means-tested benefits by lower rents are positive advantages that ought to help underpin efforts to help people move into work, where they can. It would be more constructive to build on them – as some landlords do where they see their role as being to deliver 'housing plus', not just a roof over people's heads, but other support as well.

Second, if people are better off, they may be in a position to build their lives in other ways, and to start building up assets. At the moment, the main way for existing tenants to do this is to exercise the Right to Buy, moving straight from being subsidised tenants to being owners – if they can raise the balance of the price after the discount. But there could be more – and easier – options than this, such as gradually building up an equity stake through some form of shared ownership in return for paying more to the landlord each month (which may involve lower subsidy in the long run, but may still be attractive), or more modestly, through some sort of 'save as you rent' scheme.

The changing dynamics of people's lives mean that what they need and the most effective ways of supporting them will change – but equally, the complexities of those dynamics mean that it is very easy to propose changes that end up being counter-productive.

Student finance and the delayed action means test[38]

A second example of the unintended consequences of failing to think through the ways in which policies can interact over time as people's circumstances change comes from recent reforms to the way students are supported in England, since fees were raised by many universities to £9,000 per year in the autumn of 2012.

Although the current system of repayments means that those who end up with low earnings over the following 30 years may end up paying back only part of these loans, many are concerned that the high fees could deter students from low-income backgrounds from going to university, reversing slow progress in narrowing the wide social class gap in university participation. In response, the government and universities have boosted bursaries and other forms of support based on *current* (or at least, recent) family income, supplementing the way in which the underlying repayment system relates to future *lifetime* graduate incomes.

In particular, as well as the existing national system of means-tested maintenance grants towards living costs while a student, individual universities and other higher education institutions have developed or invented their own bursary systems, using either the rules of the government's new National Scholarship Programme (NSP) or their own more generous ones. These have resulted in dramatically varying means tests based on parental income.

Ben Richards and I looked at the means-tested bursaries and other assistance such as fee reductions available to English undergraduate students going to 52 larger UK universities from September 2012.[39] The universities split into two main groups. Twenty-two of the universities from outside the more prestigious Russell Group[40] focused their bursaries mainly on the conditions of the government's NSP, under which no student from a family with an income of over £25,000 is entitled to means-tested support. Twenty-seven – including all but one of the Russell Group universities – had more extensive systems including support for those with parental income above £25,000. Three of the 52 universities did not advertise any means-tested support for English students.

The incomes used for the means tests were all based on the official government measure of 'residual household income'. For students starting in September 2012 this mainly consisted of their parents' gross earnings in the financial year *2010–11*, in addition to the student's projected unearned income for the *2012–13* academic year. The parental income used is *before* deducting Income Tax or National Insurance, but does not include tax credits or other benefits.[41] In thinking about interactions between this system and the rest of the tax and benefit system, this means that the effective marginal tax rates implicit in the university systems are *additional* to others applied to gross parental earnings in the period two years earlier.

Underlying individual university bursaries and fee reductions is the national means-tested maintenance grant. Its rules are the same for all English students whether living at home or away, or studying inside or outside London. For 2012–13 it was £3,250 per year for residual incomes up to £25,000. For those with higher incomes the grant is reduced smoothly at a marginal rate of around 18 per cent until £43,000. Above this there is no government grant.

For the universities basing their offers on the government's NSP, the most common pattern is that they offer a limited number of awards worth £3,000 per year to students whose parental income is no more than £25,000. This generally means that students either receive only the national maintenance grant or *may* receive additional support – usually £3,000 – provided that income is below a threshold, often £25,000. This creates a 'cliff edge' in entitlement: one pound of parental income over the £25,000 limit could mean £3,000 less support to go to university each year (although those applying will not know whether they will be one of the successful ones who will receive an award).

For the other universities there is a considerable range in generosity for the lowest-income students, from support worth less than £4,000 (Cardiff) to more than £13,000 (Oxford). Only two universities offer support for those with parental incomes above the government's £42,600 threshold. All the systems therefore involve significant withdrawal rates as family income rises, often with large drops – 'cliff edges' – at particular income levels. Very high marginal withdrawal rates – or effective marginal tax rates – are usually seen as undesirable:

- they can act as a disincentive to additional earnings;
- they can give an incentive to behaviour that reduces reported income (including misreporting of circumstances to slip below particular thresholds);
- they can lead to feelings of injustice, if those just below a threshold are treated much more favourably than those who are only slightly better off;
- uncertainty about which side of a threshold someone will fall once all the calculations are done can add to barriers to access.

In the case of student support, the immediate implications for work incentives may be limited. The main component of income used for the test is gross parental earnings two years *before* a student enters university. It is possible but probably generally unlikely that parents would change their behaviour having realised the impact of their earnings in one year on the potential position two years later of their children then starting sixth form if they then went on to university. But the second and third problems are more likely to apply, particularly where there are large cliff edges involved.

University bursary systems interact with other family taxes and means tests to create very high retrospective tax rates

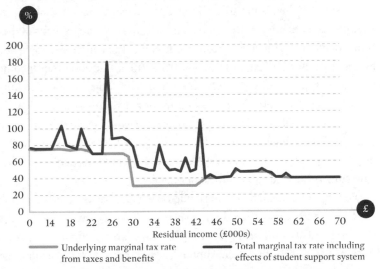

Figure 5.11 – Total effective marginal tax and withdrawal rates on £1,000 differences in parental income – average for 27 universities

But this newly important kind of means testing does not exist in isolation. Variations in gross incomes, usually earnings, will also have affected families' Income Tax and National Insurance liabilities, and entitlements to tax credits and other benefits in an earlier year. For instance, a family in the withdrawal range for tax credits in 2010–11 (the relevant year for parental incomes for students entering in autumn 2012) would *already* have been affected by a 70 per cent effective marginal tax rate from combined Income Tax, NICs, and tax credit reduction. Those with lower incomes would have faced higher marginal rates as a result of Council Tax Benefit reductions (and for tenants from Housing Benefit withdrawal). The lighter lower line in Figure 5.11 shows the effective marginal tax rates in 2010–11 from these other parts of the tax and benefit system for a two-child single-earner family paying typical Council Tax but no rent.[42]

The solid line in the figure then combines the underlying marginal tax rates that had affected a family of this kind in 2010–11, with the average effects – if income changed by £1,000 – of the student support system for first year students entering in autumn 2012 for 27 universities.[43] The results are striking. For the *entire* income range up to £43,000, the effective marginal tax and withdrawal rate exceeds 50 per cent (incidentally, the level of top rate Income Tax which was abolished by the 2012 Budget). At £30,000 and £35,000, a £1,000 rise in income only leaves the family £200 better off in the long run. At £16,000, £20,000 and £43,000, the combined marginal rate is 100 per cent or more – additional income from, say, overtime would leave the family no better off in the long run. And at the common £25,000 threshold, a rise in income of £1,000 would on average leave them £800 *worse* off in the long run, as the rate spikes at 180 per cent.

For some families the results could be even more extreme. If a child from the same kind of family had succeeded in getting a place at the University of Oxford, with the most generous bursary and fee reduction system, the loss in first year support where parents had earnings of £44,000 rather than £17,000 would be £13,050. But after allowing for taxes and for means testing of tax credits and benefits, the first family would originally have had a *net* income only £13,250 higher than the second. In effect, a family whose earnings were 180 per cent of the national median rather than 70 per cent of it would only be £200 better off as a result in the long run – effectively a *99 per cent tax rate* for the family over the bulk of the earnings distribution.

This kind of result has emerged as separate agencies – government and universities – try to protect lower-income families from the worst effects of cuts, but without coordination or thinking through the side effects of piling on more means testing within an already heavily means-tested system. In trying to take account of one kind of income variation over time – students who are currently poor, but who will be better off later on – what has emerged does not take account of how current means tests interact with those applied two years earlier.

As decentralisation extends, and more agencies become responsible for designing their own systems that may, to an extent, try to protect the poor, we are likely to see more of these kind of messy overlaps – the kinds of extreme poverty traps that the whole Universal Credit reform described in Chapter 4 was supposed to be removing.

Summary and conclusions

Data on the incomes of people who have been followed from year to year reveal a complexity that policy commentators seem to find hard to grasp. It fits neither the stereotype of rigid Britain, with an unchanging underclass and overclass, nor one of a lottery world, where people move randomly across the income distribution from year to year. Over a decade, about a quarter of people stay in much the same part of the income distribution from year to year and another quarter spend most years in a similar place, with one or two exceptional years. But things are more complicated for the other half, with more substantial movements up and down the income range, as illustrated for Jim and Tracy Ackroyd at the start of the chapter.

These movements often reflect life events. Every year household structure changes for a sixth of adults, with partnerships being formed or dissolved, children being born or leaving home, and so on. At the same time, people move in and out of work, benefit from career wage progression (although often only those with more qualifications), move home or change housing tenure, enter the labour market or retire. For many, these year-to-year changes are accompanied by more rapid short-term variations (see Chapter 4).

This has both broad and narrow implications for the way we think about public policies. For instance, most of the spells that people spend in poverty are, in fact, short, rather than long. This is good in making long-term poverty rarer, but it also means that far more people are affected by poverty at some point over a number of years than at any one moment – for instance, half of all children were in families that were poor in at least one year between 1998 and 2006. At the same time there are significant numbers that remain persistently poor – for instance, one in twenty children were in families that were poor in at least seven of those nine years. On the positive side, the extent of persistent poverty was much lower in the mid-2000s than it had been a decade before.

In broad terms this kind of fluctuation should give pause to thought for those who advocate, for instance, restrictions on the number of children in a family who should be supported by benefits on the grounds that people should trim their family sizes to what they can afford at that moment. Most people poor or out of work at any one moment were in work before, with children who arrived when they would have fitted into the approved category of 'hard-working families'. What happens afterwards is hard for anyone to predict – which is precisely why we have social systems that protect people at times when things go wrong.

More narrowly, those designing policy need to think about how to cope with circumstances that change over time, particularly if we are to avoid setting up systems with unhelpful incentives or unfair results. This chapter looked at two examples. With social housing increasingly scarce, and entry to it usually dependent on proving high levels of 'need', some have suggested that those no longer in need should have to move out. But the message of 'get a job, lose your home' would be a foolishly unhelpful one. Equally, however, the fact that people's circumstances can change suggests using the stability of social housing to help people change things for the better, and adapting and extending what is on offer to them as that happens.

Second, this chapter looked at the example of the interaction between two separate parts of policy, thought about in different places and applying at different dates. When universities were encouraged to increase student fees in 2012, many of them introduced or improved systems of bursaries of fee reductions for poorer students depending on family incomes two years earlier. Many designed systems incorporating sharp 'cliff edge' losses of thousands of pounds in support if parental income had been just a few pounds higher. In combination with the effects of Income Tax, tax credit and benefit reductions that would already have affected families, these systems have created total marginal tax rates far above the top Income Tax rate over wide income ranges – and over 100 per cent at particular thresholds. This kind of result – and there are other examples – has emerged as separate agencies have added yet more means testing to an already heavily means-tested system.

Although there are exceptions at both the top and bottom of the income distribution, we mostly do not live our lives along economic parallel lines. As a result, public policies affect many more of us over a run of years than at any one moment. By the same token, that complexity makes it easier to get the design of that policy wrong. It also means that the effects of policy changes can be over-stated if the underlying dynamics are ignored. If a percentage of people would be getting jobs anyway, for instance, the total of those who get work (or move home, in the case of housing policies) cannot be claimed as the result of a reform.

But while there is considerable change, this does not mean that people's chances are the same. If people start poor, they are more likely to end a particular period poorer than others, and if they start rich, they are more likely to end rich. Jim and Tracy Ackroyd's relative prosperity changed a great deal from year to year over the 1990s, but it would have been highly unlikely that they would have changed places with Stephen and Henrietta Osborne.

THE LONG WAVE

Stephen and
Henrietta Osborne

Jim and
Tracy Ackroyd

Osbornes

Ackroyds

£700,000
FINANCIAL
ASSETS

+

£700,000
HOUSE

+

£700,000
PENSION
RIGHTS

=

ASSETS
(PERSONAL
POSSESSIONS,
FURNITURE, CAR,
£6,000 IN A
BUILDING SOCIETY
ACCOUNT)

=

TOTAL
£2,100,000

TOTAL
£16,000

LEVEL OF WEALTH

LEVEL OF WEALTH

OF HIGHER PROFESSIONAL
PEOPLE AGED 55–64

OF COUNCIL TENANTS
AGED 55–64

JUST INTO WEALTHIEST 10%

MIDDLE OF GROUP

OF ALL HOUSEHOLDS

OF ALL HOUSEHOLDS

TOP 2%

BOTTOM 13%

6. The long wave

Wealth and retirement

Like many middle-class couples, Stephen and Henrietta Osborne are firm believers in the importance of saving to cope with whatever shocks life might throw at them, to build up assets to see them through what they hope will be a long retirement, and eventually to pass something on to their children. And the state gives them strong encouragement and help to do so. After all, if people provide for their own old age and other risks, there will be less call on scarce tax-funded spending, and at a national level saving should be good for investment and growth – in 'normal' times, at least, even if not in the depths of a recession.

Stephen and Henrietta are owner-occupiers and have quite a lot of their capital tied up in their house. Even with the children having left home and now having several spare rooms, that makes sense in tax terms. Unlike on other investments, capital gains on their main home are tax-free. With the doubling in real house prices since the mid-1990s, that has been a huge advantage. Nor is there any tax on the value to them of being able to live in their own home rent-free – whereas if they invested the money and then rented, they would have to pay tax on the investment returns that they then paid rent out of. It is true that Council Tax is a little higher for the big house they live in than it would be for a smaller one, but not by very much. And when they were first buying, they were able to claim help from mortgage interest tax relief, although that has since been abolished. If they did move, they would have to pay quite a lot in stamp duty, but that has not happened very often as they – like most owners – have only moved house infrequently. All in all, their investment in their home is close to being tax-free – particularly valuable given that Stephen is otherwise a 40 per cent taxpayer.

Their second most important asset is their pension rights. These are treated even more favourably by the tax system. Everything they have paid into them has been tax-deductible (at his 40 per cent income tax rate for Stephen), and the accountancy firm Stephen works for, and the schools Henrietta has worked for, do not have to pay employer NICs on the amounts they pay in for them.[1] So what goes in is tax-free. The funds that pensions sit in largely accumulate investment returns tax-free.[2] That might balance out, and leave pension saving as effectively tax-free overall, if the pensions that came out were going to be taxed at 40 per cent. But up to a quarter of their pension rights can be drawn out as a tax-free lump sum when they retire, and a significant part of their monthly pensions will eventually be taxed at the basic rate of 20 per cent, with no National Insurance to worry about. Putting it all together, the state effectively adds to the return on people's pension saving, with the concessions being most valuable for higher rate taxpayers, and for those who pay the most in.

For their cash savings, quite a large part is now in tax-free ISAs – they can each pay in £15,000 in 2014–15 (with no restrictions any more on how much goes into interest-bearing accounts or into stocks and shares, although they have usually mainly put them in stocks and shares), and almost as much in earlier years. They have been able to take full advantage of these since ISAs started – and were using their predecessors, known as PEPs and TESSAs, back in the 1980s and 1990s (when they were able to shift over most of the inheritance Henrietta had received into tax-free forms).[3]

That leaves only a small proportion of their wealth exposed to the taxman. In theory, capital gains tax could be quite heavy on their other stocks and shares, as the gain subject to tax no longer has an inflation allowance built into it. But the tax rate is only 28 per cent (although up from the 18 per cent it used to be before 2010), and each year they can each realise £11,000 of gains tax free, so that's not so much of a problem.

In their most prosperous times they had also dabbled in some more exotic 'tax-efficient' saving, such as the Business Expansion Scheme for rented housing Stephen helped set up in the late 1980s, which was tax-deductible on the way in, but free of capital gains tax on the way out. Unlike Henrietta's very wealthy parents they have not had to bother with things like putting money offshore – besides which, they do not think that such 'aggressive' tax avoidance is quite right.

The two of them have done well with their investments. By 2010 their financial assets (and physical property such as furniture, cars and valuables) were worth £700,000, their house as much again, and their pension rights another £700,000. The total of £2.1 million put them already just at the edge of the wealthiest 10 per cent of 'higher professional' families aged 55–64.[4] Despite this high level of wealth – putting them within the top 2 per cent of all households – nearly all of it was in tax-free, or even tax-augmented forms. They have been successful in putting money aside – and the state has helped them generously to do so.

Jim and Tracy Ackroyd also believe in saving – when they can. As things have turned out, that has been hard, although with a small nest egg Tracy inherited in the 1980s they have managed to save a little. By 2010, their total wealth, including all their personal possessions, furniture, the car Jim uses to get to work, and £6,000 in a building society account came to £16,000. Half of (slightly older) council tenant households aged 55–64 had more physical and financial wealth than this, half had less.[5]

It was only in the last few years that they transferred their savings into a 'cash' ISA, so although interest rates are now at rock bottom, they are no longer paying tax on what they do get. In the 1990s, with their savings in a standard building society account, they paid tax on the nominal returns they received. With inflation that often meant they were paying tax, even though in real terms their savings were getting little return or even losing value, making the tax rate on their real return above inflation way over normal income tax rates.

But that was not the biggest penalty that public policy can put on small savers like them. Having savings can count heavily against social security entitlements. In fact, if working-age people had savings of more than £3,000 (in nominal terms) in the years from 1984 to 2005, any Income Support or means-tested Jobseeker's Allowance entitlement they had would have been cut back by £1 per week for every £250 of savings over the threshold – effectively treating people as if they were getting annual returns of more than 20 per cent (or, in reality, expecting them to run their savings down at that rate). Luckily for the Ackroyds, in 2005 Jim was on the non-means-tested version of Jobseeker's Allowance, and by the time they were on the means-tested version in 2006, the threshold had been raised for the first time in more than 20 years to £6,000 (where it has been since), so it did not affect them.[6] Savings of more than £16,000 would rule working-age people out of means-tested benefits entirely.

An even bigger potential penalty for savers who do manage to build up more comes from the capital rules for assistance with long-term care, if someone needs it. Under the 2010–11 rules in England (still applying in 2014–15), for instance, those with savings (not including a house in which a partner still lives) of more than £14,250 would have to contribute towards care costs, again on the assumption that they could pay more than 20 per cent of the excess towards them each year. Savings of over £23,250 would rule someone out of getting any help entirely – until they were run down to that level. So, if either Jim or Tracy did end up needing residential care later in life, they could find that a lifetime of saving would have done them little or no good. As this chapter discusses, however, these rules are set to change from 2016.

But it could have been different for them. With a bit more capital or ability to borrow at the right moment, they might have been able to buy their council house at a very substantial discount. A 50 per cent Right to Buy discount in the 1990s on a property now worth, say, £120,000 would effectively have represented being given equity of £60,000 today. And capital tied up in housing would not affect means-tested benefits or assistance with care (if the other partner is still at home). The state would have greatly added to any capital they could have put together back then.

At their levels of pay, and working in the private sector, the chances were that Jim and Tracy would not have been in private pension schemes. But if they had been working for one of the bigger companies that offered a pension back in 2001, when both Gary and Paul were at school, any pension contributions they made then would have meant higher tax credits (as contributions are deductible in assessing income). Someone paying Income Tax and receiving means-tested tax credits would then only have had to sacrifice about £41 of income to put £100 into a pension pot.[7] Even allowing for some tax on the pension on the way out, this would be an even better pension deal than the tax relief from which higher rate taxpayers benefit.

As THINGS HAVE turned out – and this would be the case for many small savers – far from rewarding or encouraging their saving in the way the state does for the Osbornes, the returns on Jim and Tracy's savings have been more heavily taxed, and in some circumstances could be very harshly treated by means testing for benefits or support for residential care. But some people in fairly similar circumstances to them might have been treated much more favourably – to some extent that would be the luck of the draw (depending on whether they had bought under the Right to Buy or ended up needing residential care, for instance). As the first part this chapter describes, that is now a very big draw indeed, given the much greater importance of wealth and differences in it than in the past.

So far this book has looked at how public policies – the welfare state and taxes – affect people's flows of incomes from week to week and year to year. But policies also have a big effect on how much people can accumulate through their lives as a stock of wealth or assets, especially in particular forms such as building up pension rights or buying a home, and they are the focus of this chapter.

Overall wealth inequalities[8]

The inequalities in income described in Chapter 2 are put in the shade by inequalities in wealth – the level of a household's assets (or debts).[9] Wealth can be measured in different ways, depending on what is included. Sometimes the figures only allow for people's *financial* assets and liabilities – their savings or debts. Or they can include physical wealth – their personal possessions such as furniture, cars, and even car number plates.[10] They can include property – the value of houses and flats less any mortgage debts on them. The total of all these gives the 'non-pension wealth', shown in Figure 6.1 for the period from July 2008 to June 2010 (that is, in the two years after the crisis started). It shows how much wealth households had at each percentile of the distribution – from the first percentile (below which 1 per cent of households come), up to the 99th percentile (above which comes the top 1 per cent). It

thus shows the distribution of wealth in the 'Pen's parade' form used for
showing income distribution in Chapter 2.

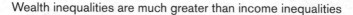

Wealth inequalities are much greater than income inequalities

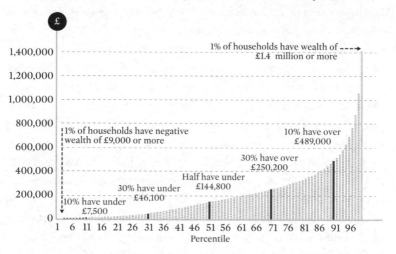

Figure 6.1 – Pen's parade of household wealth (excluding pensions), 2008–10, GB

Again, this shows how averages can be deceptive. On *average*, each
household had non-pension wealth of £220,000. But nearly two-thirds
of households had wealth below this average. Half of them had less than
£145,000 – two-thirds of the average or less. A tenth of households had
wealth of less than £7,500, and 2 per cent had 'negative' wealth – that is,
debts bigger than assets, even when those assets include all their personal
possessions. At the other end, one in ten households had non-pension
wealth of more than £489,000 and 1 per cent more than £1.4 million.

However, these days one of the biggest forms of wealth is not so much
cash in the bank or stocks and shares, but the rights some people have
accumulated to a pension paid by their employer's or another pension
fund. The value of these is very large – particularly for the wealthiest. If
these are included, you get the picture for total wealth shown in Figure
6.2. Now household wealth adds up to £360,000 on average,[11] but 68 per
cent – more than two-thirds – of all households have assets below this.

The top 1 per cent had wealth of more than £2.4 million each, adding up to around 14 per cent of the national total.

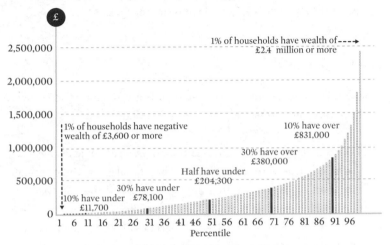

Figure 6.2 – Pen's parade of household wealth (including pension rights), 2008–10, GB

In Pen's parade terms – where it is imagined that people march past in a parade with their heights squashed or stretched in relation to their wealth compared to the average – nearly half of the households would be less than 3 feet tall (comparing the median wealth of £204,000 with the average), and many much smaller. On the other hand, 1 per cent of households would be more than 37 feet tall. The average height of the top 1 per cent (with more than 10 times the overall average) would be over 70 feet, albeit an average dragged up by the very wealthiest – wealth is highly unequal even within the super-rich.[12] Indeed, the richest 200 families included in the *Sunday Times Rich List* had wealth said to average more than £1 billion each between 2008 and 2010. In Pen's parade, they would glide past in the last three-hundredths of a second of an hour-long parade, stretching up to 15,000 feet, 15 times the height of London's Shard.

Even ignoring the billionaires and the wealthiest 1 per cent, these differences have profound implications for the life chances of people with wealthier and less wealthy parents, and present a huge challenge for attempts to create 'equality of opportunity', which the next chapter returns to. But one of the most striking features of wealth inequalities is how great they are between people of different ages.

Wealth and age

In looking at how people's levels of wealth are related to their ages, there are three important factors to keep in mind:

- There is a *life cycle* pattern to wealth and saving. People usually start their adult lives with little wealth. They build up savings through their working lives, including buying a house, if they do that, and accumulating pension rights, if they are lucky. In retirement people may run down their financial assets, perhaps downsize their housing, and the value of their future pensions will fall as the likely number of years they have left diminishes.
- There can be big differences between particular *generations* or age cohorts. With economic growth – in the past, at least – each generation has had higher incomes in real terms than its parents, and so more ability to save and accumulate more valuable pensions, especially when these have been based on final earnings. Given the wild swings in house prices, some generations have had more members who bought housing at the bottom of the market and then gained from the upswings, but other generations were not so lucky. When we look at a snapshot of how wealth relates to age at one moment we are not, therefore, looking at pure age or life cycle savings effects: some of the patterns will result from differences between generations.
- There are very large differences *within* age groups as well as between them. These differences are so large that it is not always helpful to lump them together, as if all members of the 'baby-boom' generation now nearing retirement were in a similar position, for instance.

Wealth inequalities are very large within age groups, not just between them

(a) Financial and physical wealth (excluding housing)

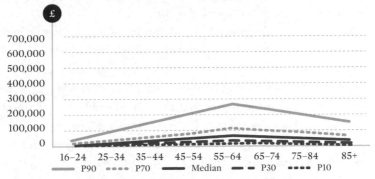

(b) Non-pension wealth (including housing)

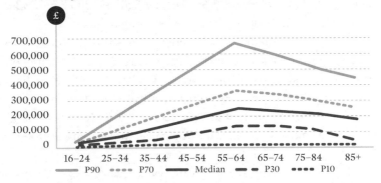

(c) Total wealth (including non-state pensions)

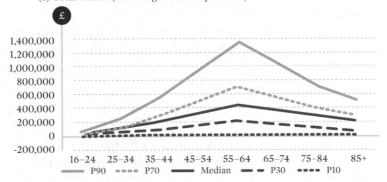

Figure 6.3 – Wealth by age of household, 2008–10, GB

Against that background, Figure 6.3 shows how wealth levels in Britain varied by age, using the same survey as used in Figures 6.1 and 6.2. It confirms that there are very big differences between age groups,[13] but also shows even larger ones within them.

The top panel (a) shows the reported value of people's net financial and physical wealth – that is, money in bank and building society accounts, stocks and shares, and so on, deducting any debt (apart from mortgages), plus the value of their personal possessions from consumer durables and cars to jewellery and fine art. Overall average (mean) wealth of this kind was £85,000, but most households at most ages had less than this. The central line in the panel shows median – middle – wealth for each age group. This was only £8,000 for the very youngest households and £25,000 for those aged 25–34, but had the highest value, £67,000, for those aged 55–64. The figure was lower for older households, just £37,000 for those aged 85 or more.

But Figure 6.3 also shows the wealth for those who were more or less wealthy within each age group. For instance, 10 per cent of households aged 55–64 had financial and physical wealth of £264,000 or more (shown by the 'P90' line), but 10 per cent had £10,000 or less (shown by the 'P10' line). A tenth of those aged 25–34 already had £88,000 or more, but a tenth less than £2,500. The ranges *within* each age group are much bigger than the differences between them.

The second panel (b) adds in the value of people's net housing assets – usually the house or flat they live in, net of any outstanding mortgage. For many this makes the numbers far bigger – their house is their largest asset, often the only one of substantial value. Doing this takes the average value of household non-pension wealth to £220,000, but again most households in nearly all the age groups have less than this. The median for those aged 25–34 is £44,000, but for those aged 55–64 it is £231,000. Again, within each age group there are very large ranges – a tenth of those aged 55–64 have £670,000 or more, but a tenth less than £15,000. A tenth of those aged 25–34 have less than £2,500, but a tenth already have eighty times as much, £197,000 or more.

Finally, the bottom panel (c) (on a larger vertical scale) adds in the value the ONS puts on the pension rights people have accumulated (not including those coming from the state) to give their total wealth. For those who have them, pension rights can be the largest part of their wealth. Indeed, average household wealth rises to £360,000 when they are included – although, as we saw in Figure 6.2, only about a third of all households have this much, and half have under £204,000. The value of people's pension rights varies hugely. This is not just because those who are older will have had the chance to work more years to accumulate them and higher-paid employees have more valuable rights, but also because some employers have provided much better schemes than others, and many employees have not been members of an employer scheme at all.

The differences both between and within age groups are now very large indeed. Half of those aged 55–64 have wealth of over £400,000, and nearly a tenth more than £1.3 million, including Stephen and Henrietta Osborne. But a tenth even of the age group nearing retirement have – like Jim and Tracy Ackroyd – total assets of all kinds of £27,000 or less to see them through retirement, apart from the state pension or benefits. This ratio between those near the top and those near the bottom of nearly fifty to one gives a measure of how great inequality is even within the same age group. Meanwhile, half of households aged 25–34 have £60,000 or more, and a tenth of them more than £244,000, but a tenth of them have £4,300 or less.

Figures of this kind, where all the assets of household members are put together, tell us little about inequalities *within* households. Husbands and wives may often be joint owners of their homes, and hold financial assets in joint names, but when partnerships break down, who acquired which assets when may become part of divorce and other settlements. A reality where assets were not truly jointly controlled and owned may emerge, and with them, gender inequalities not apparent in the 'household wealth' figures.

Baby-boomers versus the 'jilted' generation?

These differences both between and within generations have profound implications for policy and for society. Think first about those between the generation aged 25–34 in 2010 (and so born between 1976 and 1985) and those aged 55–64 born 30 years earlier, in the decade after the Second World War. Median total wealth for the first group was £60,000; for the second group it was £400,000. The difference between the two was £340,000. For the younger generation to catch up with the older one by the same age would require them to save (or get investment returns) of more than £11,000 every year for 30 years. But that is approaching *half* of typical pre-tax earnings or of typical household incomes after tax (for a couple without children).

It is highly unlikely that the younger generation will – or even could – bridge this gap through their own savings. Indeed, recent analysis by Andrew Hood and Robert Joyce shows that the opposite is happening. First, while in the past, each successive generation has had higher real incomes at any given age, over the past decade this has stalled. Indeed, the incomes of those born at the start of the 1970s were *lower* in real terms in their early forties than those for their predecessors born 10 years earlier at the same age; indeed, they had almost fallen back to those of the generation born in the 1950s at the same age.[14] Second, compounding this, the generations born in the 1960s and 1970s are saving less than their predecessors did at the same age; indeed, those born in the 1970s have been spending greater amounts than their incomes – running up debts – even in their twenties and thirties, unlike earlier generations.[15] They are also entering home homeownership more slowly than their predecessors, and the employer pension rights they are accumulating are usually of a much less valuable kind.[16]

It is hardly surprising, then, that these differences are highlighted in debates about 'intergenerational equity'. Books such as (former Minister for Higher Education) David Willetts' *The pinch: How the baby-boomers took their children's future – and why they should give it back* and Ed Howker and Shiv Malik's *Jilted generation: How Britain has bankrupted its youth* tell the story in their sub-titles alone.[17]

But another look at Figure 6.3 suggests that the story is more subtle than this. Baby-boomers aged 55–64 do indeed have very high *average* or even median levels of wealth. But there is huge inequality within the age group. Thirty per cent of them have total wealth of less than £207,000, and 10 per cent of them less than £27,000. Meanwhile, 30 per cent of those aged 25–34 already have £113,000 or more, and 10 per cent of them more than £244,000. Not all baby-boomers are wealthy and not all of those born in the 1970s and 1980s are poor – far from it.

Reinforcing this is inheritance. Look at the middle panel of Figure 6.3, showing non-pension, and therefore inheritable, wealth. Half of households aged 75–84 have more than £200,000 of non-pension wealth, and around 40 per cent of those aged 85 or more. Over the coming years, much of this wealth will be inherited. In the first instance, the inheritors may well be the next generation down, the baby-boomers, but either immediately if the money is passed on, or with a lag, much of the benefit of this will filter down to grandchildren. The scale of this will be very large – for some. For instance, a fifth of those aged 25–34 with middle wealth for their age already expect an inheritance of £100,000 or more.[18] These inheritances will be very unequally spread, as Chapter 7 discusses, and more likely to go to those already advantaged in other ways, but they have to go somewhere – eventually to many in the 'jilted generation'.

The equity issue – and the challenge for policies in a range of areas – is not simply of one fortunate generation versus another. It is about the advantages of the better-off half of baby-boomers compared to *both* poor baby-boomers *and* to those members of younger generations who do not stand to inherit. It is one thing to be one of a small number of grandchildren of owner-occupiers living in the South East of England, and quite another to be one of a large number of grandchildren of tenants or even of owners in parts of the country with low house prices.

The right house at the right time[19]

Within all of this, house prices loom large. In particular, who was in a position to benefit from the house price boom from the mid-1990s to mid-2000s? Using longitudinal data we can examine how (non-pension) wealth changed, tracking the same households from 1995 to 2005. The first thing this allows us to do is to look at how wealth changed over the 10 years – during which house prices doubled in real terms – for people in particular age groups as they grew older. Figure 6.4 uses data for a panel of households drawn from the BHPS. The wealth shown is restricted to net housing wealth and financial assets, and the coverage of this survey is not as good as the ONS Wealth and Assets Survey for the wealthiest households or for financial wealth, but it does allow us to track people over a whole decade.

The top panel (a) may surprise some at first. Much of our discussion of wealth distribution is based on the idea that people accumulate wealth in their working lives, but then run it down to some extent after retirement. But this shows no such pattern. Average wealth increased for *all* age groups over the period – even rising from £61,000 to £95,000 for those initially aged 75 or more in 1995 (at 2005 prices). This group was £34,000 wealthier at the end of the period than the start, even though it was 10 years further into retirement. The biggest increase was for those initially aged 45–54 – from an average of £73,000 to £190,000. Again, it is worth thinking of this in terms of annual incomes – the growth of £117,000 was not far off five years' worth of typical household income after tax. And average wealth increased almost as much for younger households.

But most of this was a result of the house price boom. In the lower panel (b), we give an idea of what these wealth levels would have looked like if the house price boom had never happened, and prices had been at the same level (adjusted for general inflation) in 2005 as in 1995. This is an imperfect exercise – we adjust mortgages taken out between 1995 and 2005 downwards to reflect the lower house prices people would have been paying, but we cannot allow for all the other things that would have been different in this boom-less world (for instance, how they might have saved more money in other ways).

The house price boom swamped the tendency for people to reduce
their wealth after retirement

(a) Actual house prices

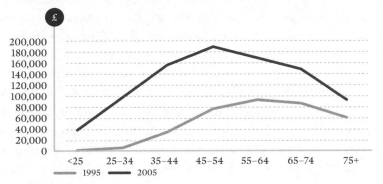

(b) Adjusted house prices

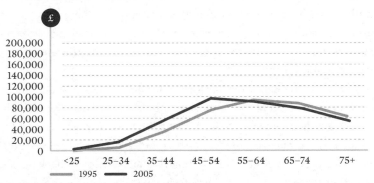

Figure 6.4 – Wealth in 1995 and 2005 by initial age of household

This picture is a little more in line with what the idea of life cycle saving
would predict. Those initially aged under 55 would have increased their
wealth, but only by around £2,000 per year for those aged 35–54, for
instance. At the same time, those initially aged 65 or more would have
reduced their wealth on average – but only by a little under £1,000 per
year. There is no sign of them reducing their wealth towards zero by the
time they reach the likely ends of their lives.

That the main driver of wealth changes over this decade was the change in house prices does not mean that nothing has changed. In one sense these are all 'paper gains', with many households occupying exactly the same houses they started in, and nothing else having changed in their lives other than the startling numbers they see in estate agents' windows. But in the long run, the change is profound.[20] Even with the economic crisis, house prices fell only a little from their peak (and in London they rose). Nothing is certain with the swings of the British house price cycle, but for the moment there looks to have been a permanent shift upwards in the value of people's housing wealth relative to other assets and, crucially, to people's annual incomes. The effect of this is most obvious for those who were not already homeowners as the boom gathered strength, and who would need many more years of saving to get onto the housing ladder, if they ever can. But in the longer run, this means larger amounts of available cash, if older households eventually downsize, and much larger inheritances going to someone. The paper gains mean some big winners, but also some big losers, for whom wealth differences have become unbridgeable.

Analysing the data from the survey in more detail, it is possible to see what sort of people were most able to boost their wealth over the period, and how much of that related to the house price boom.[21] For instance, those who were owners with a mortgage in both 1995 and 2005 increased their wealth by £127,000 more than tenants of the same age and otherwise with the same characteristics. In the absence of the house price boom, this would only have been £18,000. Adding to this, those with degrees or higher qualifications increased their wealth by a further £72,000 compared with those with no qualifications but otherwise similar characteristics. In the absence of the house price boom, this would only have been £33,000. Living in London and the South East (compared to the West Midlands) added a further £30,000 or more, but this would only have been £11,000 without the boom.

We would in any case have expected those who were most economically advantaged to have saved and increased their wealth most.

But many within the same groups were also the big winners from the house price boom. This leaves people with very different capacities to cope with the demands on them in later life, changing the contexts for policies towards both pensions and for coping with needs for potentially very expensive long-term care.

Pensions policy and problems

Pensions policy would matter less – and the state would have less to do – if most people approached retirement with enough other resources of one kind or another to see them through retirement. But that is far from the case. Putting even £130,000 into an 'annuity' that pays out through the rest of someone's life from 65 (plus half carrying on for a surviving spouse and with some annual increase for inflation) might generate around £100 per week of income at best, given rates early in 2014[22] – enough to nearly double income from the basic state pension. But the top panel of Figure 6.1 suggests that less than a quarter of households approaching retirement have financial assets of this amount. The number might rise a little if part of some people's housing equity could be released through downsizing, but not to much more than a third.

For any significant income in retirement and to have any more than this minimal amount most people will depend on state or private pensions, or a combination of the two. Given that by 2011 only around 8 million people were actively saving in an occupational pension scheme (down from 12 million in 1967),[23] for many people, state pensions will be crucial. It is hardly surprising, therefore, that more than half of the social security budget is spent on pensioners.

But the UK pension system, as it had emerged by the mid-2000s was, in the words of the Pensions Commission, 'not fit for purpose' in meeting the needs of future pensioners.[24] Many people retiring around then were benefiting from the most generous provisions of both private and state pensions, but there were gaps even then, and the outlook for many of those in younger generations was much bleaker. The evolution of pensions at the time implied inadequate pensions for many, and an increasingly unequal distribution of pension rights.[25]

The Commission identified a whole series of problems with the UK system:

- The state pension system was – and still is – one of the *least* generous in the industrialised world,[26] and had evolved into one of 'unique complexity'.[27]
- While occupational pensions provided more for some workers, only about half of the working-age population were building up an occupational pension, or had a partner who was doing so.[28]
- The value of the basic state pension, the foundation of the system, had been adjusted only in line with prices, rather than earnings, since the early 1980s, and so had become much less valuable in relation to current incomes. It was then assumed by government that this would continue, allowing state pension spending to remain the same share of national income, even as the number of pensioners is set to increase rapidly in future decades.
- To protect those at the bottom, and to reduce pensioner poverty, means-tested benefits (by then called Pension Credit) had been increased by the Labour government and kept up with earnings; again, it was assumed that this would continue. But the effect of this was that a larger and larger proportion of pensioners would face means testing in retirement – perhaps three-quarters by 2050.[29]
- This sharply reduced the prospective benefit to people from saving towards retirement, and made calculating what they would gain from doing so very hard. Both made it unlikely that the decline in private sector provision would be reversed in the way government had hoped.
- Older members of private pension schemes (and those working in the public sector) benefited from 'defined benefit' pensions, which pay out what is promised regardless of what happens to investment returns and life expectancy. But younger employees and new recruits, even if they were in a scheme at all, were now in less generous

'defined contribution' schemes, where the risks of what happened to investments and future life expectancy are carried by individuals, not by the employer.

• Particular groups were particularly poorly served by the system, especially women and others with interrupted careers, as well as those with lower incomes, and the self-employed in general.

Pensions and changing lives

At the heart of some of these problems was what is actually good news: that we now expect most people to live longer than we used to. Until recently governments had reacted to this by planning for the relative value of the basic state pension to continue to fall. Private employers have reacted by switching to less generous pensions for new employees and for future additional pension rights for existing ones.

Men reaching 65 are now expected to live seven years longer than was expected for them in the 1980s

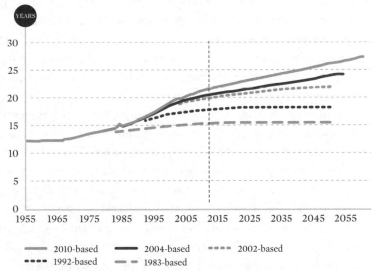

Figure 6.5 – Projections for remaining years of life for men reaching 65 between 1955 and 2055

It is only relatively recently that policy-makers (and private companies) have realised quite how rapidly life expectancies appear to be increasing. Figure 6.5 shows how big the change has been in official projections of the life expectancy of men reaching age 65 in particular years (similar changes have happened for women). The top line gives the latest estimates, and the lower lines those produced using data from earlier years. These projections are for what is known as 'cohort' life expectancy, that is, taking into account what we expect to happen to mortality in future years, giving the best estimate of how long each generation will be around to collect its pensions.[30]

When projections were being made in the 1980s about how much longer men reaching 65 in 2013 might be expected to live, it was about 14 years. By the mid-2000s, using '2002-based' projections, this had reached 19 years. The latest projections suggest that – for the same group – it will actually be 21 years, half as much again as thought before. And for those of us who are younger, the projected improvement is even bigger. For those born in 1985, and so reaching 65 in 2050, the projection in the mid-2000s was around 21 more years of life (what we now think we have already reached); now it is more than 25. For women, the life expectancies are even higher. The pace of the improvement we have seen implies that estimated life expectancy at 65 has increased by five years between those reaching that age in 1990 and those reaching it in 2010.[31] Every day has added six hours to life expectancies at later ages.

Of course, the very fact that such projections have changed so fast gives an idea of how uncertain all this is. Improvements in mortality rates at particular ages might now slow down, in which case the latest projections would be too optimistic for how long younger people might live on average. But there has been little sign of a flattening out over the last few decades. The latest projections assume a *slower* rate of improvement from now on than the experience of the last 40 years; if that trend actually continued, the current projections would be too pessimistic. Either way, uncertainty means that policy design needs flexibility.

What is – normally – good news at an individual level, is, however, a problem for designing pensions, if they assume that people draw their pension at the same age. Since the Second World War until 2010, the state pension age for men had been 65 and 60 for women. But that meant that the proportion of adult life prospectively spent above pension age rose from 23 per cent for men in 1982 to 30 per cent in 2012. The proportion for women rose from 28 per cent to 34 per cent.[32]

These differences may not sound so much, but if 25 per cent of adult life is spent in retirement, that allows three years of working life to finance each year in retirement through contributions or taxes; if 33 per cent of adult life is spent in retirement, that means only two years to finance each year of retirement. That already implies either higher tax or contribution rates than used to be the case to support a similar relative income in retirement, or spreading the jam out more thinly over a longer period if those rates are kept down – which is essentially what was happening to state pensions up to 2010.

A partial solution to this is for pension ages to rise in some way in proportion to life expectancy, which is what the Pensions Commission recommended, and both the last Labour government and the Coalition accepted. Indeed, the Coalition announced in the 2013 *Autumn Statement* that as a guiding principle, in the long run, state pension age should be formally adjusted to keep the proportion of adult life above it (averaged for men and women) constant at a third (subject to a review process, and with 10 years' notice for any change).

Thinking through the implications of this with the kind of picture shown in Figure 6.3, that implies that the state pension age could reach 70 for those now in their twenties. Waiting an extra five years for a pension compared with their grandparents (an extra 10 years for women, following equalisation of pension ages) may sound alarming, but the suggested formula implies that the pension age would only reach this much if average life expectancies for that generation reach 95, that is, still implying 25 years of pension receipt, both a longer time and a bigger proportion of adult life than earlier generations.

The quid pro quo for the Commission's recommendation was that it would allow the basic state pension to return to being linked to earnings, rather than prices. The deal for younger workers was 'a better state pension at a later age', which is what the last government legislated for in 2008. Subsequently, the Coalition has implemented something more generous than simply linking pensions to average earnings, the so-called 'triple lock', under which pensions increase by the *higher* of earnings, price inflation, or an annual rate of 2.5 per cent. In the long run, this implies pensions rising faster than earnings.[33]

On the other hand, part of the Coalition's austerity programme was to bring forward increases in the state pension age to reach 65 for women by 2018, and 66 for both men and women by 2020. For one particular group of women this has meant a very rapid change in pension ages, with little notice. For instance, a woman born in April 1950 would have been able to draw her pension from April 2010. A younger sister born four-and-a-half years later in September 1954 will not be able to draw hers until September 2020 – ten-and-a-half years later. This is a very sudden change in treatment (although as an offset for some, many women of that age will benefit from some of the other reforms under way, particularly the proposed new 'single tier' pension for those reaching state pension age after 2016).

Increasing pension ages in proportion to expected lengths of retirement makes sense, but does not solve Britain's pension problems. First, the proportion of the population above pension age will continue to rise, and with it the share of national income that will be needed for pensions, if their generosity is not to fall relative to other incomes. This is because there are two demographic drivers of the ageing population – not just individuals living longer, but also the larger size of the baby-boomer generation by comparison with its successors. This reflects the smaller number of children that women have been having since the 1960s, a decline in fertility. This is often thought of as being a problem caused by the large size of the baby-boom population. In one way it is, but another way of thinking about it is that the size of the post-war baby-boom has made pensions *easy* for the last 40 years, meaning more workers per pensioner than there would otherwise have been. If the baby-boom had not happened, we would have had to adjust to a smaller number of workers per pensioner steadily over the last 30 years. Instead, that adjustment was postponed, but will now happen all at once over the next 25 years.[34]

In talking through the consequences of demographic change, the Pensions Commission argued that there was no escape from some combination of four 'unpalatable' options:

- pensioners becoming poorer relative to the rest of the population
- working longer
- higher taxes to finance state pensions
- greater contributions in people's working life to other funded pensions.

The Commission, and all those we consulted, rejected the first. On *average*, as we have seen, pensioners are not as far behind the rest of the population as they used to be (see Figure 3.9), but they still have lower incomes, and in international terms, UK pensions are far from generous. That leaves a combination of the other three, and that is the direction policy has taken. Pension ages are rising, the share of national income going to state pensions will rise, and people who are not members of their employer's pension scheme are now being 'automatically enrolled' into it (or the new low-cost National Employment Savings Trust, NEST), unless they consciously decide to opt out.

All of this will *slow* the fall in pensions for younger generations compared with those who have retired recently. It will not reverse it. For instance, the minimum contributions from employer, employee and tax relief under Automatic Enrolment, eventually adding up to 8 per cent of earnings above a threshold once they have been phased in, are still well below – probably half – what would be needed in addition to state pensions to give people the kind of income in retirement that they regard as an absolute minimum.[35] With much lower long-term interest rates in the wake of the economic crisis than before – a product of the

Bank of England's 'quantitative easing' – this has only got worse. With low long-run returns on investments, you need to save more to get the same end result.

Nor does raising pension ages automatically mean that people will, or can, work longer. First, not all of the longer lives people are enjoying on average are spent in good health – there is a difference between life expectancy and *healthy* life expectancy. What has happened to the balance between the two is not entirely clear, due to changes in the definitions used in the official statistics. Over the 1980s and 1990s, the proportion of life after 65 that men and women could expect to spend in 'fairly good' or 'good' health stayed much the same, so most of the increase in life expectancy was in 'healthy' years, but part – a quarter or more – was not.[36] The more recent statistics are based on years in 'good' or 'very good' health. On this basis, between 2001 and 2008, healthy life expectancy increased for both men and women, but for men, this was at a slower rate than total life expectancy.

The government's proposed formula is that pension age should rise by two years for every three years' increase in prospective adult life expectancy. In terms of the long-term trends, that would imply an increase in the length of working life by roughly the same amount as the gain in years in good health. But if the most recent trends were continued, the rise in pension age would be somewhat faster for men than gains in years of good health.

A second issue, partly related to this, is that people do not necessarily retire at the same date as they become entitled to the state pension. In fact, between 1950 and 1990 average ages at retirement fell by around three years for both men and women.[37] Working lives became a smaller proportion of people's total lives, even though there were no changes in state pension age. Since the mid-1990s, this has reversed, with increases of two years in each case, to reach about 62.5 for women and 64.5 for men by 2010. Even in the first years of the recession, comparing 2006–08 and 2010, employment rates of women in their early sixties *increased*, while full-time employment of men in their early sixties fell at only around a quarter of the rate for all men.[38] Recent research has linked a continuing rise in older women's employment (and of their partners) to the rise in women's state pension age that started in 2010.[39] All of this suggests that increasing pension ages *may* be associated with people actually working longer, although that is by no means guaranteed.

Finally, as we return to in the next chapter, different kinds of people have different life expectancies. Using data from 2002–06, the ONS suggests that 65-year-old men who have had 'higher managerial or professional' jobs have life expectancies that are 3.5 years longer than those who have had 'routine' jobs. For women, the difference is 3.2 years. While the social class difference for women had stayed about the same over the previous 20 years, for men it had widened by a year.[40] There remain wide gaps in mortality rates and life expectancies between the most and the least deprived areas.[41]

This does not mean that it would have served the interests of those with lower incomes to have left the state pension system developing the way in which it was, with an ever-less valuable state pension available at the same age, even as lengths of retirement increased for all. The more fundamental issues are the relationships between working conditions and incomes earlier in life and later health, and the overall progressivity and equity – or otherwise – of the ways in which public policy treats the accumulation of wealth in different forms, of which pension rights are one, which is discussed in the next section.

The specific pensions policy dilemma is that taken as a whole, or on average, pensioners do not have particularly high incomes by comparison with the rest of the population; in fact, they are lower. But some *do* have high incomes, and they are more lightly taxed than non-pensioners, for instance, in that they are not subject to NICs. Also, as the middle panel of Figure 6.3 showed, the wealthiest quarter of pensioners have non-pension wealth of £300,000 or more, including financial wealth of more than £100,000.

One response is to argue that pensions – and other extra payments to pensioners, such as Winter Fuel Payments or free TV licences for the oldest pensioners – should become means tested. But we have just been through a series of major pension reforms designed, with widespread support, to reduce the spread of means testing in old age. This was for good reasons, given the public interest in there being clear benefits to people from providing for part of their own income in retirement. For some of the extra benefits, such as Winter Fuel Payments, rather than means testing them, it would make sense to raise the age at which people become entitled to them, and use the revenue saved for more effective ways of tackling fuel poverty, specifically greatly increasing the resources available to insulate the homes of people with low incomes.[42]

Another, and more obvious, response is that while it makes sense to protect state pensions, better-off pensioners could contribute more through the tax system. But the politics of this are fraught – when George Osborne announced the end of the extra tax-free allowance for those aged over 65, it was instantly condemned as a 'granny tax'. Other proposals that might affect better-off pensioners often face objections where some low-income pensioners who would be affected are held up in front of them as a kind of political and fiscal human shield.

Policies towards wealth accumulation – inequity and incoherence

This kind of political problem with changing arrangements that are at once economically inefficient and regressive, favouring the wealthiest most, pervades public policy towards wealth accumulation. As the stories at the start of the chapter illustrated, there are aspects of public policy that strongly encourage saving and wealth accumulation, while others penalise it. The details of this can be complicated, but some of the features illustrated by the treatment of the Osbornes and the Ackroyds include the following.[43]

Taxes on capital assets

In general, wealth and income from wealth are lightly taxed, say by comparison with income from earnings. The UK does not have an annual tax on wealth holdings in the way some other countries do, and when this was proposed by a Labour government in the mid-1970s, the idea fell foul of a combination of administrative and political objections, some of them mobilised by powerful, and wealthy interests.[44] The closest we have is the Council Tax on domestic property. But this varies only a little between more and less valuable properties, and is based on valuations made more than 20 years ago. And it can be argued that it should be seen not as a capital tax, but as a tax on 'housing services', a partial proxy for the VAT that is not levied on the rents paid by tenants or on the services enjoyed by owners living in their own homes.[45]

Instead, we have relied on periodic taxes on transfers of wealth through Inheritance Tax and stamp duty. An argument for this is that it is administratively far more efficient to collect taxes in a large lump once a generation, for instance, than on the basis of small percentages of wealth assessed in a complicated way every year. But even as personal wealth has grown in relation to national income, inheritance taxes have fallen. In real terms, Inheritance Tax raised half as much in 2010, £2.7 billion, as it had 60 years earlier, in 1948.[46] As a share of national income, it fell from 1.5 per cent in 1948 to 0.2 per cent in 2010. With a threshold now of £325,000 before an estate becomes liable, and effectively twice that – £650,000 – for a couple, few households in reality need to worry about it, even before they get involved in complicated tax-avoiding trust arrangements. As a result of this – and of the way in which transfers made more than seven years before death are exempt – only about 3 per cent of estates have been subject to Inheritance Tax in recent years. But the tax remains politically charged. The concession that couples should get two tax-free allowances was introduced by the last Labour government in reaction to the popularity of the then Shadow Chancellor George Osborne's promise in opposition to raise the threshold to £1 million. Indeed, every time in the last 50 years that the value of a 'family home' (in the South East, at least) has approached it, the threshold has been sharply raised.[47]

The more important tax these days is the stamp duty charged on capital transactions, including stocks and shares, but particularly purchases of owner-occupied property. The yield of this varies with house prices and the number of sales – dropping from £15 billion in 2007–08, for instance, to £9 billion in 2010–11 (at 2010–11 prices), but forecast to be back up to £16 billion in 2014-15.[48] Focusing on stamp duty on residential property specifically, the amounts raised annually have represented between 0.1–0.2 per cent of the net value of owner-occupied property. This is not negligible, but does little to offset the other tax advantages of owner-occupation, namely, that it is exempt both from capital gains tax and any kind of Income Tax on the value (the 'imputed rent') that owners derive from living in their own home.

Pension saving

Saving towards a pension is even more favourably treated by the tax system than owner-occupation. As illustrated for Stephen and Henrietta Osborne, pension contributions are tax-deductible on their way into a pension fund. But up to a quarter of people's pension rights can be – and usually are – drawn out as a tax-free lump sum, while for higher rate taxpayers the rest of a pension that is paid out is often taxed at a lower rate than the rate at which tax relief was originally given. There are now some (complicated) limits on the value of these tax reliefs, including a £1.25 million lifetime limit on the value of a pension pot that can get the full benefit (from 2014–15). But the overall effect remains that the tax system *adds* to the value of people's pension savings, rather than charging tax on them. The Pensions Policy Institute estimates that the value of pension tax reliefs, net of the tax paid on pensions in payment, came to £24 billion in 2010–11.[49]

Up to a basic level, it can be argued that there are public benefits from encouraging pension saving, as otherwise the state and taxpayer could end up having to do more of the job. But tax relief is worth most to the highest paid and goes disproportionately to them. For instance, a higher rate taxpayer putting £1,000 into a pension pot at age 40, and paying basic rate tax in retirement, would get an eventual net return back of £5,550, compared to only £4,150 for a basic rate taxpayer, or £3,900 if either had invested in a *tax-free* ISA getting the same underlying return on investment.[50]

As discussed at the start of the chapter, some of those receiving tax credits (or benefits such as Housing Benefit) are also favourably treated if they make pension contributions, and this advantage will be carried through in the planned Universal Credit system. But in general, it is the best paid who get the most out of the system. Seventy per cent of all tax relief went to higher and top rate taxpayers in 2010–11, for instance, while they made only 50 per cent of pension contributions,[51] and were only just over 10 per cent of all taxpayers.[52] Restricting tax relief is not entirely straightforward, however, as witnessed by the complexity of some of the rules that now limit, for instance, the annual amount individuals and their employers can contribute to a pension each year.[53]

Historically the argument for such generous tax relief has been that it is in the public interest to encourage people to tie up their assets in a way that guarantees that they have a flow of income in retirement, but that to do this there needs to be something to offset the perceived disadvantages of doing so. But the proposals in the 2014 Budget that people should no longer have to use their pension saving to guarantee a lifetime income – to 'annuitise their pension pot' in the jargon – substantially weaken this justification. For many, pension saving may be little different from any other kind of saving, so why treat it so much more favourably? Few will have enough to blow it on a Lamborghini sports car, as Pensions Minister Steve Webb suggested he still would be relaxed about when defending the proposals,[54] but there must be concern that some people would run their retirement savings down too quickly, given that, for instance, men in their sixties underestimate their future life expectancies compared to official projections by three years and women by four-and-a-half years.[55] Others might run them down too *slowly*, lowering their standard of living in retirement through being too optimistic about their own life expectancy. The proposals also remove what had been an advantage to women from the way in which annuities – promises of income for the rest of one's life – have to be sold on a 'unisex' basis, giving women the same monthly income despite their usually higher life expectancy.

Other kinds of saving

After houses and pensions, the next best treated form of savings are simply tax-free, such as ISAs. By 2006–08 42 per cent of households had some form of ISA, and their total value represented about a sixth of all net financial wealth.[56] Some forms of National Savings are also tax-free.

Many other financial assets generate a return that comes as a mixture of income (such as dividends on shares) and capital gains. The capital gains tax rate is lower than that paid by higher (and additional) taxpayers on their other income. Neither form is liable to NICs. While there is a penalty in that capital gains liabilities no longer incorporate an allowance for inflation, the annual allowance and lower rate of tax mean that investment income of this kind is more lightly taxed than earnings. This is a long way from the days when there was an 'investment income surcharge' in Income Tax (up to 1983), or 'earned income relief' in Income Tax (up to 1972).

Some landlords can be fairly heavily taxed if they fully own the properties they rent out, and they end up paying capital gains tax on the nominal, not just the real, return on their investment, as well as Income Tax on the rent they receive. On the other hand, landlords who finance their investment through loans – such as 'Buy to Let' mortgages – are lightly taxed, as their interest payments are tax-deductible.

Some financial assets are heavily taxed – notably regular interest-bearing accounts with banks and building societies. The full, nominal return on these is taxable, even though there are many periods when in real, inflation-adjusted, terms, the return is negative. But a more serious issue for some is their treatment by the benefit system, as explained at the start of the chapter.[57] While people are allowed to have a certain amount of savings (currently £6,000 if they are of working age) without it affecting their entitlements, once savings go above that level the system assumes that they can get a return on the excess at an annual rate of 20 per cent. As this is unlikely, for most people that implies running down their 'excess' savings by a fifth each year. Savings above £16,000 rule people out from means-tested benefits entirely.[58] It could be argued that the point of means-tested benefits is to help those without other resources to get by, and so it is right to take capital into account. But doing so in such a stringent way could act as a deterrent to save for some, and perhaps to make having saved a matter of regret when people realise how they have been affected.

Paying for long-term care

This has been an even bigger issue for the contributions people are expected to make towards the cost of personal care, including residential care, if they have assets. Rather than such care being available free without a means test, as with healthcare through the NHS, in England, Wales and Northern Ireland, people with assets are expected to contribute.[59] Under current rules, those with assets over £23,250 have to pay full fees for residential care. If a partner is still living in it, residential property is exempt from this, but for someone who is single or who has been widowed, it is included. This is not a new rule – the system has been like that since 1948, and before that, back to the Poor Law. But as the generation of mass owner-occupation reached the ages where care needs became more intense, more found they had to contribute. Rising house prices have brought more people further above the limit – if the capital limit for receiving help with long-term care had moved in line with house prices since the early 1960s, it would now be more than £80,000, not £23,000.[60]

This has all become highly contentious. The majority of a Royal Commission set up by the 1997 Labour government recommended that nursing and personal care should become free without a means test, but this was only implemented in Scotland. Other ideas came and went over the following decade, some shot down in political cross-fire, with, for instance, ideas of deferring costs when people were alive and recovering them from estates when they died branded as a 'death tax' in the run-up to the 2010 General Election. But in 2011, a Commission under Andrew Dilnot produced a set of reforms that will, with some modification, be implemented from 2016.

At the heart of the case made for reform by that Commission was that needing substantial care in old age is now for most people by far the largest uninsured – and uninsurable – risk that they face. On their estimates, half of people aged 65 will need to spend little on care, and three-quarters will need care costing less than £20,000 over the rest of their lives. But one in ten would face costs of more than £100,000.[61] This means that most people face a very large gamble, and one which private insurers are ill-equipped to insure against. Instead, the Commission suggested that the upper limit for assets ruling people out of means-tested help should be raised to £100,000, and there should be a limit on anyone's total lifetime costs of somewhere between £25,000 and £50,000, to cut out the worst risks that anyone faces.

In response, the Coalition government announced that from 2016, there will be a cap of £72,000 on people's lifetime liabilities for care costs, and that assistance would be available on a sliding scale from full support for those with assets of £17,000 or less, reducing for those with higher assets, and removed entirely for those with assets over £118,000.[62] This gets rid of the cliff edge ceiling that currently affects those with assets of only £23,000, but people with assets above the lower limit will still be expected to contribute at a rate equivalent to 20 per cent of the excess over it.

There are two kinds of beneficiary from this change. First, those receiving – or fearing that they will need – expensive long-term care now have a limit put on what they might have to contribute, and more will receive assistance. This brings actual help to some and presumably reduces worry to many others. The other large beneficiaries are the heirs of those who would otherwise have found the 'family home' sold and much of the proceeds eaten up by care costs.

Its costs are being met in two ways. First, the government said that the Inheritance Tax threshold will be frozen, rather than adjusted for inflation. This part of the cost would be carried by those who would benefit from inheriting some of the largest estates. The larger part of the cost is being met, notionally at least, through part of the (much larger) benefits to the Treasury through reforms to the treatment of some employer and employee pension contributions.[63] This will result in higher National Insurance payments, particularly by workers in the public sector and their employers, such as schools and hospitals (unless they are compensated in some other way that has not yet been announced), a budgeting time bomb that has so far received little attention.

Something that will have general benefits for many in terms of peace of mind, and specific benefits for some of those benefiting from significant inheritance, will be paid for by a combination of a little more tax on significant inheritors, and from public sector workers and organisations (and therefore their clients) in general. It is not entirely clear where the balance of advantage of this will lie in distributional terms. What is clear, however, is that these reforms do not in themselves increase the overall resources going towards meeting the escalating care needs of an ageing population,[64] and do nothing about the immediate pressures on local authorities struggling with rising demands for adult social care, but falling resources.

Help to accumulate

At the same time as policies that reduce support for those with more savings, other aspects of public policy have tried to help people build them up through what has sometimes been called 'asset-based welfare'. Notably, Child Trust Funds put a voucher worth £250 into a savings account (realisable at age 18), to which people could and did add, for all children born between September 2002 and January 2011. A 'Savings Gateway' scheme was, after successful piloting, going to be rolled out nationally in July 2010 to offer a government 'match' of 50 pence for every £1 saved by low-income households, but this too was abolished as an early austerity measure after the 2010 General Election. Rather than these short-lived schemes, by far the most important example of public policy boosting wealth, beyond the tax advantages described above, is the Right to Buy council (or former council) housing at a discount. These accumulated discounts now represent perhaps £150–200 billion, or about 3–4 per cent of all non-pension wealth.[65]

In the other direction, recent and future students face escalating debt from student loans, albeit debt of a particular kind that they only have to repay when earnings are above a certain level, and which many will never repay in full. At the level of university fees since 2012, many future graduates will now have student debt approaching £40,000. This is a large amount compared to other wealth for those early in their careers – a median of £76,000 for total wealth of the previous generation of households aged 25–34 in 2010, for instance, and median financial and physical assets of only £25,000 (see Figure 6.3).

Summary and conclusions

Wealth inequalities dwarf those in income discussed earlier in the book. Some of these inequalities are simply the product of a process under which people smooth their living standards over their lives through saving and building up pension rights when at work, and then drawing their pensions and running down their assets in retirement. But only a small part of the differences between households are due to this life cycle effect. For households of all ages, total wealth for those near the top (with only 10 per cent wealthier) is 70 times that for households near the bottom (with only 10 per cent poorer). But just looking within those aged 55–64, the same ratio is still nearly fifty to one.

Looking across the whole population there are differences between generations that could not be bridged through saving alone. But the issue is not just between a lucky generation of baby-boomers now approaching retirement who got the best pension deals and benefited most from the house price boom, and a younger 'jilted generation' who have little. Many baby-boomers have little wealth, and only a minority enough to see them through retirement without state pensions playing a major role. And a significant proportion of younger people stand to gain a great deal from inheritance and lifetime help from parents and grandparents. The conflict of interest is ultimately between the more affluent half of the baby-boom generation and poorer members of their own generation and younger households with the 'wrong' relatives, for whom advantage will not cascade down the generations.

Because public policies are so closely related to age, as discussed in Chapter 3, demographic change lies at the heart of some of the largest policy debates and reforms that are currently underway, notably around pensions and the treatment of pensioners. Raising state pension ages to keep a balance between the proportions of adult life spent at work and in retirement in the long run is one way to prevent the jam of available resources being spread ever more thinly and ineffectively. Trying to stem the falling tide of occupational pension rights and to fill in the gaps in coverage through 'automatic enrolment' into employer pensions schemes is another. But substantial inequalities will remain in the resources that people have to face retirement, both between and within generations. Those differences now represent many more years of income than they did 20 years ago. And with restrictions on how people use their pension saving proposed for abolition, inequalities in what is left for later old age may become even greater.

Looking across the range of public policies towards wealth, two things stand out. First, that the treatment of different kinds of assets and kinds of people varies widely, from strong encouragement and assistance to penalties that must lead some to query why they ever bothered saving. Second, it is often those who start with the highest incomes and greatest wealth who are the biggest beneficiaries of the most favourable treatment. There is little sign of a coherent approach towards narrowing the kinds of inequalities in wealth within and between generations described at the start of this chapter; often the effect is quite the reverse. Those wealth differences are part of what drives the links between advantage and disadvantage in one generation to those of its children that are discussed in the next chapter.

THE LONGEST WAVE

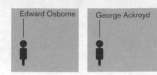

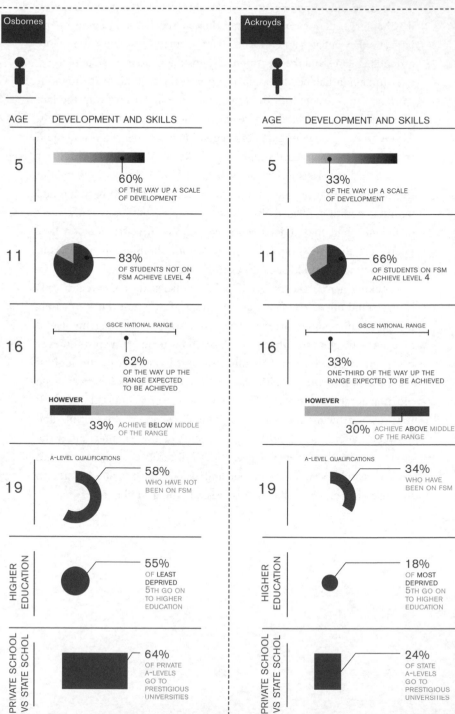

Osbornes

AGE	DEVELOPMENT AND SKILLS
5	60% OF THE WAY UP A SCALE OF DEVELOPMENT
11	83% OF STUDENTS NOT ON FSM ACHIEVE LEVEL 4
16	GSCE NATIONAL RANGE — 62% OF THE WAY UP THE RANGE EXPECTED TO BE ACHIEVED. **HOWEVER** 33% ACHIEVE **BELOW** MIDDLE OF THE RANGE
19	A-LEVEL QUALIFICATIONS — 58% WHO HAVE NOT BEEN ON FSM
HIGHER EDUCATION	55% OF **LEAST DEPRIVED** 5TH GO ON TO HIGHER EDUCATION
PRIVATE SCHOOL VS STATE SCHOL	64% OF PRIVATE A-LEVELS GO TO PRESTIGIOUS UNIVERSITIES

Ackroyds

AGE	DEVELOPMENT AND SKILLS
5	33% OF THE WAY UP A SCALE OF DEVELOPMENT
11	66% OF STUDENTS ON FSM ACHIEVE LEVEL 4
16	GSCE NATIONAL RANGE — 33% ONE-THIRD OF THE WAY UP THE RANGE EXPECTED TO BE ACHIEVED. **HOWEVER** 30% ACHIEVE **ABOVE** MIDDLE OF THE RANGE
19	A-LEVEL QUALIFICATIONS — 34% WHO HAVE BEEN ON FSM
HIGHER EDUCATION	18% OF **MOST DEPRIVED** 5TH GO ON TO HIGHER EDUCATION
PRIVATE SCHOOL VS STATE SCHOL	24% OF STATE A-LEVELS GO TO PRESTIGIOUS UNIVERSITIES

7. The longest wave

From generation to generation

At the end of July 2013 new grandchildren were born into both the Ackroyd and Osborne extended families. Gary and Denise Ackroyd's baby, seven years younger than his brother Ryan, was a boy, quickly named George. After a little thought Henry and Clare Osborne rejected the same name, and their son, five years younger than his sister Lucy, was eventually named Edward.

We do not know how the lives of these two boys will turn out. First, we have only a rough idea of how anyone's life might turn out over the coming decades, even on average: nothing is fixed in stone; the world changes. As a guide, however, we can look at what has happened in the recent past and see how people's chances of different outcomes vary depending on their backgrounds, but within that they could be a lot luckier or less lucky than such average chances. So when looking at how their life chances compare as things have been recently, in either case there is a wide range around any average figures.

Given how things have been for those born recently (around the start of the millennium), by the age of five, children with the most affluent fifth of parents are on average 60 per cent of the way up a scale assessing their development, but children with the poorest fifth of parents are only a third of the way up it.[1] So on that basis, Edward may already be several months of development ahead of George by the time he is in the first year of primary school.

And so, in recent experience, it goes on. At the age of 11, 66 per cent of children receiving free school meals (because of low parental income) achieve 'Level 4' in English and maths, compared to 83 per cent of other pupils.[2] At 16, as a boy from an affluent neighbourhood, one might expect Edward to have GCSE scores 62 per cent of the way up the national range, but for George as a boy from a poor neighbourhood, only to be one-third of the way up the range. On the other hand, 30 per cent of boys from the poorest neighbourhoods come above the middle of the range, and more than a third of boys from the most affluent neighbourhoods come below the middle.[3] By the age of 19 the proportions of young people achieving any qualification equivalent to two A-levels ('Level 3') are 34 per cent for those who have been on free school meals, but 58 per cent for those who were not.[4] On average at each stage boys from backgrounds like Edward's would be expected to do better than boys from backgrounds like George's.

Driven mostly, but not entirely, by school results, it is already more likely than not that Edward will go on to higher education, with more than three times the likelihood of doing so than someone from a lower-income family, even if he goes to a state school.[5] But given what we know of his family's traditions, the chances are that he will be sent to a private school. If so, he would have nearly a three times greater chance of going to one of the most selective universities than an A-level student from a state school.[6]

It is not that George will inevitably end up with low qualifications – after all, his uncle Paul was already the first in the family to go to university. But all the way along, Edward's chances are better. And this will make a huge difference to what kind of job each of them ends up in, and what sort of income he receives. If things stayed the same as they were for men born in 1970 – which, of course, they almost certainly will not – we would expect nearly half of the difference in their families' incomes when they are older children in the 2020s to be reflected in what George and Edward might be earning in their late thirties, in 2051.[7]

So, simply knowing that Edward's family have incomes that are, say, four times as high as George's when they are growing up and nothing else, we might expect Edward to end up earning nearly twice as much as George. That would mean Edward earning the equivalent of £41,200 and George £21,900 per year (in terms of what men in their late thirties were earning in 2010).[8] And Edward's chances of marrying a higher-earning graduate, perhaps met at university, will also be higher, further increasing differences in total family income. Of course, within each generation with particular backgrounds, some will do better and some worse than that, and the links between the incomes of parents and children being born now may well be different from what we see for today's adults. But in the absence of a better crystal ball, their economic chances are already very different.

And their life chances differ in other ways, too. From what we know of their families, Edward is much more likely to benefit from a significant inheritance than George – either indirectly, if Stephen and Henrietta Osborne leave their money to Henry and Charlotte when they die (most likely in the 2030s), and they then use that to help the Osborne grandchildren, or directly, if the estate skips a generation. As we saw in Chapter 6, Jim and Tracy Ackroyd will have little to pass on. Actual inheritance of cash and property will have come on top of all of the other ways in which higher income and wealthier parents will have been able to help their children earlier on, from buying houses in the catchment areas of the most favoured schools, or paying private school fees, or helping children with deposits to get on to the owner-occupied housing ladder.

And so the wealth cycle carries on. Half of today's 'higher professional' households in their late fifties and early sixties had wealth (including pension rights) of more than £890,000 (in 2008-10); for 'routine' workers the equivalent was £144,000.[9] If their educations do diverge in the way the averages suggest, and their occupations follow, those tracks take Edward towards a wealth level that might be more than six times George's by the end of their working careers.

It is not just their life chances that vary, but also their chances of a long life. The higher wealth Edward might expect to end up with is one of the best predictors of surviving longer when people are over 50. At the start of their lives, even if all we knew about them was which local authority area they were born in and nothing else, on average we would expect Edward to live nearly four years longer. As things stood when they were born, George Ackroyd's life expectancy, born in Salford (taking account of ONS central estimates for how mortality rates will change over the next century) would be just under 88 years; Edward Osborne's, born in Stockport, would be over 91 years. If he had been a girl, we would have expected her to live to 94, even though Stockport is not even very far above the English average. In other areas, life expectancies are now even higher.[10]

NEARLY ALL POLITICAL parties across the spectrum aspire to the idea that there should be 'equality of opportunity'. What people mean by equality of opportunity varies, however, sometimes concentrating on relative chances of ending up at the top or bottom of a social or economic ladder, sometimes on their absolute chances of reaching some level of attainment or outcome. What is needed to achieve the former is much tougher politically than to achieve the latter – in relative terms, increasing one person's chances of going up also increases another's of going down. But as George and Edward's prospects illustrate, and this chapter describes, we are currently very far from equality of opportunity, whatever definition we use.

Background and life chances[11]

As anyone who has seen the film *Titanic* knows – and other readers should look away now – people's life chances a century ago were related to their background. Kate Winslett's character, travelling first class, survives. Leonardo di Caprio's character, travelling steerage, drowns. That was about right. In fact, 97 per cent of all the women (and their female servants) travelling first class survived, but only 86 per cent of women in second class and 49 per cent of women in third class. All of the children in first class (probably, with one possible exception), and all children in second class made it, but only 34 per cent of those in third class. Despite the idea of 'women and children first', men in first class had nearly as high a chance of survival (33 per cent) as children in third class. But only 8 per cent of men in second class and 16 per cent of men in third class survived.[12]

Figure 7.1 shows something much more recent, but not so different. It shows the (age-adjusted) survival rates over not the minutes and hours following the sinking of an ocean liner, but over the following six years for the older people (aged over 50) interviewed for the English Longitudinal Survey of Ageing in 2001. The results are divided according to the respondents' wealth levels from the top fifth to the bottom fifth. The differences are stark, not just by gender, but also by wealth. Ninety-five per cent of women with the highest fifth of household wealth survived the six years, but only 81 per cent of women with the lowest fifth of household wealth. Ninety-one per cent of the wealthiest men survived, but only 76 per cent of the least wealthy. A woman with low wealth had nearly four times the chance of dying in the six years as a wealthy woman.

Wealth is a strong predictor of longer life expectancy for older people

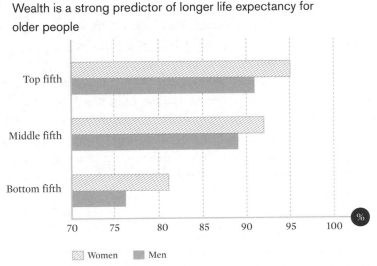

Figure 7.1 – Six-year survival rates (%) for men and women aged over 60 by wealth

Differences set in early

Variations in life chances – ultimately reflected in life expectancy – reflect an accumulation of differences in experiences across whole lives, starting from the earliest years. It is, of course, very hard to tell when children are young how they and their abilities may develop later on, and any attempt to measure different types of 'ability' (in terms of a score on some kind of assessment or test) is subject to wide margins of error. None the less, clear differences emerge early on between children from different backgrounds. Figure 7.2 gives some examples drawn from the Millennium Cohort Study (MCS), which has been following a group of children born in 2000–01. In this case, assessments are shown for children aged three (the left two clusters) and aged five (the third cluster). The average results are shown for children whose families were in each of five income groups. They show how high up the range, out of every 100 children, the average ranking would come for each group. If there were no differences between poorer and better-off children, all the bars would have a height of 50 – the average ranking for each group would match the overall average.

In fact, there were substantial differences. In terms of 'school readiness' at age three,[13] there was a difference of 31 places between the children from the poorest group of families and those from the richest – a third of the measured ability range. The gradient in vocabulary ranking at age three with income was almost as great. By the age of five, the difference in ranking of vocabulary scores was even greater than at age three. For assessments of conduct and hyperactivity at age five (not shown), the poorest fifth of children had an average ranking 26–27 places higher – that is, with *more* problems – than the richest fifth of children.[14]

There are already clear differences in assessments of children at 3 and 5 years old, depending on their parents' incomes

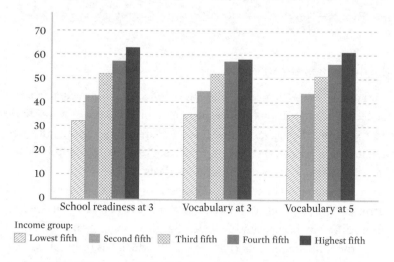

Figure 7.2 – Differences in 'school readiness' (average position out of 100) by parental income

There are, of course, many reasons why child development and parental economic position should be linked like this. Some differences relate to genetic links between parents and children, or to the ways in which the potentials of different children are expressed depending on the environments in which they grow up.[15] As well as the resources available to them, parental behaviour and parenting style may differ, both because of the different pressures on and opportunities open to parents with different incomes, or because more educated parents may both earn more and interact with their children in different ways. The MCS also shows strong links between parental income and resources and factors known to affect child development. The children of poorer mothers had lower average birth weight (which affects later development) and their mothers were far more likely to suffer post-natal depression than the children of richer parents, both of which have direct links to relative resources. In terms of behaviour, there were strong gradients by income in whether three-year-olds were read to every day and had regular bed times.[16]

When the MCS children reached the end of Reception year, aged around five, teachers assessed them for their Foundation Stage Profile (FSP). Because assessments were made in the summer term, the children were different ages when assessed, with up to a year's age difference. This gives a helpful benchmark for understanding the variations between other groups. For instance, the gap in assessment for children in England analysed by mothers' highest qualification was more than 20 points – equivalent to 15 *months* of typical development – between those whose mothers had no qualifications and those with the highest qualifications (degree and equivalent vocational qualifications). Dividing the children into groups by other characteristics also shows very large gaps. These were equivalent to: a year's development between those with no parent in paid work and those with two parents working; eight months between those whose parents were in poverty and those who were not; six months between those in lone-parent and two-parent families; and, remembering that there may be language issues involved, 10 months between those with a White and with a Pakistani or Bangladeshi mother.[17]

Mother's education and family incomes are associated with
differences in assessment at age 5, equivalent to several months
of development

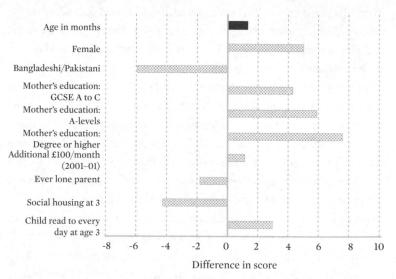

*Figure 7.3 – Factors related to differences in teachers' assessment of children at the
start of primary school*

Of course, each of these factors is related. For instance, those with low
qualifications are more likely to have low incomes. The differences
between groups defined in one way may actually be the result of
variations between them in other, more important, ways. Figure 7.3
shows the results of analysis by Andy Cullis and Kirstine Hansen, which
looks at the relationship between the children's scores and various
child, family and parental choice factors, after allowing for the effect
of the others.[18] It shows, from a wide range of factors, which ones
remained most statistically significant after allowing for other factors. A
child may be affected by more than one factor at once, so the effects are
cumulative. For instance, it shows that:

• girls had an assessment equivalent to over three months of
development more than boys;

- children whose mothers had degrees were assessed six months ahead of those whose mothers had no qualifications above Grade D at GCSE;
- every extra £100 per month in family income when the child was first surveyed (2001–02) was associated with a difference equivalent to a month's development. Given incomes at the time, differences in income could be many hundreds of pounds;
- if children were in social housing at age three, the difference in development was more than three months.

On the other hand, a child read to regularly at age three had assessed development, controlling for other factors, which was the equivalent of two months' extra development.

Where families have low incomes, children's test scores are most closely related to those of their parents

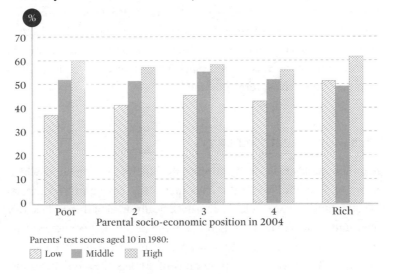

Figure 7.4 – Children's test scores (aged 5–16 in 2004) by parents' socio-economic position and parents' test scores in childhood (aged 10 in 1980)

These factors interact in complex ways. One example of how they do so is shown in Figure 7.4. This uses data from a survey that has followed people from when they were born in 1970 and has also looked at their children. It relates how high up the ranking the children came in a range of tests of their cognitive abilities in 2004 when they were aged 5 to 16 (and their parents were 34), both to assessments of the *parents'* abilities when they were 10 (in 1980), and to the family's socio-economic position. Looked at separately, both parental ability and family resources matter. But looking at both together, it is the socio-economic gradient for the children of *low* (measured) ability parents that is strongest. Where parents had *low* assessments when they were aged 10 and had low income when they were aged 34, the children came 37 per cent of the way up the assessment range. Where the parents had *high* assessments at 10 and the family had low income when they were 34, the children were 60 per cent of the way up the range on average. For children of the high and middle ability parents, income differences appear to matter less. There are, of course, many other factors that affect the relationship between children's performance in tests and their parent's performance in similar ones, such as differences in the 'home learning environment' that parents provide. But after allowing for a wide range of such factors, the authors found that about a sixth (but only a sixth) of the variation in children's test scores was related to what we know of parental abilities when they themselves were children.[19]

Does money really matter?

Such interactions make it extraordinarily difficult to disentangle which factors in a child's life are the ones that really have an effect. Kerris Cooper and Kitty Stewart looked systematically at all of the studies they could find available internationally (for OECD and EU countries) that might have a bearing on whether income mattered in itself for children's outcomes. Out of the many thousands of studies they screened, just 34 used techniques such as experimental research or sophisticated statistical analysis that allowed some confidence that what they showed was a *causal* effect of income differences, not possibly just the result of some other association.[20] Taken together, the results of these robust studies were striking. They showed that, 'Low income affects direct measures of children's well-being and development, including their cognitive ability, achievement and engagement in school, anxiety levels and behaviour,'[21] and nearly all the studies pointed in the same direction, finding positive effects of higher income.[22] The studies also found effects of income on other factors that affect children, such as parenting style, maternal depression and smoking in pregnancy.

The studies suggested that a given amount of extra income would have more effect on outcomes for poorer children than on richer ones. Putting a scale on the effect is even harder, but the relationships which some researchers had found suggested that the effect of a given amount of money boosting income was 'comparable in size to effects calculated for other interventions, including studies of school expenditure and early childhood intervention programmes', with income having an effect across a wider range of outcomes.[23]

This kind of finding matters. If the effects of a given amount of government spending on schools or early years were much larger than that of spending the same amount on raising the income of a poor family, an argument could be made that it was tough, but in the long run better for the child, to divert money from benefits to services. The evidence does not seem to support this. For those trying to economise on public spending, the uncomfortable conclusion is that *both* income and services matter, and both can make a difference.

The school years

The gap between income groups already seen in the early years does not seem to narrow over the school years, as can be seen in Figure 7.5. This presents a summary of evidence on the comparative performance of children who are and who are not receiving free school meals at each age in England through the school years. Whether or not a child is receiving free school meals is an imperfect measure of low income, as not all children from low-income families are entitled to free school meals, and not all those entitled actually claim or receive them, but it is the most easily available indicator. The results shown are for children of different ages in 2011–12, rather than for the same cohort of children as they get older.

Differences between children from poorer and other families persist all the way through school

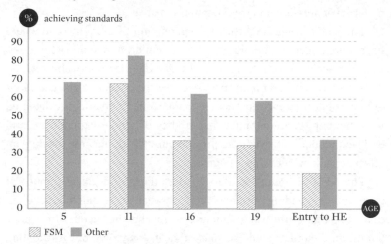

Figure 7.5 – Attainment gaps between children receiving free school meals (FSM) and other children at different ages, 2011–12, England

As we saw above, fewer children from low-income families are assessed as having a 'good' level of development at the start of primary school. In 2011–12 the difference was 19 percentage points between children receiving free school meals and others. By age 11, the gap between children achieving 'Level 4' in English and maths was a similar 17 percentage points. At age 16, 37 per cent of children receiving free school meals passed five or more GCSEs including maths and English at grades A*–C, compared to 63 per cent of other children, a gap of 26 points. By the age of 19, the gap between those achieving at least a 'Level 3' qualification was 24 points, and on leaving school, 38 per cent of those not receiving free school meals went on to higher education (HE), but only 20 per cent of those receiving them, an 18-point gap.

Although these gaps are wide, they are a little narrower than they were just a few years ago. The attainment levels of all children have risen, but those of poorer children have risen slightly faster. For instance, the free school meals gap at age 5 was 21 percentage points in 2006–07, falling to 18 points in 2010–11, before a small rise in 2011–12.[24] The gap at age 16 was 28 points in 2006–07, falling to 27 points in 2010–11 and 26 points in 2011–12.[25] Only 14 per cent of young people who had received free school meals went on to higher education by age 19 in 2006–07, increasing to 20 per cent by 2010–11, while the rise for others was from 33 to 38 per cent, so this gap fell too, by more than one percentage point.[26]

Some of the most striking improvements have been in London, some of them coming at the same time as the policies and resources associated with the 'London Challenge'.[27] These have been particularly striking for children from poorer families. One result of this was that by 2011–12, the children in state schools from the *poorest* neighbourhoods in London were achieving the same results (an average C grade) in GCSE maths and English as children from *average* areas in the rest of the country. Children from the poorest neighbourhoods elsewhere were only achieving a grade D on average for the two subjects.[28]

There are many different ways of measuring gaps in attainment of children depending on indicators of how well-off their parents are. Some studies compare poor children with all other children; others look at differences across composite indicators of parental resources. Some look at proportions meeting a particular threshold; others at average scores within a range. And the age at which children are assessed can vary from primary school entry all the way up to degree-level attainment. Jo Blanden and Lindsey Macmillan have combined a whole series of these to produce the summary measure of the relationship between educational attainment and family resources for children born in different years, shown in Figure 7.6. This suggests that attainment gaps between those from poorer and richer families widened between those born in 1958 and in 1970, and again for those born in 1978. But after that, they started falling again, with the gap early on for those born around 2000 back down to around the size for those born 40 years earlier (who were among the first to be affected by the school leaving age being raised to 16, and the abolition of 'secondary modern' schools, which generally only taught up to age 15).

Some of these results are drawn from national tests, such as GCSEs, where there have been accusations that the upward trend in results is no more than the result of 'grade inflation'. Combined with the 'ceiling effect' on higher income groups where pass rates are already high and cannot improve much, that could be a source of what otherwise looks like good news. But confirmation of a reduction of the social gap for school-age children comes from the international PISA (Programme for International Student Assessment) tests of 15-year-olds run by the OECD. The performance of British children is notoriously more affected by socio-economic background than elsewhere. For instance, 14 per cent of the variation in how well pupils do in the PISA tests in England is related to family background, but only 8 per cent in Finland and 9 per cent in Canada.[29]

But differences in children's attainment related to background have been falling for those born in the 1980s and 1990s

Figure 7.6 – Trends in attainment gaps between children by background, by year of birth

But here there is also good news. Comparing the results of PISA reading tests taken in 2009 with those taken in 2000, the gap in England between advantaged and disadvantaged children has fallen by what is measured as the equivalent of a term's worth of education. The biggest narrowing is at the bottom of the attainment range, where the gap has narrowed by the equivalent of two school terms.[30]

Given that educational achievement is such an important factor in how people then fare in the labour market, the recent reduction in the extent to which family background is associated with how well children do at school could point to the relative life chances of lower-income children such as George Ackroyd having improved compared to those of his parents born in the 1980s. But we will not know how that really plays out in the labour market for several decades. For instance, will the catching up of children from poorer backgrounds in school attainment and going on to university for a first degree be trumped by those from more affluent backgrounds obtaining further degrees, and these then being the key entry barrier for higher-level jobs?

Averages are not destiny

In all of this, it is important to remember that there is a large range around the average results for any group. Figure 7.7 shows one way of looking at this. The lines in the diagram show how well girls (in state schools) did at their GCSEs in 2010, arranged by the deprivation level of the neighbourhood in which they lived. The middle line shows the median (middle) result for a girl from each kind of area, in terms of how high up her overall GCSE results put her within the national ranking for all state school pupils (boys and girls).[31]

Thus the median result for girls from the most affluent areas was 72 per cent of the way up the national ranking, but for those from the most deprived areas, it was only 43 per cent of the way up. This is a very large gap (although slightly narrower than it had been even in 2008). But other lines give an idea of the range of results within each kind of neighbourhood. Looking at the top line, nearly 30 per cent of girls from the poorest neighbourhoods came in the *top* third of national results. Looking at the bottom line, nearly 30 per cent of the most affluent girls came in the *bottom* half of the national distribution. The chances are that a girl from an advantaged area will do better than a girl from a disadvantaged one, but this is not necessarily so. Just because the average for one group is below that of another, this does not imply that the same will be true of particular individuals.

School results are correlated with are a deprivation and affluence, but there is a big spread within all kinds of area

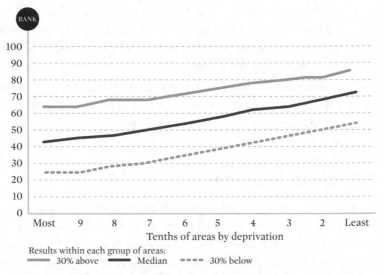

Figure 7.7 – GCSE results for girls (rank in national distribution) by area deprivation, 2010, England

After school

Despite a slow narrowing over recent decades, there is still a large social class gap in whether children go on to higher education. As Figure 7.5 showed, in 2010–11, 20 per cent of young people who had been receiving free school meals went on to higher education by age 19, but nearly twice as many, 38 per cent of other children. Looking more widely across the population divided into five groups by socio-economic status, Jo Blanden and Lindsey Macmillan showed that among those born in 1991, 18 per cent of the least advantaged fifth of young people from state schools were in higher education by the time they were 19, but 55 per cent of those from the most advantaged fifth.[32] For participation in particular 'higher status' institutions, the relative chances were even wider: 3 per cent of those from the most deprived fifth, but 22 per cent from the most affluent backgrounds.[33] And this is just among those who went to state schools. Of all A-level students going to independent schools, 64 per cent went on to what the Social Mobility and Child Poverty Commission described as the 'most selective' universities in 2010–11, compared to 24 per cent of all A-level students from state schools.[34]

Students with professional parents and those who went to private school are more likely to go to higher status universities

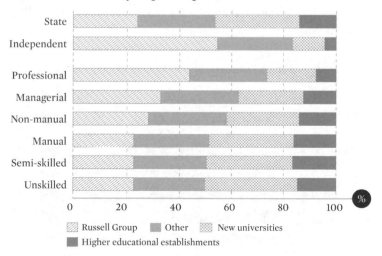

Figure 7.8 – University attended by background, UK-born students, UK universities

This is not just a difference between the most and least advantaged, but a gradient right across the social scale. Figure 7.8 shows what kind of university those who completed higher education in 2002–03 with different backgrounds had gone to. As was still the case for more recent entrants, more than half of students who had attended private schools went on to the research-intensive Russell Group universities, but only a quarter of those from state schools. There was an equally strong gradient by parental social class – more than 40 per cent of those with professional parents went to universities from the Russell Group, but less than a quarter of those with manual, semi-skilled or unskilled parents. Nearly half of the latter went to 'new' (post-1992) universities or other higher education establishments.

Eventual degree results follow almost as strong a pattern. Figure 7.9 shows that those who had been to private schools were rather more likely to get first or upper second class degrees than those from state schools. However, when factors such as the subject being taken and the university attended are allowed for, those from private schools were actually *less* likely to get good degrees than would otherwise be expected.[35] The figure also shows a strong gradient by class. Two-thirds of those with professional parents achieved firsts or upper seconds, but only half of those with unskilled parents.

And there is a social class gradient in class of degree achieved

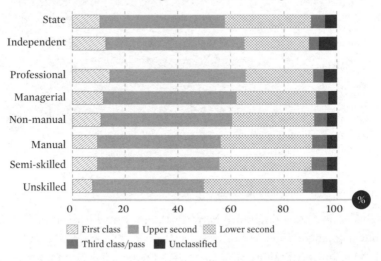

Figure 7.9 – Class of degree achieved by background, UK-born students, UK universities

Many of the differences in whether people go on to higher education can be predicted from the qualifications that young people achieve earlier on in the educational process. Haroon Chowdry, Claire Crawford and colleagues found that most of the social class differences in entry into higher education in 2004 and 2005 could be explained by the results they had achieved by age 16 and the types of school they had attended. In terms of going on to higher education at all, there was a 40 percentage point gap for men between the top and bottom fifths by socio-economic status, and a 44 percentage point gap for women. But type of school (state or independent), factors such as ethnicity and performance in tests at age 11 and 14 accounted for more than half of the differences. If GCSE results were also allowed for, the unexplained gaps fell to 9 and 11 percentage points for men and women. If age 18 results were allowed for too, the gaps fell to 4 and 5 percentage points.[36] Looking specifically at going to higher status universities, the gap between the top and bottom groups was 31 percentage points for men, and 32 percentage points for women. But all but 2.5 percentage points for men and 4 percentage points for women could be explained by their prior attainment up to age 18.[37]

However, the fact that who goes to university and what kind of university they go to is mostly 'explained' by factors such as ethnicity and how young people have done by the time they are finishing school rather than by other ways in which universities are selecting them does not remove the very large differences between those from different social backgrounds, or the onus on universities to make sure that they are selecting fairly. But it does mean that many of the differences in life chances between people from different backgrounds are driven by things that are visible while they are still at school. By implication, action to close social class gaps in going on to higher education would have to begin early, and not just when children are taking A-levels or when universities are choosing between applicants. This is not just a matter of the 'early years', however: quite a lot of the social class difference relates to what happens at secondary school, between the ages of 11 and 16.

And so to work

How people do at school, whether they go on to higher education and how they get on while they are there, all have powerful effects on the kind of jobs they go on to do and what their incomes will be. But as we have seen, there are strong differences in educational attainment between people from different backgrounds. This makes it unsurprising that there are strong links between how much people end up earning and what kind of family they come from. What may be more surprising, however, is quite how strong those links are, and how much stronger they are in the UK and the US than in many other industrialised countries.

Just at the start of people's careers, gaps widen out. This is not just between graduates and others with lower levels of qualifications, or with no qualifications, but also between graduates from different backgrounds. The researchers who carried out the analysis used in Figures 7.9 and 7.10 used information on the group of students who had graduated in 2002–03 to examine what earnings levels looked like three-and-a-half years after their graduation. Despite achieving slightly *lower* degree classes than women, 22 per cent of male graduates in full-time employment were earning more than £30,000 (that is, already within the top 30 per cent of full-time earners) compared to only 12 per cent of women. There was an even greater difference by schooling: a third of those who had gone to private schools earned over £30,000, but only 14 per cent of those who went to state schools. A quarter of graduates who had professional parents had high earnings, but less than 15 per cent of other socio-economic groups.[38]

The researchers were able to look at what was most important in determining wages. Allowing for other factors, including the class and subject of degree, the region the university was in[39] and the sector and region of employment, men who had been to private schools earned 8 per cent more than those who went to state schools. That is, *on top* of their greater chances of high performance at GCSE-level, and greater chances of going on to higher education, male graduates who had gone to private school were already earning 8 per cent more within four years of graduation than one would have expected given their gender, ethnicity, degree class, subject taken and occupation.

In more recent work, Lindsey Macmillan, Claire Tyler and Anna Vignoles looked at what kind of job people who completed university (either a first degree or a postgraduate degree) in 2007 were doing three-and-a-half years later. They found that graduates who had been to private schools were a third more likely to enter high-status occupations than state-educated graduates from similarly affluent families and neighbourhoods. Part of the difference was related to attainment levels at A-level and to taking subjects that have greater value in the labour market. But a large part was down to the kind of university attended, with those from private schools being more likely to attend 'elite' universities (as seen in Figure 7.8). In turn, part of these differences related to the use of personal networks in finding a job, but this only explained part of the link between socio-economic background and a high-status job.[40]

Chapter 5 has already shown how the wages of men and women with different levels of education follow very different tracks across their working lives. For women with low educational qualifications working in the private sector there is very little difference in their pay by age (see Figure 5.3). By contrast, highly qualified men in their forties are paid three times as much as those in their early twenties. 'Career progression' is something that makes a big difference for highly qualified men and women (although it eventually goes into reverse for older women working in the private sector). Wages for men and women with mid-level qualifications (and for men with low qualifications) are higher for people in their thirties than for those at the start of their careers, but then no higher – or even lower – for older workers.[41] This sort of comparison is based just on a snapshot of people of different ages. The different tracks (on average) by education levels can also be seen when following the same generation of workers as they aged through the 1990s and 2000s (see Figure 5.4). It was the best qualified men whose real earnings grew most rapidly, although all education groups saw rising real wages as a result of the growing economy, even if little or none of that reflected career progression for the less well-qualified.

The benefits associated with higher levels of qualifications therefore build up over time, are very large and, as we have seen, are strongly associated with social background. Given this, it is therefore no surprise that children's earnings when in adulthood are related to how well-off their parents were when they were growing up. It is easy to see how that might make a difference, and why the research evidence suggests that 'money matters' on top of all the other factors that later outcomes might be associated with.[42] While there are, of course, many things that 'money can't buy' (in the words of the title of Susan Mayer's book[43]), there are lots of things that money *can* buy, such as:

- high-quality pre-school care
- houses in the catchment areas of the best-regarded state schools (which then command a significant premium)
- after-school activities, private tutors, etc
- private schooling
- parental support in going on to tertiary education (and reduction in the worries associated with student loans)
- support in taking a Master's degree (for many better-paid careers this now represents the same basic required qualification that a first degree did a generation ago).[44]

Parents, if they can afford it and choose to do so, can also provide support with living costs at the start of careers, including during the unpaid internships that often act as an entry barrier into particular professions. The Social Mobility and Child Poverty Commission reports that, 'Graduates who have completed internships are three times more likely to get a job than those with no work experience, but 90 per cent of placements are unpaid in professions such as journalism.'[45] Beyond that, parents (and grandparents) may provide substantial help with housing costs – allowing their children to afford to live in the areas where there are jobs, including help with deposits for house purchase, without which few young adults now become owner-occupiers.

The scale of intergenerational links

To understand how big these intergenerational links are, we need to know not just how much people are earning today, but also how much their *parents* were earning when they were growing up. This is only possible from surveys that have been following particular groups of children since they were born (or which can track down information on the parents of today's earners).[46] In the UK case these data are for a group of children born in 1958 and another born in 1970. From these we can measure how strong the relationship is between adult earnings and family incomes in childhood. Figure 7.10 shows the results of recent work by Paul Gregg, Lindsey Macmillan and Claudia Vittori. It shows how strongly children's earnings when they were in their twenties, thirties and forties were related to family incomes when they were 16 – that is, in 1974 for the older cohort born in 1958, or in 1986 for the younger one born in 1970. If children's earnings were completely unrelated to parental incomes, the coefficients shown would be zero; if children's incomes were directly in proportion to those of their parents, the coefficients would be equal to one. In between, they show roughly what percentage of children's earnings appears to be associated with their parents' incomes. As with much (although not all) of this kind of analysis, the results shown are for men, as the relationships are more complex for many women with career breaks and more varied labour market histories.[47] Note that the results here compare children's *earnings* with family *incomes* when growing up, which come from other sources, whereas other studies (such as those summarised in Figure 7.11 below) compare children's earnings with a parent's *earnings*, which may give a different strength of relationship.

Two things stand out from this analysis. First, the strength of the relationship builds up as people become older. At age 30, only about 20 per cent of earnings differences for men born in 1958 were associated with family income; by age 42, nearly 30 per cent of them were. Given what we have seen about career progression and the chances of getting into the best careers, this is unsurprising. After that age, however, the parental income effect appears to wear off somewhat, looking at the latest figures for when the group reached 50.

But second, the association appears to be *stronger* for those born in 1970 than for those born in the 1950s. It matters *more* how well off their parents were for those born later.[48] This can also be seen if the family incomes for those entering particular professions from the two generations are compared. The parents of those born in 1970 who became doctors, lawyers, journalists or bankers were on average much better off relative to others at the time than the parents of those born in 1958 who entered the same professions.[49]

Earnings of men born in 1970 appear more strongly linked to parents' incomes than for those born in 1958

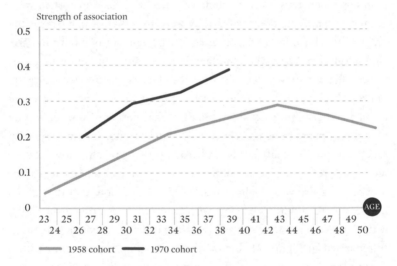

Figure 7.10 – How much of the variation in children's earnings is associated with parental income? (Men born in 1958 and 1970)

The result of this can be seen from the strength of the association when those born in 1970 had reached age 38. By then nearly 40 per cent of earnings variation between those in this cohort was associated with family income when they had been 16. If the same trend continues into their forties, as for the older group, by their mid-forties, we would expect the relationship to be stronger still.

In fact there are two reasons for supposing that this kind of analysis *understates* the importance of parental incomes. First, what we know about parents' incomes is imprecise, and an observation at one moment (as we saw in Chapters 4 and 5) may only give a rough measure of what incomes were like throughout childhood. If the average of parents' incomes when the children were 10 and 16 is used, which should give a better measure of childhood circumstances, 46 per cent of the variation in men's earnings at age 38 is explained by parents' income rather than just the 39 per cent shown in Figure 7.10.[50] Second, the estimates rely on the earnings we can see for those who were actually in work when they were interviewed. But those who had poorer parents who had longer periods out of work were themselves more likely to be out of work at any particular moment, and so left out of the calculations. Allowing for this would push the strength of the relationship up, perhaps by a further 5 percentage points.

Putting both of these issues together suggests that for men now in their forties around *half* of the differences in their earnings may be associated with how well off their parents were when they were teenagers. As we saw for the young George Ackroyd and Edward Osborne at the start of the chapter, if this carried on in the same way, it makes a huge difference to how well-paid we would expect them to be in 2040.

But note that this also implies that half of the variation in earnings is *not* related to family background. We may live in a society where people's life *chances* are systematically different from one another, but this is not one where people's destinations are *determined* by their origins. A key implication of this is that it would be hard, for instance, for today's better-off parents to be completely confident that their children, and especially their grandchildren, would also be as well off, and so would never need the kind of protection and insurance offered by a tax-funded welfare state.

The kind of picture shown in Figure 7.10 lies behind the frequent observation that 'social mobility' has declined since the 1950s, with the blame put variously on the abolition of (most) grammar schools in the 1970s to the alleged failings of the last Labour government in the 2000s.

But two words of caution are needed. First, members of the 'younger' cohort we can examine were born in 1970, went to school in the 1970s and 1980s, and were already 27 and well into their careers by the time the Blair government was elected in 1997. We simply do not know what has happened to this kind of intergenerational mobility for those born more recently. What has been happening through the education system, shown in Figure 7.6, suggests that the educational outcomes for those born in the 1990s and up to 2000 are *less* clearly related to parental background than for those born in the 1970s. If that narrowing of socio-economic gaps is carried through into earnings, the links between children and parents' incomes may already have weakened again for younger adults. But it will take until they, too, are in their late thirties before we can say anything definitive about more recent trends.

Second, what this kind of analysis shows is the relationship between the earnings or *incomes* of parents and of their children. This is not necessarily what people mean when they talk about 'social' mobility. Other kinds of analysis look at the strength of the relationships between the broad kind of *occupation* of parents and children: are today's professionals and managers relatively more likely to have parents who were in high rather than low-status occupations than a generation ago? The evidence here also suggests that these links are strong – we do not live in a perfectly mobile society – but that there was *no change* in relative occupational mobility for those in their late twenties between the early 1970s and mid-2000s (allowing for the changing composition of jobs, with more white-collar ones now than in the past).[51]

There is a fierce – and at times acrimonious – academic debate about how to reconcile these two contrasting findings. One sort of explanation is that the kind of differences shown in Figure 7.10 are just the random effect of comparing two sets of data, possibly affected by imprecise measurements of income when the older cohort were children. A second kind of explanation is that they are looking at two different things, one concerned with links between parents and children's incomes, and the other with links between the broad kinds of occupation they have.

Given that income inequality has increased *within* occupations as well as between them, it is perfectly possible that both observations are correct: what matters more now for your income is that your parents were *well-paid* white-collar workers, even if your relative chances of becoming a white-collar worker, given your parents' broad kind of occupation and the jobs available, has not changed.

It matters more in the UK (and the US) to choose the right parents

The strong association between parental incomes or earnings and sons' earnings is not only seen in the UK – it is also strong in Italy and in the US, despite the rhetoric of the US being a 'land of opportunity'. These three countries have had high levels of income inequality. By contrast, the links between fathers and sons' earnings are weaker in Scandinavian countries, which have had lower income inequality. Looking internationally at the countries for which comparable analysis can be made, Miles Corak and colleagues have shown that there is a general association between high income inequality and low intergenerational mobility in earnings, as shown in Figure 7.11. In the countries where income inequality was relatively low when those born in the 1960s entered the labour market, parental earnings (family income in the UK case) were half as important in explaining sons' earnings as in the countries with high-income inequality.[52]

This relationship is so striking that Alan Krueger, Chairman of US President Obama's Council of Economic Advisers, has dubbed it the 'Great Gatsby curve'. It may be that the 'rich are different from you and me', as the original book's author, F. Scott Fitzgerald once (almost) wrote, and not just in that 'they have more money' (as Ernest Hemmingway is said to have riposted). But in an unequal society the life chances of the children of the rich are also very different.

More inequality is associated with lower earnings mobility across the generations

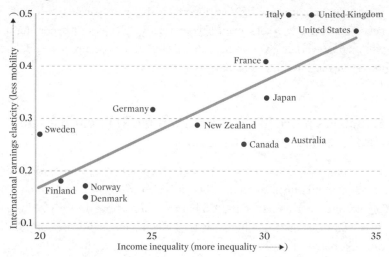

Figure 7.11 – The Great Gatsby curve

Source: M.Corak (2013) 'Income inequality, equality of opportunity and intergenerational mobility', *Journal of Economic Perspectives*, vol 27, no. 3, Figure 1

One of the reasons for this lies in the combination of two factors. First, income inequality is associated with higher returns to education – those who are better-qualified end up with much higher earnings relative to everyone else than in societies with more equal incomes overall. And second, if incomes are unequal, better-off parents have more resources available to invest in their children's education, so building their 'human capital'.[53] This combination feeds stronger links between parents' and children's earnings, and lower intergenerational mobility, as suggested in Figure 7.12. Countries where graduates earn much more than others, such as the US and UK, have strong intergenerational links. The reverse is true in Scandinavia – although note that the relationship does not appear to hold in Italy, whose reported graduate premium is low, despite its high overall income inequality.

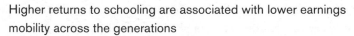

Higher returns to schooling are associated with lower earnings mobility across the generations

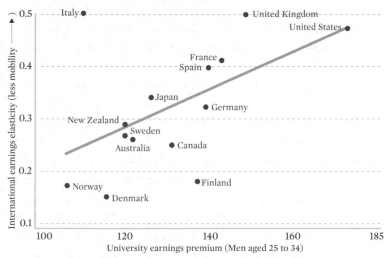

Figure 7.12 – Education earnings premiums and earnings mobility

Source: Corak (2013), Figure 4 (see Figure 7.11)

It isn't only income

If money matters, it does not just come in the form of annual flows of income and earnings, but also in the form of wealth, where inequalities are even starker, as described in the last chapter. Indeed, by the time people are nearing retirement, the income differences between those in different kinds of occupation discussed above and in Chapter 5 have congealed into massive differences in wealth. In 2008–10, half of households aged 55–64 who had been in higher professional or higher managerial jobs had total wealth (including pension rights) of more than £890,000. A tenth had wealth of more than £2.1 million. Ninety per cent of them had more than £260,000. By contrast, half of those who had been in 'routine' occupations had total wealth of less than £144,000, and a tenth of them less than £7,500.[54]

Parental *wealth* as well as parental *income*, and having access to one's own assets early on may also boost people's life chances. But it is difficult to disentangle the effects of parental wealth or wealth holding early in adulthood from all the other things that affect how people get on in adulthood, given how closely related they all are. As better educated parents have both higher incomes and higher wealth, separating out a separate 'asset effect' is difficult. Using data from the BHPS and from the study of people born in 1958 used above, Eleni Karagiannaki and Abigail McKnight have recently tried to do so.[55] Their results – which control for a wide range of other factors in people's background that will also be associated with their outcomes – suggest that there are additional effects from wealth. In particular, having parents with at least middle levels of wealth rather than low wealth is associated with a higher probability of getting a degree and with higher levels of employment and higher wages at age 25. Having some financial assets of one's own by age 23 is associated with higher levels of employment at 33 (for men) and 42 (for both men and women), even after allowing for other factors. Having assets at age 23 is also associated (for both men and women) with significantly better wages at both ages 33 and 42.

And, of course, family wealth leads on directly to people's own wealth through inheritance. Annual flows of inheritance are now very large indeed. Eleni Karagiannaki estimates that the amount being inherited by people other than spouses had reached around £35 billion annually by 2005.[56] And those inheritances are very unequally distributed. Between 1995 and 2005, about 2.4 per cent of adults received an inheritance each year, but for only around 1.4 per cent was the value more than £2,000 (at 2005 prices).[57] Among all those who inherited between 1996 and 2005, around half of the total of all inheritances in the decade went to the top tenth of inheritors, that is, to around 2 per cent of all adults.[58]

All sorts of people inherit, including some who have low incomes or who previously had little wealth. But those who are already economically more advantaged are both more likely to inherit, and inherit more when they do. Allowing for other factors (such as age), the chances of receiving an inheritance are greatest for those with degrees and least for those with no qualifications, and are much higher for homeowners and those who already have financial wealth. In each case, the amount that inheritors receive is also greater for the better qualified and for homeowners and those with financial wealth.[59]

This is borne out in what people currently expect for the future. Using data from the 2006–08 Wealth and Assets Survey, Andrew Hood and Robert Joyce have looked at how people's expectations that they would inherit related to how much wealth they already had. The most telling differences are for those in their early thirties, when they had already started to build their own savings (if they could), but would not yet have received most of their likely inheritances. They found that 78 per cent of the already wealthiest third expected a future inheritance, and that 35 per cent of them expected that it would be above £100,000. For those in the least wealthy third, only 45 per cent expected any inheritance, and only 12 per cent that it would be over £100,000. These figures are just for individuals; they are compounded when looking at partners' expectations. For all those in their thirties who expected to inherit more than £100,000, nearly all (87 per cent) of partners expected an inheritance, and more than half of their partners (52 per cent) an inheritance of more than £100,000.[60]

The only downside (in one unfeeling sense) for those with wealthier parents is that, as we saw in Figure 7.1, children are likely to have to wait longer before they inherit, because their parents are likely to live the longest. But not all financial transfers come through inheritance – parents also make cash gifts while they are still alive. Unsurprisingly, it is the better-qualified, homeowner, and higher-income parents who are most likely to be making transfers. At the receiving end, the chances of ever having received a gift in their lifetime are greatest for those who are better qualified and who end up with higher incomes. But those gifts – especially help with education – tend to arrive *before* they have got their qualifications and at a time when they have lower incomes. The gifts help them along their way, but are less important later on in their careers.[61]

What does all this mean for the aims of policy?

Political perspectives and politicians differ in the extent to which they believe that their role is to reduce inequalities in economic *outcomes*. But almost all agree that an aim of policy should be to create greater equality of *opportunity*. For Deputy Prime Minister Nick Clegg in the Coalition government,

> "The over-riding priority for our social policy is improving social mobility.... There is no more potent investment in the future than investment in the early years."[62]

He has argued even more strongly that it is whether there is mobility that determines whether any level of income inequality is fair or not:

> "Social mobility is what characterises a fair society, rather than a particular level of income equality. Inequalities *become* injustices when they are fixed; passed on, generation to generation."[63] (emphasis added)

For Prime Minister David Cameron,

> "I agree ... that we need a far more socially mobile country. That is something we need to do far more about.... We are making some progress but it's not fast enough.... I want to see is a more socially mobile Britain where no matter where you come from, what god you worship, the colour of your skin, what community you belong to, you can get to the top in television, the judiciary, armed services, politics, newspapers.... Don't just open the door and say we're in favour of equality of opportunity, that's not enough. You've got to get out there and find people, win them over, raise aspirations and get them to get all the way to the top."[64]

But this is not so different from the leaders of the last government. As Gordon Brown put it in 1996, before Labour was elected, "The essence of equality is equality of opportunity."[65] After becoming Prime Minister in 2008, he continued to argue that,

> "Raising social mobility in our country is a national crusade in which everyone can join and play their part.... At its core, this is a great moral endeavour."[66]

In fact, it is hard to find many people who argue against equality of opportunity. Even US President George W. Bush took an Act through Congress entitled, 'No child left behind'.

The phrase often used to describe the aim is that of achieving a 'meritocracy'. In a paper in 2001, a Cabinet Office official under the last Labour government explained this as follows:[67]

> By a meritocracy is meant a society in which the most able and committed people can succeed in attaining *the most desirable, responsible and well-rewarded positions*. Unless one believed ability and commitment were (either in whole or in part) determined by one's social class origins, the features of such a society would include high rates of social mobility and the absence of any association between class origins and destinations, ie equality of opportunity. (emphasis added)

There are two points to note within all this discussion. The first is the assumption, highlighted above, that getting the most able and committed people into the most responsible positions (which is hard to argue with) also means that these are the most 'desirable' and 'well-rewarded'. Second, the earlier quotations suggest that social mobility is a sufficient condition for social justice, and that the scale of differences in rewards for those who end up at the top and bottom of a meritocratic society is of no further concern.

But there are two issues with this. First, within a market society it may be necessary to pay those you want in particular jobs *some* more, but that does not tell you how *much* more. Second, much of the evidence in this chapter has described how, all through life, having access to greater resources reinforces advantage and disadvantage. What happens in the 'early years' is clearly important, but advantage and disadvantage reinforce themselves at successive stages *throughout* the life cycle. As the 'Great Gatsby curve' relationship suggests, this makes it extremely hard to achieve equality of opportunity for future generations in societies where there are large differences in economic outcomes within the current generation.

What is often forgotten is that Michael Young's 1958 book, *The rise of the meritocracy*, which introduced the word, was a satire, not a blue print. Its point was the smugness of those who rose to the top of such a society and believed not only that they deserved whatever rewards flowed from that, but also that their own children would deserve them too, reflecting the advantages of their inherited abilities, as well as the way they would be brought up.

Summary and conclusions

The evidence described in this chapter suggests that Britain is marked by unusually strong links between the affluence of parents and the life chances of their children, and that these links are also strong in other unequal societies. These links are reinforced through the education system, through inheritance, and through transfers throughout life. Once people find themselves on a favourable economic trajectory, those advantages tend to compound themselves through their working lives, into retirement, and even into life expectancy.

As the evidence also shows, however, there is nothing deterministic in this. Some children from disadvantaged backgrounds do well through the education system; it is just that at each stage, their chances of doing so are lower than those starting from more affluent backgrounds. It may be that up to half of the variation in earnings between men currently in their late thirties directly relates to differences in family income when they were growing up, but half does not. As with the shorter-range, higher-frequency dynamics of people's lives discussed in previous chapters, what both policy-makers and individuals are dealing with is the awkward complexity of a situation where there is mobility and change over time, but where some people's chances are systematically different from others. One implication of this is that even the comparatively affluent cannot be sure that their children and grandchildren will be quite as secure as they are themselves, widening the share of the population who have an interest in the collective forms of protection and insurance offered through the welfare state.

It maybe should not be a surprise that there is a symbiotic relationship between high inequality in a society and low social mobility. In a highly unequal society, many advantaged parents will do all they can to ensure that their children do not slip down the economic ladder – they know that it goes a long way down. And if incomes and wealth are unequally distributed, they have the resources to help them. At the same time, they may realise that higher rates of social mobility, in relative terms, cannot be a one-way street. If policy helps increase the chances of someone starting in a less privileged position to go up the social scale, that must mean that someone else's chance of going down has to rise, which may include their own children, and does not then seem so attractive. While many favour increased upward mobility, few seem to mention the increased *downward* mobility that has to go with it (in terms of relative positions, at least).

If children's prospective outcomes were closer together, parents could be more relaxed about where their children might end up, and about policies that might really boost social mobility. Equally, if high rates of social mobility were really achieved, more advantaged parents would have stronger reasons for insisting that the outcomes for children, whether they stayed at the top of the ladder or slipped down it, were more equal.

What that means for policy is that achieving more equality of opportunities and of resources go together. Failing to achieve one will make the other harder, and breaking through where inequalities in both are high, as in Britain and the US, is very hard indeed.

A MOVING BACKDROP

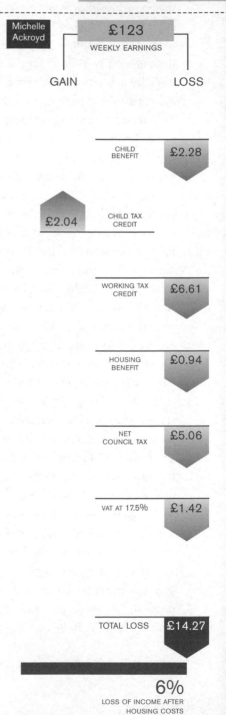

Stephen Osborne

£96,840
YEARLY EARNINGS

GAIN   LOSS

£29 TOTAL NICS

TOTAL INCOME TAX £926

£59,241
NET AFTER PC/TAX

Henrietta Osborne

£8,608
YEARLY EARNINGS

GAIN   LOSS

£113 TOTAL NICS

£547 TOTAL INCOME TAX

Stephen and Henrietta Osborne

£297 COUNCIL TAX

VAT £698

TOTAL LOSS £638
(= £12.20 PER WEEK)

0.7%
LOSS OF DISPOSABLE
INCOME PER YEAR

Michelle Ackroyd

£123
WEEKLY EARNINGS

GAIN   LOSS

CHILD BENEFIT £2.28

£2.04 CHILD TAX CREDIT

WORKING TAX CREDIT £6.61

HOUSING BENEFIT £0.94

NET COUNCIL TAX £5.06

VAT AT 17.5% £1.42

TOTAL LOSS £14.27

6%
LOSS OF INCOME AFTER
HOUSING COSTS

8. A moving backdrop

Economic crisis, cuts, growth and ageing

So far this book has discussed how both rapid and longer-term changes in the lives of individuals and families interact with the operation of the welfare state and other parts of public policy. But all of that takes place within an economy and society that are changing – and seldom as dramatically as over the last few years since the start of the economic crisis.

All of the extended Ackroyd and Osborne families have been affected by the crisis itself in terms of work and pay since their situations around 2010 described in earlier chapters. They have also been affected by the austerity measures – spending cuts and tax changes – brought in both in the last years of the Labour government and by the Coalition since 2010.

Stephen and Henrietta Osborne are the most affluent. By the summer of 2014 both were paid a little more in cash terms than they had been four years earlier, with their total pay rises in line with the national average over the period (7.6 per cent) since the situation described in Chapter 5. This took Stephen to just under £97,000 annual earnings and Henrietta to £8,600 for her part-time job.[1] But that lagged behind inflation – in real terms their pay was down by 4.1 per cent over the four years.[2]

But they, like most other people, were affected by the series of tax changes introduced since 2010. The scale of this can be seen by comparing the taxes actually due on their income in 2014–15 with what they would have had to pay if the 2010–11 system had been left unchanged, but simply uprated for inflation.[3]

National Insurance Contribution (NIC) rates rose over the four years (particularly for people who are 'contracted out' of the state second pension, like Henrietta). But the threshold for payments was £1,520 per year higher than it would have been if only adjusted for inflation. Together this meant Henrietta was paying £113 a year less NICs than without reform. For Stephen, a further adjustment to the upper limit to contributions meant that he did not get most of the benefit of the rise in the lower threshold, and he ended up paying only £29 a year less as a result of the reforms.

Henrietta was a big gainer from the rise in the Income Tax personal allowance to £10,000 per year – this took her earnings out of Income Tax altogether, saving her another £148. Indeed, it left some of her tax-free personal allowance to set against part of her investment income (which had now reached £19,400 after tax), saving her £400 more. On the other hand, Stephen was paying £926 more Income Tax than he would have done.

This is not because the rates of Income Tax have changed for him. Although a high earner, he is paid much too little to be affected by the new top rate of 45 per cent (or 50 per cent for a while) for those with incomes over £150,000. Rather, it is because less of his income is now charged at the basic 20 per cent rate, and more at 40 per cent, more than removing the benefit of the increased personal allowance from higher earners like him. He was now drawing £10,000 per year from his property trust, but the tax treatment of this has not changed – and his total taxable income after allowing for pension contributions was not enough to take him above the £100,000 level where the tax-free personal allowance is now phased out.

Taking all of this together, between the two of them they were paying about £236 more direct tax in 2014–15 than they would have done under the old system, or less than £5 per week, 0.2 per cent of their disposable income.

But two other major factors affected their taxes in different directions. First, East Cheshire District Council had frozen its part of their Council Tax for the last four years, so they were paying £297 less on their Band H house than they would have done if this had risen with inflation.[4] At the same time, the VAT rate was 17.5 per cent in 2010–11, but rose to 20 per cent from 2011–12 onwards. Allowing for the proportion of income that ends up spent on items charged VAT by people with their kind of income, this means that the Osbornes were paying around £700 per year more than if the rate had not risen.[5]

Other things will have affected them and others as well, but as far as these biggest tax items are concerned, the net result is that the couple were paying £638, or £12.20 per week, extra tax in 2014–15 compared to what they would have done without the combination of austerity measures and increases in tax thresholds. This was a little under 0.7 per cent of their income.

That will be fairly typical for very affluent but not super-rich 'empty-nesters' like the Osbornes, although some others would have lost more. For instance, if they had still had two children at home they would no longer receive Child Benefit for them under new rules given the level of Stephen's pay, which would have meant a further loss of nearly £2,000 compared to the 2010–11 system, or about 2.1 per cent of their income.

Single parent Michelle was the poorest of the Ackroyds in 2010. In 2014–15 she was still in much the same position as described in Chapter 2, working 16 hours a week at a rate which had also risen with the national average to £7.68 per hour, again well below general inflation. Comparing her actual tax and benefit position in 2014–15 again with what it would have been under the 2010–11 system adjusted for inflation, she is also worse off.

At that earnings level (lower in real terms than in 2010), she would not have had to pay Income Tax or NICs in any case, so she did not gain at all from the increases in the thresholds for liability since then. However, she lost out through the freeze in Child Benefit up to 2013, and then below-inflation increase in it in 2014, costing her £2.30 per week. Part of her Child Tax Credit had increased with the retail price index (RPI) measure of inflation, faster than inflation measured by the CPI. But the other parts of her tax credits had increased by much less than inflation. Overall, her tax credits were £4.57 less than they would have been under the old system, if it had been linked to inflation.

Her Housing Benefit was also 94p per week lower than it would have been, as it was now being cut back from a lower income level in real terms than before.[6]

But a bigger loss for Michelle came from the changes to what had been Council Tax Benefit, run by central government until April 2013, and until then giving a full rebate of the tax for those on the very lowest incomes. After that, responsibility for means-tested support was passed to local councils, but with the budget for it cut by 10 per cent, and councils instructed not to reduce support for pensioners, so all of the saving had to come from non-pensioners.

On the positive side for Michelle, Salford Council had, like East Cheshire, frozen its part of Council Tax since 2010–11 in cash terms, so her total Council Tax had risen by less than inflation, saving her £1.80 per week.[7] But at the same time, Salford's system of Council Tax support for those on low incomes now requires a minimum payment of 12 per cent of the tax from all non-pensioners, no matter how poor, and the rate it is cut back at if incomes (like Michelle's) are above a threshold increased from 20 to 25 per cent. This is actually less harsh than many councils, which now require a minimum 20 per cent payment, but still left Michelle having to pay an extra £5.06 per week compared to the 2010–11 system adjusted for inflation, even allowing for the Council Tax freeze.

All of these benefit changes left Michelle £13 per week worse off than she would have been under the old system. But she also had to pay higher VAT on part of her spending, now at 20 per cent, rather than 17.5 per cent. Even though the other benefit changes mean she has less to spend, she was spending £1.42 more per week on VAT than she would have done.[8] This took her total loss from tax and benefit changes to £14.30 per week, or £744 per year.

This is a greater loss in cash than for the much wealthier Osbornes, and is a much greater proportion of her income – 6 per cent of her income after deducting housing costs, more than eight times as much as they were losing. And that was all before allowing for the cuts in public services, which were much more important to families like hers than to those near the top of the income distribution.

There have been others with low incomes who have faced much larger losses for particular reasons. These include, for instance: social tenants affected by the 'Bedroom Tax' (which Jim and Tracy now would be, if they ended up on benefits again); private tenants affected by tighter limits on rents eligible for Housing Benefit (especially in London); people affected by the overall limit on benefits people can receive; people affected by disability benefit reforms; or those affected by the much greater use of 'sanctions' suspending people's benefits.[9] But as discussed below, Michelle's experience is fairly typical for what has happened to low-income families with children in general.

Overall, Michelle's total net income after allowing for her housing costs and inflation was more than 5 per cent lower than it had been back in 2010. This was not just because her pay had not kept up with inflation, but also because her tax credits and benefits had been cut even more. By contrast, excluding their investment income (which had done quite well since the bottom of the market), the Osbornes were 4 per cent worse off, but their slightly higher taxes were only a small contributor to this.

LIKE PEOPLE'S OWN lives, the economy, society and the welfare state change over different timescales. This chapter looks first at recent changes, such as those affecting Michelle, Stephen and Henrietta, particularly over the last four years. Are their patterns of losses from austerity – including measures which are coming but not in place yet – typical of people with their income levels? And how does what has happened in the UK compare with other countries in the crisis? Second, how should we think about the level of benefits, pensions, and the key features of the tax system over the longer term, in relation to prices and to incomes? Finally, given the way in which spending on the welfare state is so closely related to the life cycle, as described in Chapter 3, how will the ageing of the population affect those costs?

Fairness in a changing world

In thinking about all of this there are two critical issues on which approaches and attitudes vary: what constitutes 'fairness' in adapting to change, and, closely related to this, against what benchmark should we measure how policy has changed?

As an example of the first, what would constitute an 'equitable' way of rebalancing the public finances and reducing the public deficit[10] in the wake of the current economic crisis? People might take a number of positions, running roughly from the least to the most distributionally progressive:[11]

- In coping with an unexpected national shock, all households should make an *equal contribution* – for instance, through effectively lump sum (Poll Tax) tax increases, or through losses in services or cash benefits that have an equal value to each household.

- Governments should *withdraw gains* that people had previously made as a result of its activities that were unsustainable in the long run – for instance, by reversing public spending increases and tax cuts that were made at a time when there was what turned out to be an over-optimistic view of the public finances. That is, we were living beyond our means, and now need to adjust back to what was always the underlying reality.

- Contributions through higher taxes or losses of services should have an *equal proportionate impact* on each household depending on its resources, such as disposable income – that is, the effects should be neutral across the income distribution as measured at the start of the process.

- A related requirement could be that impacts should be neutral between *generations*, either in absolute terms, or in proportion to their relative resources.

- Contributions should be *progressive*, with 'the broadest shoulders carrying the largest burden'.

- Fiscal adjustment should be carried out in a way that *offsets* the distributional effects of other aspects of the crisis, such as rising unemployment or changes in real wages, that is, restores levels of inequality to pre-crisis levels.

- Contributions should come from those who had the largest gains in the years *before the crisis*, on the grounds that it was the whole operation of the economy, and the accompanying growth in inequality, that was unsustainable, rather than necessarily taxes and public spending.

- The burden should be borne by those believed to have *caused* the crisis, such as those in the financial sector.

Each of these interpretations would suggest a different evaluation of a particular package of measures. It might be noted, however, that in the current context only in the first two cases might a regressive set of changes (with the poor losing a larger share of income than the rich) be consistent with the notion of social equity.[12] The other concepts of equity imply that the impact of adjustment should at least not be regressive, and half of the concepts that it should be progressive.

This, combined with what we saw in Chapter 2 about the distributional effect of the welfare state and the taxes that pay for it, has important implications. Suppose we needed to close the government's budget deficit by £1,000 per household (or by £26 billion overall) – an amount equivalent to 3.3 per cent of the total of all households' disposable income. One way of achieving this would be to cut all of the services and benefits from the welfare state (shown above the line in Figure 2.10 in Chapter 2) by around 8 per cent. Figure 8.1 shows what a cut like this, spread equally across all of this spending, would be equivalent to for poorer and richer households as a share of their net incomes. The poorest tenth of households would lose benefits and services equivalent to more than 12 per cent – an eighth – of their net incomes. For all of groups in the bottom half it would be more than 5 per cent. But the loss for the top tenth would be equivalent to less than 1 per cent of their incomes.

An alternative way to try to reduce borrowing by the same amount would be to raise all household taxes in proportion by around 8 per cent. For instance, the main rates of Income Tax and VAT would each have to rise from 20 to 21.6 per cent, and so on. This would cost the higher-income households much more in cash than lower-income ones. But the second line in the figure shows that the sacrifice would, using ONS estimates, be much the same proportion of net incomes across all income groups – just over 4 per cent at the bottom, around 3 per cent in the middle, rising to around 3.5 per cent for the top three groups.

It is very hard to escape from the fundamentals of Figure 8.1. General cuts in the welfare state bear much more heavily on those with low incomes at the time than on those with high ones, while general tax increases tend to hit people in rough proportion to their incomes. We discuss below some of the ways in which the Coalition government has actually tried to close the deficit since 2010. Some of the tax rises introduced at the end of the Labour government's term were skewed towards the highest earners, and some of the cuts have attempted to protect the poor. But there are tight limits to how much the latter can be done sensibly within an already heavily means-tested system, as we saw with the effects of means-tested university bursary schemes in Chapter 5. And with the Coalition's decision that 80 per cent or more of deficit reduction should come from spending cuts and only 20 per cent from tax rises, it is virtually unavoidable that austerity will hit the poor much harder than those with higher incomes, as we saw at the start of the chapter, even before allowing for cuts in services.

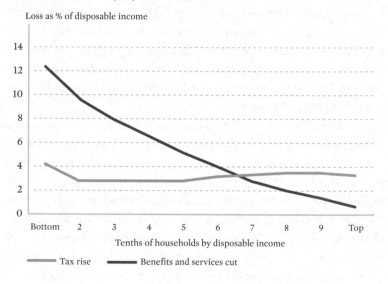

General cuts in social benefits are sharply regressive; general tax increases have a proportional effect

Figure 8.1 – Losses from general cuts in social benefits and services or general tax increases averaging £1,000 per household

What does 'unchanged policy' look like?

In describing how Stephen and Henrietta Osborne and Michelle Ackroyd had been affected by tax and benefit changes since 2010 at the start of the chapter, the main comparison used was between the actual tax and benefit system as it had been put in place by the Coalition government for 2014–15 and the 2010–11 system, with all its elements increased in line with price inflation. In other words, a standstill policy would have been to have increased all benefits and tax allowances by just under 13 per cent.[13]

But measuring the redistributive effect of tax and benefit reforms can be done in a number of different ways. The key issue is what is assumed to constitute an *unreformed* system – that is, what would have happened in the absence of structural changes. There are two main choices. One is that the initial system would have been uprated in line with *price* inflation – then any real increases or cuts in benefit levels show as a gain or loss to the income groups affected, for instance.

But over the long term, if incomes are growing, following this kind of benchmark would mean that the relative generosity of benefits and values of tax allowances would be falling in relation to incomes, and so other things being equal, relative poverty rates would increase over time. The public finances would also improve substantially as benefits became easier to finance and 'fiscal drag' increased direct tax revenues as a share of GDP (as a greater proportion of income became taxable). An alternative therefore is to compare the end system with what the initial one would have looked like if all its elements had been uprated in line with a measure of *income* growth, such as earnings or GDP per capita.

To show the difference that the choice between these two benchmarks can make, Figure 8.2 shows analysis by Stuart Adam and James Browne from the IFS of what happened as a result of the tax and benefit changes of the last government. It compares the effects of the system in place in 2009–10, just before the 2010 General Election, with the system Labour had inherited in 1997. As well as benefits, tax credits, and direct taxes like Income Tax and NICs, the analysis includes the impact of *indirect* tax changes, such as in VAT rates, which offset some of the progressive effects of the last government's direct tax reforms.[14] The two bars show the comparison against, first, a price-indexed base, and then, against one where the inherited system was uprated in line with average incomes (per capita GDP).

If the comparison is between the 2009–10 tax benefit system and the 1997 system just adjusted for price inflation, Labour increased the incomes of the poorest two tenths by around 15 per cent, while the higher income groups were comparatively unaffected. But if the benchmark is taken as the inherited system adjusted in line with income growth, gains were more modest (3–4 per cent) for the bottom four income groups, while there were modest losses (up to 2 per cent) for the top four groups. On this basis, what Labour did emerges as more clearly redistributive.

Labour's tax-benefit reforms boosted incomes most at the bottom

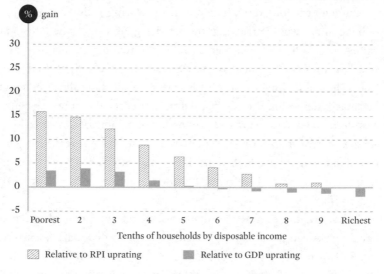

Figure 8.2 – Distributional effects of Labour's tax and benefit reforms from 1997 to 2009 compared to systems adjusted with prices or incomes

In the discussion of more recent reforms below, comparisons are currently only available compared to a price-linked base. It should therefore be remembered that the effects may be smaller when compared to a base linked to incomes. For instance, in the cases discussed at the start of the chapter, an alternative comparison would have been with what would have happened if the old system (including Michelle's housing association rent) had been adjusted in line with *earnings* growth rather than price inflation. Compared with that tougher (over this period) assumption, the reforms only reduced Michelle's income by 3.0 per cent, although that would still be more than seven times as great as the also reduced 0.4 per cent loss for Henrietta and Stephen calculated on this basis.

Coalition impacts

What has happened since 2009 has been far more dramatic, as first the Labour government at the end of its term in office and then the Coalition government have brought in tax changes, benefit cuts and reforms, and cuts in public services designed to reduce the deficit in the public finances that opened up in the wake of the financial and economic crisis. Some of these were mentioned at the start of the chapter, as they affected Stephen and Henrietta Osborne and Michelle Ackroyd. The full list is too long to include here, but some of the most important since the start of 2010 include:

- increased rates of NICs, but combined with above-inflation increases in the threshold for liability;
- an increase in the real value of the tax-free Income Tax allowance to reach £10,000 by 2014–15, but a cut in the amount of taxable income taxed at the basic 20 per cent rate, so the higher 40 per cent rate comes in earlier;
- removal of the tax-free personal allowance (on a tapered basis) from individuals with taxable incomes over £100,000 per year;
- a new top rate of Income Tax for incomes above £150,000 set first by Labour at 50 per cent from 2010–11, but cut to 45 per cent by the Coalition from 2013–14;
- reduction in the value of pension contribution tax reliefs for those with the highest earnings;

- the rate of VAT increased from 17.5 per cent to 20 per cent, together with changes in most other indirect taxes, such as delays to increased duties on petrol;
- penalties on councils that increased their Council Tax by more than a small percentage and encouragement for the tax to be frozen in cash terms, but combined with a reform to what had been Council Tax Benefit, reducing its value for those with low incomes by many local authorities;
- below-inflation increases in tax credit amounts and the income levels above which entitlement is cut back;
- a three-year freeze on Child Benefit, and tapered withdrawal of it from households where one member has taxable income more than £50,000;
- announcement that most working-age benefits will be linked to CPI in future, which increases less rapidly than RPI. However, the state pension is now increased in line with the 'triple lock' (see below), meaning that it rises at least as fast as the higher of prices or earnings;
- steadily tighter limits on private sector rents eligible for Housing Benefit and the introduction of the 'Bedroom Tax' (referred to by government as 'abolition of the spare room subsidy') for working-age council and housing association tenants receiving Housing Benefit and with more bedrooms than the officially set limit;
- an overall cap on the amount of benefits that one household can receive;
- a series of reforms to benefits for people with disabilities, including tighter tests for eligibility for the most generous ones;
- announcement that Universal Credit will be phased in (by 2017, according to current plans), replacing a number of existing working-age benefits (see Chapter 4);
- substantial cuts to funding for most public services, particularly those delivered by local authorities, but with some protection for the NHS and school education.

The distributional impact of many of the reforms to taxes, tax credits and benefits (but not other public services) has been analysed by David

Phillips and colleagues from the IFS, and their results are summarised in Figure 8.3. They examine the effects of measures announced since January 2010 (and so include the effects of Labour's pre-election Budget such as the new top rate of Income Tax) up to the March 2014 Budget statement, looking at their cumulative effects by April 2015. As discussed in Chapter 4, although the introduction of Universal Credit is a major part of the Coalition government's reform package, its implementation has been delayed. This analysis and that in the following two figures therefore do not allow for its future effects. The effects are shown against a base system uprated in line with price inflation.

Broad comparisons of this kind exclude some of the things that have had the greatest effects on individual households, such as the reclassification of people between kinds of disability benefit, or the much increased use of 'sanctioning' for those deemed to have violated conditions for receiving benefit, discussed in Chapter 9.

Reforms to taxes and benefits since January 2010 have been regressive, except right at the top

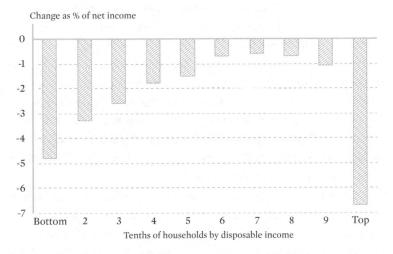

Figure 8.3 – Institute for Fiscal Studies estimates of effects of tax and benefit reforms, January 2010 to April 2015

Overall, the changes are equivalent to an average reduction in household income by just under 3 per cent. Unsurprisingly, given the importance of benefit cuts in measures described above, for most of the income distribution the net effects of the changes are regressive. On average, those with the lowest incomes lose most – more than 4 per cent of their incomes. Michelle Ackroyd, losing 6 per cent of her income already by April 2014, does a little worse than this, but as the breakdown in Figure 8.4 shows, that is not far above the average for families with children like her in the bottom three-tenths of the distribution. In fact, the same analysis suggests that the average loss for lone parents in work across all income groups is 5.4 per cent (and 9.7 per cent for out-of-work lone parents).[15]

There is more of a puzzle in the figures for the top tenth, where the *average* loss is shown as more than 6 per cent, greater than for any other income group. This is a surprise if one thinks of how little the changes have affected Stephen and Henrietta Osborne, losing only 0.7 per cent of their income by April 2014. They are, after all, well within the top tenth of the income distribution. Part of the explanation is that they do not have children – if they had, the loss in Child Benefit for people with their incomes would have taken their loss to more than 2 per cent.

But the main reason for the discrepancy is the inequality *within* the top tenth of the income distribution, and the ways in which the Income Tax increases brought in by the last government affect the very top, with incomes of over £100,000, or over £150,000 so far as the new top rate of tax is concerned. It is the top 1 per cent, and within this those with the very highest incomes, who have had a sizeable increase in their tax bills (to the extent that they have not been able to avoid them, which is not taken into account in the figure).

Averaging out these very large numbers (because the highest incomes are very high) with the much more modest contributions of the simply well off like the Osbornes produces the high percentage contribution from the top tenth as a whole. The net effect of the reforms does eventually become progressive at the very top, but for the overwhelming bulk of the population, including the lower part of the top tenth, they are regressive, with people losing a greater proportion of their income the closer to the bottom that they are.

Another feature of the reforms is how they vary between different kinds of household, as can be seen in Figure 8.4, which breaks down the same results as Figure 8.3 between pensioner households, those without children, and working-age households with children.

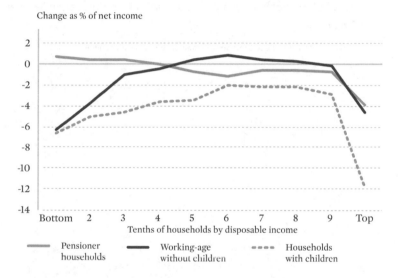

The biggest losers in each income group are families with children

Change as % of net income

Figure 8.4 – Institute for Fiscal Studies estimates of effects of tax and benefit reforms, January 2010 to April 2015, by household type

With favourable indexation of state pensions, the pensioners in the bottom 40 per cent break even or even gain on average, and in all income groups except the highest, pensioners lose less than 2 per cent of their incomes. By contrast, the poorest working-age people without children – whose incomes are most dependent on out-of-work benefits such as Jobseeker's Allowance – are more than 6 per cent worse off. However, households without children in the top half of the distribution gain, or lose very little, except right at the top. The biggest losers in nearly all income groups are families with children – losing over 5 per cent of their income on average, and more than 4 per cent for those in the bottom three-tenths of the distribution. Again the average loss for those with children in the top group is very high – nearly 12 per cent. Part of this comes from things such as the withdrawal of Child Benefit and tax credits from those with high incomes, but most is driven by the higher income taxes on those of working age and with the very highest earnings.

Adding in the effects of some cuts in services reinforces the losses at the bottom

Change as % of 2010–11 net household income including benefits in kind

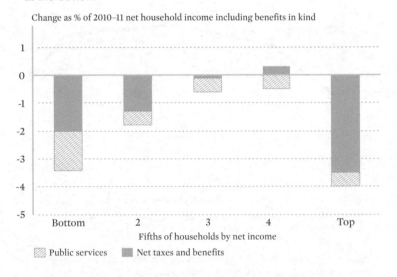

Figure 8.5 – HM Treasury estimates of distributional effects of tax, benefit and public service changes by 2015–16

These figures are based on very detailed analysis of all of the tax and benefit changes that have been announced, but they do not include the effects of cuts to public services. The effect of including these can partly be judged from Figure 8.5, giving the Treasury's own estimates of the distributional effects of reforms between 2010–11 and 2015–16. These are done on a different basis from those given by IFS, with more limited coverage of some of the tax and benefit changes. In particular, the losses are shown as percentages not of net cash incomes, but of net cash incomes *plus* benefits in kind from public services, which gives a smaller number. However, the differences between the bars with and without the effects of service cuts give an idea of their distributional effects. These suggest that for most households, the effect of the cuts identified by the Treasury is equivalent to about 0.6 per cent of income using this wider concept. However, for the poorest fifth the loss is nearly three times this, 1.4 per cent. For the other groups, the loss is just below the overall average. The top group is shown as having the largest average percentage loss from changes in taxes and cash benefits, but that is again the product of averaging out the losses for the small very high-income group right at the top across the whole of the top fifth, most of whom will have done much less badly.

Within all of these changes women might be expected to have done worse than men – given that the changes in taxes and benefits most severely affect families with children (and single-parent families in particular) and that cuts to public services have larger effects on families and on older pensioners using social care. According to analysis by the Women's Budget Group, that is indeed the case. Using a wider definition of cuts in public spending than the Treasury does, single women (with and without children) lose most – the equivalent of 12 per cent of their net income on average, compared to 9 per cent for single men, and 7 per cent for couples. Within particular groups – single working-age people without children, single pensioners, and lone parents – the loss as a share of net income is larger for women than for men in each case.[16]

How did other countries react to the crisis?

The UK is not the only European country to have carried out 'fiscal consolidation' – tax rises and spending cuts – in reaction to the economic crisis. Using the EUROMOD model of tax and benefit systems in different European countries, Paola de Agostini, Alari Paulus, Holly Sutherland and Iva Tasseva have looked at the distributional effects of tax and benefit changes introduced since 2008 and that were in effect by 2013 in 12 EU countries. The comparisons that can be made so far relate to the early phases of government responses, which tend to include changes to things such as tax rates which are more likely to be progressive and take effect more quickly rather than changes to benefits and their annual adjustments that take longer to affect people's incomes. They also exclude the effects of cuts in public services of the kind shown in Figure 8.5, which are likely to be more regressive. In the UK case, they include the effects of the tax and benefit changes implemented before 2010 (in contrast to Figures 8.4 and 8.5).

Figure 8.6 shows the patterns of effects in six of the larger countries examining measures that include changes to direct taxes and cash benefits. The results show the difference in net incomes for each income group under the 2013 systems, compared to what would have happened if the tax brackets and benefit levels had been either uprated in line with price inflation or in line with household income growth since 2008. One measure of how severe austerity has been in other countries is that over this time period, compared to a price-indexed base, this narrowly defined set of changes emerge as roughly neutral (apart from the very top) in the UK case, but generate losses in Ireland, Italy and Spain for all income groups and for some income groups in Germany and France.

The countries divide into four groups:

- In Germany, the changes were clearly regressive compared to either a price-indexed or an income-indexed base, with lower-income groups losing and richer ones gaining.
- The reverse was the case in France, where lower-income groups gained and higher-income ones lost.
- In Spain (apart from the bottom tenth), Ireland, and Italy, all income groups lost, but higher-income groups lost most as a share of their income.
- In the UK compared to a price-indexed base, most groups break even, but the top group loses. Compared to an income-indexed base (which would have involved real cuts in benefits and tax thresholds as real earnings fell), the changes emerge as progressive, with all groups gaining apart from the top one.

In the early stages of the crisis countries made different choices on how to spread the pain

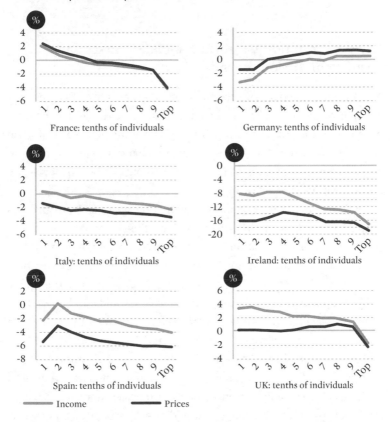

France: tenths of individuals

Germany: tenths of individuals

Italy: tenths of individuals

Ireland: tenths of individuals

Spain: tenths of individuals

UK: tenths of individuals

Income   Prices

Figure 8.6 – Distributional effects of direct tax and benefit changes in six countries, 2008–13

If changes in VAT are included, losses are greater (or gains smaller) in Ireland, Spain, Italy and the UK, and the distributional effects are less progressive.[17] If public service cuts were included, one would expect the effects to be more regressive again, for the reasons given above.

It will be some time before we can unpick how the effects of policy change play out over the longer term, and adjustments have clearly been much more dramatic in some other countries than they have been so far in the UK. But the differences in response in the early phases at least suggest that there is nothing inevitable that means that they have to bear more heavily on those with lower than with higher incomes.

The power of doing nothing: social security and taxation in the long term[18]

When thinking about how tax and benefit systems are changing, our thoughts are dominated by the headline changes in things like the rates of VAT or of Income Tax, or by big reforms like the plans for Universal Credit. But over the long term much bigger changes can occur through the glacially slow process of how tax thresholds or benefit levels are adjusted (or not) from year to year.

In September 1971 pensioners reaching the age of 80 were given an extra 25 pence (five shillings) per week on their state pension. Forty-three years later, the addition is still 25 pence – no government has had the heart (or the courage) to abolish it, but none has thought it worth adjusting to allow for inflation or changing living standards. If its value had kept up with average earnings, the addition would now be £5.60 per week – not such a lot, but not nothing compared with the basic state pension of £113.10 per week (from April 2014).[19]

Back in November 1978 the basic state pension itself was equivalent to 26 per cent of average earnings. For most of the period from then until 2010, its value was adjusted only in line with prices, not with earnings. If it had kept up with earnings, it would now be worth £168 per week. Even more dramatically, the single rate of Jobseeker's Allowance (then Unemployment Benefit) was nearly 20 per cent of average earnings. Today it is only 11.3 per cent. If its value had kept up with earnings, it would now be £119 per week, nearly £50 per week more than its actual £72.40 now.

As a final example, the single person's tax-free allowance for Income Tax was £595 per year when the modern system of Income Tax was brought in from 1973. If that had kept up with earnings, it would now be £10,370. In other words, the major reforms of the last three years that have taken the allowance to £10,000 in 2014–15 have simply taken the allowance back almost to where it was relative to people's earnings 40 years ago.

Views vary on how features like these should be adjusted from year to year. At the moment state pensions are being adjusted in line with the 'triple lock' – that is, by the *higher* of price inflation (as measured by CPI), earnings growth, or 2.5 per cent in cash terms. The philosophy behind this is that pensioners' basic living standards should not fall behind that of others – roughly caught by earnings growth over the long term. But at the same time, we have not wanted pensioner incomes to fall in relation to prices, even at times when real earnings have been falling, as in the last five years. And the Blair government was deeply embarrassed when an inflation increase one year only added 75 pence to the basic pension – our 'biggest mistake', he said once – so they now always grow by at least 2.5 per cent.

In the long run, this formula means pensions growing not only in real terms, but also relative to other people's living standards – albeit from a starting point that is less generous than it was in the late 1970s, and less generous than in most other comparable countries.

By contrast, most working-age benefits are usually increased each year only in line with price inflation and some have – as illustrated for Jobseeker's Allowance – fallen steeply in relation to earnings and other living standards over time. More recently, one of the most important austerity measures discussed above has been switching the indexation formula from one based on the old RPI to the CPI, which generally rises more slowly. This creates substantial savings from social security, and implies that benefits will fall faster behind earnings, when those start growing again. To add to this, most benefits are only being increased by 1 per cent each year for three years from 2013, well below the rate of inflation.

The rationale for this is that real earnings have fallen, but benefits were price-protected, so that gain needs to be reversed. But in effect, this amounts to a form of 'double lock' or ratchet *downwards*. When earnings grew faster than inflation, many benefits fell behind; but when earnings have fallen in real terms, the argument is that they should fall too – the exact reverse of the policy being followed for pensions.

Other parts of the system follow different rules. Under the 'Rooker-Wise' amendment, Income Tax allowances should be increased each year at least in line with inflation unless Parliament explicitly decides otherwise. Some elements – like the thresholds for the amount of savings people can have when claiming benefits – are only adjusted from time to time, as discussed in the last chapter. Others – such as the 25 pence pension addition at 80 – are never adjusted.

All of this gives governments a great deal of discretion, and the ability slowly to change the system without anyone noticing very much. But eventually, these 'non-decisions' can make a huge difference. Quite how large the scale of this is, is illustrated in Figure 8.7. This shows the changes that would have accrued over a 20-year period during which earnings grew by 2 per cent per year more than inflation from the system in place in 2006–07. From today's perspective, growth at that sort of rate looks like a pipe dream, but if the economy does eventually return to sustained growth, the same factors will come back into play, although possibly more slowly.[20] The figure compares how different income groups would fare, comparing the system which would emerge following the standard rules of indexation followed at the time with what would come from linking everything to earnings growth, a rule that would roughly leave income distribution unaltered, on this account at least.[21]

Over time, the comparison would save government a great deal – the equivalent of 3.6 per cent of GDP, or £47 billion at 2006–07 income levels. This would happen for two reasons:

- *Fiscal drag:* if tax-free allowances only rise in line with inflation each year, but incomes are growing faster, a bigger proportion of income is brought into tax each year, and the share of Income Tax in the economy will rise, other things equal. The same effect can pull more of people's income into higher tax brackets.
- *Benefit erosion:* if benefit and tax credit rates grow more slowly than earnings, their cost to government falls as a share of national income – benefits that are a smaller share of average earnings are easier to pay for.

Over time, failing to adjust benefits and tax allowances in line with growth means large losses for the bottom half

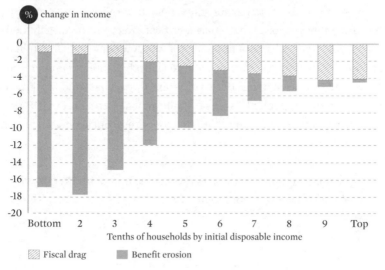

Figure 8.7 – Effects of fiscal drag and benefit erosion over 20 years, if real earnings grew by 2 per cent per year

The larger part of the overall saving, 57 per cent, comes from benefit erosion, with 43 per cent coming from fiscal drag.

The figure shows that the effects of fiscal drag are more important for those with higher incomes, reducing their incomes in this hypothetical scenario by 4 per cent. By contrast, for the bottom income groups, fiscal drag only reduces income by around 1 per cent. However, benefit erosion is far more important for those with low incomes, equivalent to more than 15 per cent of income for the bottom tenth and 17 per cent for the second group, but less than 1 per cent for the top two groups. Overall, the bottom fifth would lose 17 per cent of their income, but the top fifth only 5 per cent. As a corollary, child and working-age poverty rates would rise substantially; lower-income pensioners would be mostly protected by the decision already taken when the analysis was done that the state pension was to be earnings-linked in future. It is worth noting that even in the middle of the distribution benefit erosion effects (on things like tax credits and Child Benefit) are more important than fiscal drag.

These kinds of effect are often how chancellors – in normal times, at least – can pull rabbits out of hats on Budget day, using the unseen boost to the public finances to pay for some much more visible initiative. But how the money is 'given back' has a critical effect on the distribution. Figure 8.8 shows what would happen if a little under half (£20 billion at 2006–07 income levels, equivalent to all of the amount coming from fiscal drag) was used in one of two different ways. That would still leave a net gain to the public finances of more than 2 per cent of GDP (for instance, as one way of coping with the pressures from ageing discussed in the next section).

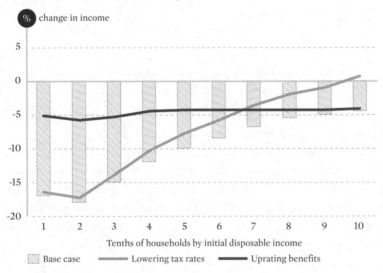

If government returns part of its revenue gain through tax cuts, the overall effect is even more regressive

Figure 8.8 – Effects of fiscal drag and benefit erosion if part of revenue used for tax cuts or benefit increases

If the returned revenue was used gradually to cut tax rates, it would, for instance, allow over the whole period the basic rate of Income Tax to be cut by nearly an eighth. For the top income group that would more than offset the effects of fiscal drag on them, and they would end up with a net gain overall. But for other income groups, and especially those in the bottom half of the distribution, cutting Income Tax rates would have little or no effect, as they do not pay Income Tax anyway. The second line shows what would happen if benefits (other than those already earnings-linked) were increased at a rate between price inflation and earnings growth (in fact, by nearly as much as earnings growth), leaving the same net gain to the public finances. In this case, all income groups would end up with a net loss of around 5 per cent of income.

This is, of course, a thought experiment, not a prediction or a recommendation. What it illustrates, however, is that what are often invisible decisions – such as the failure to uprate tax credits and benefits in line with even price inflation that caused part of Michelle Ackroyd's losses from austerity – eventually have huge effects on the structures of both tax and benefit systems, and through these on income distribution.

This kind of process is, however, potentially exactly what could be the result of the government's decision announced in the 2014 Budget to introduce a 'global cap' on the total of social security spending (excluding the state pension and Jobseeker's Allowance). The cap will increase only in line with price inflation. By implication, if the economy grows, the value of all benefits and tax credits will fall behind other incomes – or if one part of the system does not, another part has to be cut further. In the long term, that would institutionalise the effects shown in Figure 8.8 – unless something else means that demands on the benefit and tax credit system fall – for instance, if low pay rose faster than other incomes (reducing the cost of tax credits), or rents rose less rapidly than other prices (reducing the cost of Housing Benefit). In the other direction, the effects could be even more severe if, for instance, the number of people entitled to disability benefits rose or rents rose faster than other prices. That would then squeeze the resources available for everything else even more tightly.

It's all going to get more difficult

All of that is about what happens if the economy is growing steadily, and the country's demography is not changing. But in reality, demography is changing, and we are becoming an older society, as already touched on in Chapter 6. Figure 8.9 contrasts Great Britain's age structure in 2011 with the central projection from the ONS for 2051.[22] On these forecasts, there will be a smaller share of population in virtually every age group up to 50–54 and a larger share in every age group from 65 onwards. For instance, the proportion aged 80–84 is projected to grow from 2.4 to 4.0 per cent. In all, a sixth (16.8 per cent) of the population was 65 or older in 2011, but ONS projects this will be nearly a quarter (24.3 per cent) by 2051.

By 2051 the proportion of the population aged 65 or over is predicted to rise from a sixth to a quarter

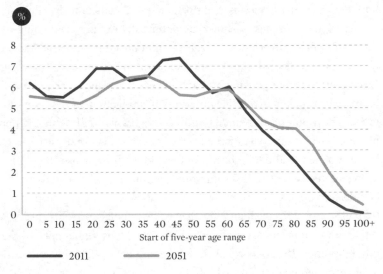

Figure 8.9 – ONS projections for percentage of population in each age range, 2011 and 2051

That people are living longer is good news. But in combination with the age-related patterns of demands on the welfare state of the kind shown in Figure 3.5 in Chapter 3, this means a large increase in what we would expect to have to spend in the future, if we carry on treating people of a given age in the same way as we do now.

The independent OBR looks each year at what pressures of this kind – alongside other factors such as pension reforms already under way – would mean for future public spending. The results of its 2013 exercise are shown in Figure 8.10. Such projections are, of course, vastly uncertain – we cannot be at all precise about how the age structure of the population will actually evolve over the coming decades, and many features of the welfare state are bound to change, as they have in the last 50 years. But the projections do give an idea of the scale of the problem. They are based on some key assumptions:[23]

- They incorporate the Coalition government's overall public spending plans up to 2017–18. Those include major cuts that have not yet happened, many of which have not yet been spelt out. As they take total (non-interest) spending down from 40.5 to 36.7 per cent of GDP between 2012–13 and five years later, they are, to say the least, dramatic. Whether they will happen is uncertain – not least because an election campaign will happen between now and then. It is what happens after 2017–18 that gives a measure of the age-related pressures in the system.
- They use the ONS's central projection for life expectancies, but a 'low' variant for net migration (which implies a somewhat older age structure in the short run than the faster net migration assumed in Figure 8.9).
- Most government spending (after 2017) is assumed to grow in line with national income.
- State pensions incorporate current plans for a 'single tier' pension from 2016, and increases in state pension age to 66 by 2020, 67 by 2028 and 68 by 2048 (less rapidly than now implied by subsequent announcements). The value of pensions is protected by the 'triple lock' (and so grows faster than earnings over the long term).
- Other benefits (including the new Universal Credit) grow in line with earnings after 2017 – a neutral assumption in understanding pressures from ageing, but one which is very different from current policy, under which they are falling behind even prices.

- Health spending reflects assumptions of needing the same care at any given age, but with productivity growing in line with the economy. Spending on long-term care is as projected by LSE's Personal Social Services Research Unit, taking account of ageing.

Having done all this, the bottom line is that total spending would be projected to grow from 36.7 per cent of GDP in 2017–18 to 40.6 per cent in 2062–63, or by 4 per cent of GDP – 1 per cent of GDP every decade. That is a great deal, but clearly not impossible. Indeed, it would only reverse the assumed cuts built into the projections up to 2017, putting us back where we were in 2012. But the intention of those cuts is to eliminate public borrowing without putting up taxes any more. Whatever the right level of the deficit in the short run, in the long run, increased spending would need to be matched by higher taxes. The same OBR projections suggest that government revenues would grow only by 1.2 per cent of GDP under neutral assumptions over the period, so there would be a big hole to fill. The difference of 2.7 per cent of GDP is, for instance, equivalent to about £43 billion at 2013–14 levels of national income. Doing this all at once would make recent tax increases look easy. On the other hand, having to find an extra £1 billion in each year's budget for the next 40 years is equally clearly not impossible.

In one way, the projections may overstate the pressures. Note first that the total is projected to be *lower* in 2022 than in 2017. Over this period the ageing pressures are less acute, and savings are already built in through rising state pension age and reforms to public service pensions. Even in 2032 the total is only put at 0.9 per cent of GDP more than 15 years before. It is after that when the totals start growing. But part of the reason for this is that the only subsequent increase in state pension age is pencilled in for 2048. If – as is now planned – pension age rises in line with life expectancies, actual increases in pension age would come much faster (see Chapter 6), and state pension spending would, in fact, rise more slowly.

It is also possible that the projections are too gloomy on the demands for healthcare in one way. They are built on assuming that each 75-year-old needs the same care in 2052, for instance, as a 75-year-old in 2012, despite the projections that people will be living much longer in 2052. This might mean that care needs would kick in at later ages. In its 2012 report, the OBR suggested that allowing for what is sometimes called 'compression of morbidity' – that is, staying healthier longer – could cut health spending needs by 0.5 per cent of GDP by 2061, or even by 1 per cent of GDP in the best case scenario.[24]

After 2020, ageing puts pressures on public spending equivalent to an extra 1 per cent of GDP per decade

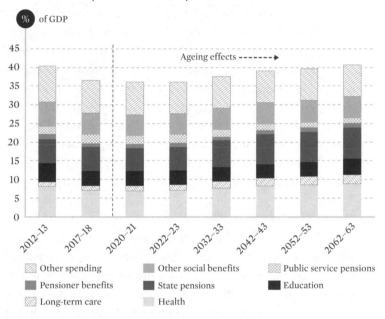

Figure 8.10 – OBR long-term public spending projections

The greater risks could be the other way, however. Some conditions are not, on current trends, being postponed in this way. Looking ahead just to 2030, compared to 2010, a recent House of Lords Select Committee investigation[25] pointed to likely increases for those aged 65 or older in England and Wales of:

- 80 per cent in people with dementia
- 45 per cent in people with diabetes
- 50 per cent or more in people with arthritis, coronary heart disease and stroke
- 90 per cent in people with moderate or severe needs for social care.

To make matters worse, the OBR projections assume that productivity in healthcare rises in line with that in the rest of the economy. But productivity gains are much harder to achieve when most of what is being provided depends on inputs of people's time for caring in one form or another. Historically this has meant that measured productivity has grown more slowly in public services than in other parts of the economy – the so-called 'Baumol effect' identified by the US economist William Baumol. The OBR suggests that between 1979 and 2009 UK healthcare productivity grew, but only by 1 per cent per year, while the rest of the economy grew faster. If this continued through the projection period, the cumulative effect would be to add 1.9 per cent of national income to the cost of providing constant services by age in 2062 – taking the overall rise by then compared to 2017 to 5.8 per cent of GDP.

A further source of risk in the OBR analysis is what happens to migration in the future. The analysis it uses suggests that migrants make a positive contribution to public finances – migrants typically make less use of public services than others (often having been educated abroad) and pay more taxes (as they are more likely to be in work). As a measure of the potential effect of this, if net migration to the UK was reduced to zero from 2016 (rather than the OBR's central assumption of 140,000 people per year), other things being equal, public spending would be 1.2 percentage points of GDP higher and current receipts 0.1 percentage points lower by 2042–43, with the effects escalating rapidly after that.[26]

There are vast uncertainties in both directions. But what this illustrates is one of the most important background factors in British politics over the coming decades. An ageing population and the structure of our welfare state means we will have to spend more just to stand still in terms of services in relation to needs and living standards. That leaves us with two choices in the long run – cutting services in relation to needs or raising more revenue.

Summary and conclusions

The complex variations this book describes in people's lives from week to week, year to year, across their own lives and from generation to generation do not take place in a vacuum. The world about them is changing too, and with it, the way public policies are structured. This chapter looked at three aspects of this.

We have been living through dramatic changes to taxes and benefits as first the Labour government and then its Conservative-Liberal Democrat successor have tried to reduce the public deficit in the wake of the financial and economic crisis since 2008. The impact of those changes has not been evenly spread across the population. One of the crucial reasons for this is the decision that the balance of adjustment should overwhelmingly come from cuts in public spending, especially on social security benefits rather than from taxation.

We saw already in Chapter 3 that pensioners have generally been more protected from this than working-age people and families with children. The analysis presented here shows that the general impact of the changes has also been regressive, bearing more heavily on people the lower down the income distribution they are. This was not so much the case at the start of the process, with many benefits continuing to be at least protected against inflation and with some tax rises, particularly for those with the highest incomes. But as time has gone on, the impact on those with lower incomes has grown. What happened to working single mother Michelle Ackroyd, losing nearly 6 per cent of her net income from the changes between 2010 and 2014, was fairly typical for lower-income families with children, and the loss of under 1 per cent for the much higher-income Osbornes fairly typical for high-income, but not super-rich, households without children at home. The difference is reinforced by the way that people with lower incomes also lose proportionately more from cuts in other public services than others. It is only when one gets into what is, in fact, the very top percentage or two of earners that the changes to top Income Tax rates and other adjustments have had major effects, with much greater effects than on others who are simply near, but not at, the top.

In the long run, the quiet and often hidden processes of how we adjust the level of benefits and tax allowances from year to year can have just as great an effect. Left on autopilot, if and when the economy returns to growth, each year benefits and tax credits tend to fall behind general living standards (although pensions are now insulated from this), and fiscal drag brings a bigger share of income into tax, and into tax at higher rates. Letting this run on helps public finances, but does so in a way that increases inequality and poverty. Recent short-term fiscal adjustments have been regressive, but so – unless conscious decisions are made to offset it – are the long-term effects of how we adjust the tax and benefit systems to allow for growth and inflation. Indeed, the idea that social security benefits (except for the state pension) and tax credits should grow no faster than prices is now being institutionalised through the planned 'welfare cap'.

At the same time the implication of the way in which so much spending is concentrated on older people – not just pensions, but also healthcare – is that the ageing of the population will mean rising costs just to stand still over the next few decades. Some of these costs can be kept under control if, for instance, state pension ages increase as life expectancy rises. But even with fairly optimistic assumptions on healthcare, one set of estimates put the trend of rising costs due to ageing as the equivalent of 1 per cent of national income every decade. That would be a huge amount of revenue to raise in one go, although clearly not impossible if adjusted for steadily. The alternative to such relentless and unwelcome pressure on every Budget is to reduce the scale of services and benefits people receive to cope with the pressures of their lives at each stage, which would also be unwelcome. The final chapter returns to the beliefs surrounding how we make this unattractive choice.

9. Conclusion

Britain's misunderstood welfare state

BRITAIN'S WELFARE STATE now accounts for two-thirds of all government spending. This proportion continues to grow as the population ages, and as successive governments have chosen to increase spending on the 'big ticket' items (healthcare, schools and pensions) in good economic times, and to protect them in bad ones. How it operates, for whom, and how it evolves are probably the most important questions in British politics – whether the concern is with public spending, taxation, inequality or economic efficiency.

It is therefore profoundly damaging that as a nation we understand so poorly what all this activity achieves, and who is affected by it. Public perceptions (and misconceptions) are dominated by two linked notions, often tapped into by politicians and then further fed by their own rhetoric and parts of the media. First, the beneficiaries of the 'welfare' system are largely unchanging and are different from the rest of us who pay for them through our taxes. Second, the bulk of this huge amount of spending goes on hand-outs to a group of people who are out of work, often claiming fraudulently. Some of the evidence on these issues is discussed in more detail below.

The lives of 'others'

A central assumption in much discussion of the welfare state is often the notion that people receiving benefits are somehow 'others'. *We* are law-abiding and pay large amounts into a system that supports a stagnant population of *them*, who are either on the fiddle or are sitting around idly when there is actually plenty of work available.

There are doubtless people who are shiftless and idle, or who at least manage to disguise their lack of idleness from benefit officials. But that group of people, and what they extract from the system, is completely unrepresentative of how most people live and of what the welfare state really does. The reality is far more complicated and ever changing.

Although the short vignettes about the members of the extended Ackroyd and Osborne families at the start of each of the last seven chapters are fictional and stereotypical, they are based on what we know of ordinary people's lives – not the very rich or the very poor, but the great majority of us in between. Their circumstances illustrate and introduce key points from the detailed analysis and evidence presented in the respective chapters.

Give and take?

Chapter 2 showed that at any one time there are considerable transfers going on between people who are richer and poorer at a particular moment. Adding in the value of what working single mother Michelle Ackroyd gets from the NHS and state schooling for her daughter, together with benefits and tax credits, she was benefiting by around £16,000 more in 2010 than she was paying in taxes. In the same year, comparatively well-paid young parents Henry and Clare Osborne were putting in almost exactly that sum through taxes over and above what they were getting out. This is a considerable amount of redistribution, but even after it, Henry and Clare were still twice as well off as Michelle.[1] This reflects one of the main challenges facing the British welfare state: compared to other countries: it has so much to do. Even though tax and social spending achieves as much redistribution as in many other countries, the UK still ends up as one of the most unequal of the industrialised countries because it starts with such an unequal distribution of income from the market (earnings and investment income).

In the last decade – predating the 2008 economic crisis – the incomes of those in the middle have come under pressure. But that squeezing of the middle has not happened because there has been greatly increased redistribution to the poor. Rather, what has happened is that the shares of all other income groups have been squeezed as the share of the very top has soared, bolstered by the ability of those finding themselves able to extract what economists call 'rents' from the particular positions they are in, and by the rising importance of returns to wealth.[2] It is the rich who have got more expensive, not, as has been alleged, that the 'cost' of the poor has risen.

To richer and to poorer

Snapshot pictures of redistribution can be very misleading, however, as explained in Chapter 3. Over our whole lives we are all – or nearly all – considerable beneficiaries from the welfare state, including affluent middle-class professionals such as Henry's parents, Stephen and Henrietta Osborne. Their prospective lifetime receipts from the system projected back in the late 1980s – including pensions over their longer lives, the best healthcare and subsidised sixth form and university education for their children – came out almost as great as those for the much less well-paid Jim and Tracy Ackroyd, Michelle's parents. The Osbornes got more, if tax reliefs and other parts of public spending were thrown in. Things have changed, and averaging out different kinds of lives suggests more of a dead heat than this, but the implications are still startling.

Generally speaking, however rich or poor, what the members of a typical household eventually get out of the welfare state at different points over their lifetimes, from pensions, the NHS, schools, care for older people, benefits and tax credits, is now equivalent to up to 25 years' worth of average annual net (take-home) income (or the equivalent of three houses at current average prices). There is redistribution between the lifetime rich and the lifetime poor, as the lifetime rich pay much more in tax, but most of what the welfare state and the taxes we pay for it do is to redistribute across our own life cycles, and so smooth out our available resources from year to year.

Living on a roller coaster

The reasons for all this moving around of resources – and why we need this to happen – lie not only in how things change over the life cycle, but also because of how rapidly changing many people's lives are from week to week and from year to year, even within the same stages of life. As illustrated in Chapter 4, income and outgoings may stay much the same across the year for a young civil servant like Henry's sister, Charlotte. For many others, such as Michelle's brother, Gary, and his wife, Denise, things are far more complicated. Varying hours each week, term time-only work and benefits and tax credits that adjust with variable and sometimes incomprehensible lags, not just periods between jobs, mean a roller coaster of circumstances from month to month or week to week for many lower-income families. With the spread of 'zero hours contracts', with no guaranteed hours each week, the uncertainties in this have worsened for many.

And far from unemployment mainly being the same people staying out of work for long periods, a million people lose their work every three months, while another million find work. Fewer than half of new claims for Jobseeker's Allowance last more than two months. Only 6 per cent lasted as long as a year before the economic crisis, and still only 10 per cent after it. Perhaps more surprising for some, becoming unable to work because of sickness or disability is not a one-way street – people's conditions do improve. Fewer than half of those starting claims for what was Incapacity Benefit in the mid-2000s were still receiving it after a year, and only a third after two years, However, for some people, the fact that health conditions (such as mental health problems) can fluctuate from day to day can make finding and keeping work hard, as employers often prefer people whose attendance is more reliable.

All of this makes the design and delivery of policies very hard. If the new Universal Credit does eventually come into being, as currently planned, the system running it would have to cope with 1.6 million changes in circumstances *every month* among the 7.5 million households receiving it. This will make the system hard to run. But the way it is intended to operate will also increase some of the pressures on low-income budget managers like Denise Ackroyd. Many are used to budgeting weekly or fortnightly, but the new system will roll all the benefits up into a single monthly lump.

The complexity of people's lives makes attempts to simplify the benefit system sound attractive, but that very complexity makes 'simplification' fraught with difficulty, threatening to make things even harder to cope with for people with little margin for errors – their own, or those of official systems.

Life cycles of ups and downs

Over the longer term, as well as changes in jobs and periods out of work because of unemployment or sickness, people's needs change, as Seebohm Rowntree observed in the 'cycles of want and plenty' in the lives of York labourers more than a century ago. Children are born, grow up, leave home, and sometimes return again, at least for a while. Looking at what happened to them in the 10 years up to 2010, we saw in Chapter 5 that with three children still at home, Jim and Tracy started in 2001 only a little above the poverty line. But after Michelle moved out for a second time in 2005, and Gary started bringing in a wage, the family reached the middle of the income distribution – but only before dropping into poverty for a time when Jim lost his job in 2006. By 2008 he was back in work again, and by the time all three children had left home by 2010, they were better off than they had ever been. Meanwhile, Stephen Osborne's heart attacks in 2002 and 2003, and subsequent downshifting in the pace of his work, meant that his and Henrietta's incomes also fluctuated considerably over the decade – although they still managed to stay within the top 2 per cent of all households.

These patterns match what we see across the whole population: people's incomes vary greatly from year to year – those counted as poor in one year are often not poor the next, and continuous poverty for several years in a row is comparatively rare (and became less common over the 2000s as persistent poverty fell). But these movements are not random: people who start poor are more likely to end poor, and people who start rich are more likely to end rich, whatever time period we look at.

This is a long way from either of the simple worlds in which policy design would be easy. There is not a rigid underclass or overclass whose members stay the same: people move up and they move down. But those movements are not random, with today's elite on the breadline tomorrow, or vice versa. One implication of this is that many more people are affected by low income over a number of years than at any one time – for instance, half of all children were in families that were poor in at least one out of the 10 years up to 2006. A second implication is that we have to take account of changing circumstances in how we deliver services and benefits, but should do so in a way that does not send out precisely the wrong signals. It does not help anyone to give the message that they will have to leave social housing if they are no longer 'in need' – 'get a job, lose your home' – for instance. Nor can we pile means test on means test in an attempt to protect the poor while keeping taxes down, if the effect of this is to leave those just above the cut-offs worse off or resentful as to why they seemed to have been ruled out of something that others get, so gaining little for 'doing the right thing'.

Wealth – and how we help some to accumulate more

So far, the evidence has looked at how people's flows of *income* change over their lives. Chapter 6 looked at how *wealth* – people's stocks of assets such as savings, houses and accumulated pension rights – changes over their lives, and at the far greater inequality in the patterns we see for wealth than there is for income. Although they live outside London, where house price inflation has had its greatest effects, Stephen and Henrietta Osborne had accumulated wealth of one kind or another worth £2.1 million by 2010, putting them in the top 2 per cent of all households. Most of this wealth accumulation had been helped (or at least not hindered) by the tax system, with favourable treatment for their pensions saving, house purchase, tax-free savings accounts, and capital gains. By contrast, the £6,000 of cash savings that Jim and Tracy had managed to accumulate had not been so favourably treated by the tax system, and if this sum had been a little higher, they would have been penalised at times when they claimed benefits. There is some luck in this – if they had been in a position to exercise the Right to Buy their council house in the 1990s, they would have been considerably helped by the system.

The sums involved when one looks at wealth are far greater than those we normally think about in terms of annual incomes. However, the way policy relates to it is also far less coherent, treating what are inherently similar things (ways of saving or kinds of asset) in very different ways, and often benefiting the already advantaged most and reinforcing inequalities. Wealth is generally lightly taxed, meaning that more tax revenue has to be collected from people's earnings and spending.

With wealth now being so much larger in relation to incomes than it was 20 years ago, it takes many more years of incomes and saving to move each rung up the wealth ladder. This has also led to members of successive generations ending up with such great, possibly unbridgeable, differences in wealth. Middle wealth households aged 55–64 have £340,000 more wealth of all kinds than those aged 25–34. That there is a difference is not surprising – older households have had more time to save, build pension rights and pay off a mortgage. It is the size of the difference that is startling. To close that gap over 30 years would require the younger group to save the equivalent of nearly half of average take-home income every year. There is no sign that this is going to happen, quite the reverse in fact. But this is not simply about uniformly rich 'baby-boomers' compared to the poor members of a 'jilted' younger generation. The inequalities within each age group are as great as those between them. Some baby-boomers benefited from the most generous kinds of 'final salary' pension and from the boom in house prices in

London and the South East, but many of them did not. Many people currently reach retirement with little by way of assets beyond their right to a future state pension. And while large numbers of younger people will benefit considerably from future help and inheritance from parents and grandparents, which can be equivalent to many years of income, this will happen in a very unequal way – being one of a small number of grandchildren of homeowners in the South East is a different proposition from being part of a large generation whose parents are tenants or who live outside the most affluent parts of the country.

From parents to children

Wealth inequalities – and the inheritances they eventually create – are just one of the factors meaning that the life chances of those born to different kinds of family vary. Chapter 7 started by looking at the differences in the life chances of George Ackroyd and Edward Osborne, both born in July 2013. Edward's chances are much better on average than George's. Given national statistics for life expectancy, if all we knew was that one was born in Solihull and one in Salford, and nothing else about their parents, we would already expect Edward to live nearly four years longer. Given what we do know about his background, Edward is also likely to enter school with a better vocabulary, and to leave it 13 years later with better qualifications, making it more likely that he will go to a good university, get a much higher paid job and end up with much greater wealth and pension rights than George.

There is nothing certain about this, however. Just as people's lives are very variable from year to year, so, too, are the links between the generations. It could turn out that George does better at school than Edward, for example. And while up to half of differences in men's earnings in middle age are currently linked to differences in their parents' incomes when they were growing up in the 1980s, the other half is not. So George could end up as the higher earner – it's just that he probably will not. That some people have gone from rags to riches does not make doing so likely or easy. And while the links between adult

CONCLUSION

earnings and parents' incomes appear to be stronger for those born in 1970 than for those born in 1958, the evidence for younger generations now coming out of school suggests that some of the social gaps in educational achievement had narrowed by 2010, which would help George's chances, if sustained.

Even so, we are a very long way from having the 'equal opportunities' that all the main political parties say they aspire to. And these differences in life chances depending on background are stronger in the UK (and the US) than they are in some other, generally less unequal, countries. This link between high inequality and low movement in economic position from generation to generation is perhaps unsurprising in political terms. Looking at what might happen to their children if they do not do well in education and a career, higher-income parents know that it is a long way down the economic ladder. And because of Britain's inequalities in incomes and wealth, they have the resources to try to make sure that their children do not fall. If income mobility is low, better-off parents can be more relaxed about the inequalities of the adult world into which their children will arrive. Boosting 'social mobility' without reducing current inequalities is hard – but doing something about the two together would mean confronting very strong interests that push in the other direction.

Lean times and future prospects

Finally, Chapter 8 looked at how things had turned out for the poorest of the families – single mother Michelle Ackroyd and her daughter – and the richest – Henrietta and Stephen Osborne – through the austerity years from 2010 to 2014. Benefits have been cut back or held back, and taxes have been increased, alongside reforms of both systems. For the Osbornes, with a combined income of more than £100,000 (but neither of them individually earning that much), the tax increases affecting them worked out at less than 0.7 per cent of their income, or about £12 per week. Stephen's Income Tax went up and they are paying more VAT, but they have gained from reduced Income Tax and National Insurance for

Henrietta, and from the freeze in most of their Council Tax. For Michelle, working 16 hours a week at just over £7 per hour, the big changes are the way that her tax credits and Child Benefit have not kept pace with inflation, and a big cut in her means-tested Council Tax support, combined with a cut in her Housing Benefit. All in all, the changes have cost her about £13.50 per week. This is more in cash than the Osbornes have lost, and is nearly 6 per cent of her much lower income.

Differences like these match the national picture – apart from the effects of Income Tax changes that have affected the top few per cent of earners, the closer non-pensioners are to the bottom of the income scale, the greater the share of income they have lost through the tax and benefit changes, reinforced by the larger effects of public service cuts on those who use them the most.

Big as these changes are, over the longer term, they – and we all – will have to cope with much larger challenges. In the long term the quiet effects of how we do (or do not) adjust benefit levels and tax allowances and thresholds within a growing economy or in response to inflation have huge, but often invisible, effects. The new 'welfare cap' is intended to ensure that total benefit and tax credit spending (excluding pensions) never grows faster than prices. This implies that living standards for many in the bottom half of the income distribution will automatically fall behind others when the economy returns to growth. If this happens, poverty will rise. This is one way of coping with some of the pressures that an ageing population will put on those parts of the welfare state – healthcare and pensions – which are both the most expensive and the most popular. But it is hardly an equitable one, and hard to see how it could be sustainable in the long run. And it still leaves the problem of how to cope with the other rising costs, leaving the unattractive (but inescapable) choice between taxes rising steadily over time or reducing the scale of services and benefits people receive to cope with the pressures of their lives at each stage.

The welfare state is not just 'welfare'

A huge political challenge lies in the way in which coping with these pressures will have to happen against a background where political and media discussion often leaps from the large and growing size of the *welfare state* as a whole, including the NHS, pensions and schools, to policy around only social security, or around the far narrower (and often pejoratively used) concept of '*welfare*', in the US sense of cash payments to working-age people who are out of work.

This feeds gross misperceptions of the issues we are dealing with. For instance, in a YouGov survey at the end of 2012, people were first told that 'the government's welfare budget pays for pensions, tax credits, benefits for the unemployed, the disabled and other groups', that is, describing the social security and tax credit budget. They were then asked, 'Out of every £100 of this welfare budget, how much do you think is spent on benefits for unemployed people?' Half of those surveyed thought that 40 per cent or more of spending was on the unemployed; a quarter thought it was more than 60 per cent. The average was 41 per cent.[3] As explained below, it is actually 4 per cent.

This is not new. Back in 2001 the BSA survey asked people which they thought were the largest, next largest, and smallest parts of social security spending divided into five categories – retirement pensions, child benefits, benefits for the unemployed, benefits for disabled people, and benefits for single parents. Forty-four per cent thought that benefits for the unemployed were the largest item on this list, and 27 per cent that they were the second largest.[4] Only 28 per cent correctly identified retirement pensions as being the biggest item.

Quite how far from the truth these perceptions are can be seen in Figure 9.1, which breaks down spending on the welfare state into its component parts. Total government spending in 2014–15 is forecast to be £732 billion, of which £489 billion, or 67 per cent, is on the welfare state. Within that, social security and tax credits together amount to £213 billion, or 44 per cent of spending on the welfare state.

Spending on out-of-work benefits and tax credits is £1 out of every £12.50 we spend on the welfare state

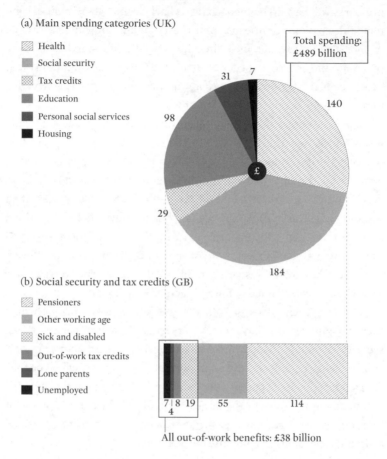

(a) Main spending categories (UK)

- Health
- Social security
- Tax credits
- Education
- Personal social services
- Housing

Total spending: £489 billion

31 7

140

98

£

29

184

(b) Social security and tax credits (GB)

- Pensioners
- Other working age
- Sick and disabled
- Out-of-work tax credits
- Lone parents
- Unemployed

7 | 8 19   55   114
    4

All out-of-work benefits: £38 billion

Figure 9.1 – Spending on the welfare state, 2014–15 (£ billion)

The breakdown of social security and tax credits in the lower part of the figure (for the £207 billion of such spending in Great Britain) brings home quite how dominant pensions are and how small benefits for the unemployed (Jobseeker's Allowance and associated Housing Benefit) are as a share of the total – less than £7 billion, or less than 4 per cent of social security and tax credits (and 1 per cent of all public spending). This is a tenth of the proportion most people think goes to unemployed people. Even if one adds in tax credits for out-of-work families and benefits for other working-age people who are out of work for other reasons (lone parents and sick and disabled people), the total comes to £38 billion, or around a fifth of all social security and tax credits.

And social security and tax credits together are less than half of all spending on the welfare state when we include the NHS, education, social care and housing. Most of the debate on 'welfare' is around what is, in fact, less than £40 billion out of the £489 billion we spend on the welfare state – just £1 in every £12.50 we spend.

Not trying hard enough

With people believing that unemployment benefits are such a large part of what we spend on social security, their other beliefs about them cloud attitudes to the welfare state as a whole. These include that the majority of people now believe that, 'around here, most unemployed people could find a job if they really wanted one'. Twenty-seven per cent of people in the UK agreed with this, even at the lowest point of a recession in 1993, but this rose to 70 per cent in 2005, and still more than half, 55 per cent, in 2012.[5] In fact, as Figure 9.2 shows, across 17 countries covered by the European Social Survey in 2008, people in the UK were the most likely to agree that the existence and level of social benefits made people lazy, with nearly two-thirds of UK respondents agreeing, compared to well under half in most of the other countries shown.

Britain's high degree of cynicism is, in some ways, surprising, given how comparatively *un*-generous our benefit system is towards those who are out of work. If we do have a low commitment to work it may come from other reasons, as can be seen in Figure 9.3. Ingrid Esser plotted responses from the International Social Survey Programme in 2005 suggesting how much people in different countries valued work against OECD calculations of the proportion of in-work income that people in each of them would receive if they received out-of-work benefits in different circumstances. Of the 13 countries, men in the UK simultaneously had the second lowest replacement rates (that is, the least generous benefit system in relation to income in work) apart from the US, and had the lowest commitment to their jobs. By contrast, Norwegian men had the most generous benefit system for the unemployed, but had the equal highest level of commitment to work. If there is causality here, it is not from high benefits to low work commitment. It could, however, go the other way. Perhaps because we believe we are lazy and do not seem to enjoy our jobs much, we may also believe we have to keep benefits down. The solution to this, however, surely lies elsewhere: what is it about British jobs and the way we regard them that is so unattractive compared to other countries?

People in the UK are more likely than any other Europeans to agree that benefits and services 'make people lazy'

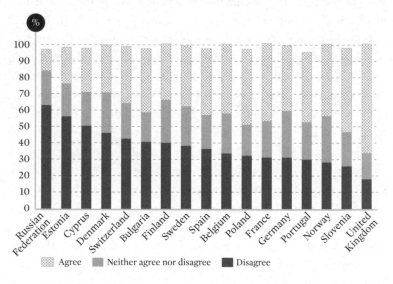

Figure 9.2 – Agreement that 'social benefits and services make people lazy', 2008

On the fiddle

The belief that people are not looking for work hard enough goes alongside widespread beliefs that a substantial minority of claimants are doing so fraudulently, including, presumably, actually working for 'cash in hand', but doing so while still claiming. The DWP's own estimate across the whole of the benefit system (including pensions), based on its detailed examinations of a random sample of cases, is that a total of £3.5 billion was overpaid in 2012–13 as a result of a *combination* of fraud and error by administrators or by claimants (without fraudulent intent).[6] Of this, £900 million was subsequently reclaimed. At the same time, official errors meant that £1.6 billion was being *under*-paid as a result of official error. These are large amounts, but they are from budgets that are very large indeed. Total overpayments were 2.1 per cent of all benefits spending (excluding tax credits). However, two-thirds of this total for 'fraud and error' – often quoted as if it measured fraud – was said by the DWP to be due to error. Just 0.7 per cent of all benefits was over-paid as the result of fraud, or £1.2 billion. For Jobseeker's Allowance, estimated fraud was 2.9 per cent, or an annual total of £150 million, for example.[7]

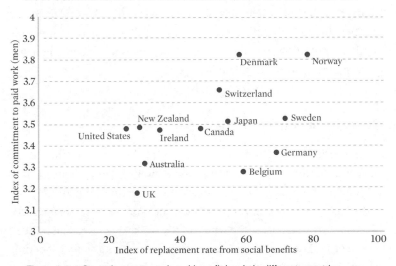

Both commitment to work and benefit levels are low in the UK

Figure 9.3 – Commitment to work and benefit levels in different countries

However, when people were asked in 2012 what proportion of the total benefits and tax credit budget was 'claimed fraudulently (that is, people who dishonestly claim more benefits than they are entitled to)', half thought that this was 20 per cent or more, and the average amount was 27 per cent,[8] equating to £58 billion. This is nearly 50 *times* the grossed-up result from the DWP's probes into random cases. A quarter thought that 40 per cent or more of benefits were being claimed fraudulently. This would require virtually *all* non-pensioner claims to be the result of fraud (such as there being no children at all in the country for whom Child Benefit is paid), or most of them plus a good proportion of pensioners to be fraudsters too, perhaps having lied about their age in some cunning way.

This belief in fraud is not new, but it has grown stronger. Back in the 1980s a little over 30 per cent of people in Britain agreed with the strong statement that, 'most people on the dole are fiddling in one way or another'. By the late 1990s this had reached nearly 40 per cent, and in 2012 it was 37 per cent, compared to only 30 per cent who disagreed.[9]

This kind of belief is also much stronger in Britain than in most other comparable countries. In the World Values Survey across OECD countries between 2000 and 2004, 61 per cent of respondents in Great Britain agreed that either 'almost all' or 'many' people were claiming state benefits to which they 'are not entitled'. This put Britain behind only Turkey, Italy, Greece and Poland in the extent to which we believed our compatriots were on the fiddle.[10]

Myths have consequences

Misconceptions about the welfare state and the way it is abused are not just a matter of harmless misunderstanding. They create serious problems in how the welfare state is run, affecting both those in or on the margins of poverty at any one time, and all of us through the choices we are making for the whole of the welfare state. Actual fraud of Jobseeker's Allowance may be less than one thousandth of all spending on social security, according to official analysis, but if we believe it to be over a tenth of the total,[11] we will demand that our politicians react accordingly.

There are two groups of people who suffer from this misconception. The first are those who are at the sharp end of 'welfare reforms' designed to cut spending and to give a signal to voters that the government is acting on their concerns. For instance, each year from 1998 to 2008, there were between 200,000 and 300,000 'sanctions' for those receiving Jobseeker's Allowance and what is now Employment and Support Allowance for sick and disabled people for failing to meet conditions such as seeking work assiduously enough or attending interviews, leading to benefits being suspended. By the end of 2013, the annual rate had reached 900,000.[12] By the autumn of 2013, the monthly rate at which Jobseeker's Allowance claimants were being sanctioned had reached 6 per cent *every month*, compared to under 2.5 per cent in the decade up to 2007.[13] More than half a million different Jobseeker's Allowance recipients had been affected over the preceding year. At the same time, where people do appeal against these decisions, the majority of those appeals are now being upheld.[14]

As well as the much harsher administration of benefit rules that this suggests, many rules have also been changed to limit entitlements or to reduce the numbers entitled to more generous treatment. These changes include limits on Housing Benefit for private tenants, set at levels that only rise with general price inflation and not the rate at which rents are rising. In London, in particular, this means widening areas of the capital where Housing Benefit recipients will only be able to live if they pay out an escalating 'shortfall' from the rest of their income.[15] For some social tenants, similar pressures come from the 'Bedroom Tax' (officially, 'abolition of the spare room subsidy'), under which tenants deemed to be under-occupying their property face cuts in benefit, even if there are no available smaller properties to move to. While there is a national issue of how well we use our available housing stock, this measure is targeted only at low-income working-age social tenants, who have between them fewer than 3 per cent of the nation's 'spare' bedrooms.[16] The old benefit to cope with the cost of disability for more severely disabled people is being scrapped, with its replacement, the Personal Independence Payment, designed to be 20 per cent cheaper, and so far with many affected by long delays in being paid. And low-income working-age households across many parts of England face (like Michelle Ackroyd, but often more acutely) the cuts in Council Tax support that have followed from responsibility for it being passed to local councils, but with a reduced budget.

What measures such as these have in common is how heavily they bear on what are often very narrow groups of people. Given that such a small share of the welfare state goes on benefits to people who are out of work, creating savings from them that actually makes a difference to overall spending requires more and more drastic action. But this comes at a cost. The hardship to those affected is most obvious in the rapidly escalating use of voluntary food banks across the country, with more than 900,000 people receiving three-day food parcels from the Trussell Trust charity in 2013–14, up from 350,000 the previous year and 60,000 in 2010–11.[17] But it also comes in the individual testimonies of those who have found themselves effectively destitute as a result of what seem to them to be unfair decisions or of changing rules.[18] What was once a national safety net, albeit not a very generous one, now has substantial holes in it.

There is no 'them and us' – just us

The second group is much larger. Many more people benefit from the operation of the welfare state than are affected by narrowly selected parts of it at any one time – indeed, nearly all of us do. For instance, when looking at people over an 18 year period, Barra Roantree and Jonathan Shaw found that nearly half had received a means-tested benefit or tax credit at some point. That was three times the number reporting this in any given year. Over whole lives – and with less under-reporting – the proportion would be even higher, just for these parts of the system before allowing for pensions, Child Benefit, the NHS and education.[19]

But if we continue to think about policy as if all its benefits, costs and problems affect a group of 'other' people, we will make choices that fail to meet our own interests, even if we never expect to be out of work or to face sickness or disability ourselves. The alternatives to it, through private insurance or through accumulating a large enough pile of cash to see our families and ourselves through all eventualities, are hugely expensive, and out of the question for most. Switching to private provision would also act strongly against the interests of younger generations who will have to continue to pay into the system for those who have already retired or who are nearing retirement, regardless of whether we call a halt to their own future entitlements. And breaking the link that this kind of 'pay as you go' system entails, where one generation pays for its parents and is then supported by its children's generation in turn, would go against the intergenerational solidarity that many in fact value.[20]

But the effect of an ageing society is that simply to stand still in terms of what we provide to meet particular needs, we will have to pay more. This creates what Peter Taylor-Gooby has described as 'the double crisis of the welfare state' – the immediate effects of cuts across many areas of social provision, and the longer-term pressures that cannot be accommodated simply by ever-tightening provision for poor minorities, unless we are prepared to countenance deeper social divisions.[21] There is what he describes as a 'more humane and more generous' alternative, but people are unlikely to agree to spending what is needed for this – and raising the taxes that this requires – if they misperceive what the system does and who benefits from it.

Those with an interest in keeping down the contribution from taxes on higher incomes or greater accumulations of wealth may continue to feed those misperceptions, so this will remain an up-hill battle, but how perceptions could be better brought into line with the reality of what is going on is now one of the central challenges facing those making and debating social policies and their future. In a situation where there are rising demands for services on the one side and the legacy of crisis and slow growth in living standards meaning tight constraints on resources on the other, we cannot afford to make choices and decisions by myth, rather than in the light of reality.

We know from our own experiences, those of our families – and from TV soap operas and nearly every novel – that people's lives and circumstances change. And yet, as I have described at the start of this book, the problems of social policy and the effects of the welfare state are presented in terms of a static group of 'them' who benefit, and another static group of 'us' who pay for it. But this characterisation is profoundly to misunderstand the implications of the dynamics of our lives that this book has explored in detail. It remains true that people starting advantaged remain much more likely than others to end up advantaged, and those who start poorer are more likely to end up poorer. But there is considerable variation and uncertainty around such average differences in life trajectories. This does not just include the long-term changes over the life cycle that we all go through, but also other variations and changes, from at one end the rapid variations many people experience in circumstances and need for support from week to week to, at the other end, the factors that affect the life chances of our children and our grandchildren.

As a result of all this variation in circumstances over our lives between good times and bad times, most of us get back something at least close to what we pay in over our lives towards the welfare state. When we pay in more than we get out, we are helping our parents, our children, ourselves at another time – and ourselves as we might have been, if life had not turned out quite so well for us. In that sense, we are all – or nearly all – in it together.

Endnotes, figure sources and figure notes

Chapter 1

1   'Spending Round 2013', Speech by Chancellor George Osborne, 26 June 2013 (www.gov.uk/government/speeches/spending-round-2013-speech).

2   'Benefits: our achievement', *The Guardian*, 29 July 2013.

3   Speech by Mitt Romney, May 2012, later published on Mother Jones website (www.motherjones.com/politics/2012/09/full-transcript-mitt-romney-secret-video#47percent).

4   'Welfare for the 21st century', Speech by Work and Pensions Secretary Iain Duncan Smith, 27 May 2010.

5   DWP (2007, foreword).

6   Beveridge Lecture, Toynbee Hall, 18 March 1999.

7   Beveridge (1942, para 22).

8   Beveridge (1942, para 19 [vii]).

9   King (1995).

10 Broadcast by Granada TV on 15 May 1989. See Woolley and Le Grand (1990) for details of the calculations on which the programme was based.

11 The programme was designed to illustrate some of the points made in Julian Le Grand's (1982) book, *The strategy of equality*, in particular the way in which, looked at over complete lifetimes, middle-class families were often major beneficiaries from the welfare state and other public spending.

12 Broadcast on Budget Day, 19 March 1991. See Hills and Sutherland (1991) for details of the calculations behind that programme.

Chapter 2

1   More details of the calculations underlying the descriptions of the incomes of the Ackroyd and Osborne families at the start of this and following chapters are available on request from the author at the LSE.

2   Hills et al (2013a, Figure 5.2) show that the average of 90th percentiles for men aged 25–29 and 30–34 in 2010–11 was around £20 per hour.

3   He was earning £39,626 and Clare was earning £17,544 for her 60 per cent of a full-time job as a secondary teacher – her £16.18 per hour also put her at the 90th percentile for women aged 25–29.

4   Henry's pension contributions (at 7 per cent) and Clare's (at 6.4 per cent) are deductible in calculating Income Tax. Being in the teachers' pension scheme, Clare pays a lower rate of NICs as she was 'contracted out' of the state second pension.

5   This was the part of Child Tax Credit that replaced what had been left of the old Married Couples Allowance when it was abolished and still went to those with earnings up to a little over £50,000. If it hadn't been for their nursery fees, they wouldn't have received this in full.

6   The ONS's analysis of *The effects of taxes and benefits on household income 2010/11* suggests that people in the eighth decile group pay indirect taxes equivalent to 17 per cent of disposable income and people in the ninth, 15.9 per cent; Henry and Clare were on the boundary between the two (ONS, 2013a).

7   The ONS analysis puts a value of £4,720 for non-retired households on average, but the Osbornes are only a family of three.

8   In the 2005 BSA survey, when people were asked how many out of every 100 people they thought were financially better off than themselves, 44 per cent thought they were in the middle fifth; only 9 per cent thought they were in the top fifth.

9   Using the income definitions used by the Department for Work and Pensions (DWP) in its *Households Below Average Income* (HBAI) analysis. These adjust for household size (dividing by 1.2 for a couple with one child), so Henry and Clare's income would be counted as £669 per week before housing costs. Looking at Figure 2.5 later in the chapter, this puts them at the 81st percentile of the income distribution – only 19 per cent of households would be classed as better off. On the DWP's definitions, their after housing costs income – allowing for mortgage payments of £125 and Council Tax of £38

per week – was £533, putting them at the 75th percentile of that distribution – only a quarter of households were better off. The DWP calculations do not allow for childcare costs.

10   In common with around two-thirds of lone mothers, Michelle was not receiving any child maintenance from Wayne at the time, as he was out of work. In better times, when he was in steady work (and in better touch), he had been contributing around £50 per week to help with Chloe's costs (close to the median amount for those who do pay; see Skinner and Main, 2013, for the national picture in 2008–09). Any payments Michelle did receive would not result in her Council Tax Benefit (since October 2010) or tax credits being cut back and so would not affect the balance between the taxes she pays and the benefits she receives.

11   Michelle's taxes and benefits calculated using the DWP's tax benefit model for 2010–11 are available on the archived website for publications from before May 2010 (http://webarchive.nationalarchives.gov.uk/+/http://statistics.dwp.gov.uk/asd/index.php?page=tbmt). The standard DWP numbers are adjusted to a Salford Council Tax of £16.95 per week (for a single person in a Band B property), rather than the standard £16. The numbers given are those that would result if the system delivered precisely the amount each week to which Michelle was entitled. As discussed later in Chapter 4, lags in the system, particularly for tax credits and Housing Benefit, make this rather unlikely, although it should have ended up roughly like this in the long run.

12   Based on 78 per cent of the average amount of indirect and intermediate taxes the ONS allocated to non-pensioner single adults with children in 2010–11, as her disposable income was 78 per cent of the average for that group.

13   Strictly speaking, this was Salford's average spending per pupil across all schools, so is likely to be an over-estimate for primary places.

14   Communities and Local Government calculations presented in Hills (2007, Table 6.4) suggest an average 'economic subsidy' of £13 per week to housing association tenants in the North West in 2004, a figure that would have risen with rising house prices by 2010.

15   This is by coincidence, rather than by construction.

16   See Figure 2.5, with her £299 income divided by 0.87 (that is, increased) to make it equivalent to £343 for two adults with no children. After housing costs (dividing by 0.78 in this case), her £212 income was equivalent to £271 for two adults.

17 See Pearce and Taylor (2013) for a discussion of the changes over the whole period, and Sefton (2009) for changes during the Labour government from 1997 to 2006.

18 Hills and Lelkes (1999).

19 Hedges (2005); see also Sefton (2005).

20 Rowlingson et al (2010).

21 See Alzubaidi et al (2013) for official analysis of the statistics, with independent commentaries in Cribb et al (2013b) and Hills et al (2013a, Section 7).

22 See Hills et al (2010, pp 180–1), for a discussion of the problems with this, but also with alternatives to it.

23 Taking the average height of all adults in England in 2009 as 5ft 6 inches (168.4cm) from the 2009 Health Survey for England (downloaded 7 October 2013).

24 The 2010–11 incomes reported to Her Majesty's Revenue & Customs (HMRC) for the top 1 per cent (which are used to adjust the HBAI statistics for this group) may have been affected by 'forestalling' to avoid 50 per cent tax by arranging for receipts to come in the previous year, when the top tax rate was lower.

25 One measure of growing inequality in the last 50 years is that, back in 1961, the median was 90 per cent of the mean.

26 It could be over 100, if one person received all the money and other people lost money during the year.

27 A detailed account of ONS's calculations for 2010–11 can be found in Tonkin and Thomas (2012). The calculations in this chapter using the ONS's results are drawn from the ONS's historical data from the series presented at www. ons.gov.uk/ons/rel/household-income/the-effects-of-taxes-and-benefits-on-household-income/historical-data/sum--historical-tables.html, Table 14 (downloaded 11 October 2013). This series uses a consistent way of adjusting for household size across all years from 1977 to 2010–11 (the modified OECD equivalence scale). Note that the ONS calculations are based on a different survey from that used in Figure 2.8, which contains less detailed information. Importantly this ONS series does not include the adjustment for incomes of the top 1 per cent (based on tax records) that the DWP makes to the main income distribution series, and so does not capture inequality at the top of the distribution so well.

28 Allowing for the varying needs of households of different sizes, that is, *ranked* by equivalent disposable income. The averages shown in Figure 2.7 (and also in Figure 2.10) are, however, amounts before any adjustment for household size.

29 Of course, in the absence of such benefits, people's behaviour would be different – for instance, trying to keep on working, if there were no pensions.

30 The definition of income used here is similar to that used in Figure 2.5, with households arranged in order of income adjusted for household size (but the totals shown for each household are not adjusted by household size).

31 Direct taxes in the ONS's calculations include Council Tax (rates in Northern Ireland), net of Council Tax Benefit.

32 The ratios here are between the average incomes of the top and bottom 10th. If you look at the cut-off points for each of these, £11,400 and £48,700 (after adjusting for household size), you get a 90:10 ratio of 4.3 to one for *households*, a little higher than the 3.9 90:10 ratio between *individuals* shown in Figure 2.5 (which uses a different data source, the Family Resources Survey, which contains more detailed income data).

33 Including estimated benefits from bus and rail subsidies.

34 The Gini coefficient for disposable incomes was 18.2 percentage points lower in the UK in 2010 than that for market incomes, compared to an (unweighted) average for the 31 countries of 16.3 points.

35 Beyond these, there are other public services that are harder to allocate to households, taxes paid by businesses and others that are not households and – especially important in this year, 2010–11 – public borrowing.

36 Measured as a percentage of their gross incomes, the poorest tenth paid *more* in direct and indirect taxes taken together than the rest of the income distribution, including the top tenth – 48 per cent compared to 33 per cent for the top tenth and 34 per cent overall.

37 Sefton (2005).

38 Where answers on pensions and unemployment benefits differed, they were combined as follows. If one was earnings-related and the other flat-rate, they were classed as earnings-related. If one was means-tested and the other flat-rate, they were classed as means-tested. If one was earnings-related and the other means-tested, they were classed as flat-rate.

39 Fifty-eight per cent agreed with this in the 2008 European Social Survey, fewer than in all but 3 of 22 other EU members (interestingly including the Netherlands and Denmark).

40 Korpi and Palme (1998).

41 Kenworthy (2011, Figure 6.1, p 55).

42 Marx and van Rie (2014, pp 239–64).

43 Own calculations based on the ONS's effects of taxes and benefits on household income database, Tables 14 and 16A.

44 Hills (2013a, Figure 9), based on DWP's HBAI analysis.

45 This is because the effect of non-retired households having more people in them more than offset higher NHS spending per individual pensioner.

46 Using DWP's figures for the distribution of disposable income adjusted for household size, as in Figure 2.5.

47 Downloaded 15 April 2014. These figures are not completely comparable with those drawn from the HBAI-based series shown in Figure 2.14, as they refer to income after income tax of the top 1 per cent of 'tax units' (couples and single people in 1979, but single people since 1990), rather than being based on household disposable income.

48 See Piketty (2014) for a detailed discussion of this internationally and over the long term.

Figure sources and notes

2.1 Should government redistribute income from the better-off to those who are less well-off?

Source: BSA survey, 1986–2013 (www.britsocat.com).

Note: Respondents answering 'don't know' and refusing to answer are included in the base.

2.2 Would you say the gap between those with high incomes and those with low incomes is too large, about right or too small?

Source: BSA survey, 1983–2013 (www.britscocat.com).

Note: Respondents answering 'don't know' and refusing to answer are included in the base.

2.3   Should it be government's responsibility to reduce income differences?
        Source: BSA survey, 1985–2013 (www.britsocat.com).
Note: Respondents answering 'don't know' and refusing to answer are included
        in the base.

2.4   Should government spend more money on welfare benefits for the poor,
        even if it leads to higher taxes?
        Source: BSA survey, 1987–2013 (www.britsocat.com).
Note: Respondents answering 'don't know' and refusing to answer are included
        in the base.

2.5   Pen's parade of incomes in the UK, 2010–11
        *Source: Hills et al (2013a, Figure 7.1). Derived from DWP analysis of HBAI
        dataset based on Family Resources Survey (UK). Distribution is for individuals
        based on household disposable income adjusted for household size and
        composition.*

2.6   Inequality in disposable incomes in industrialised countries, 2010
        *Source: OECD statistical database on income distribution and poverty,
        downloaded 17 October 2013.*
Note: Gini coefficients of income after taxes and transfers across whole
        population. (*) indicates 2009 figures.

2.7   Distribution of household incomes, 2010–11
        Source: ONS (2013a, Table 14). Benefits in kind exclude rail and bus subsidies.

2.8   Inequality of market incomes in industrialised countries, 2010
        *Source: OECD statistical database on income distribution and poverty,
        downloaded 17 October 2013.*
Note: Gini coefficients of income before taxes and transfers across whole
        population. (*) indicates 2009 figures.

2.9   Inequality before and after redistribution in the UK and Sweden, 2010
        (*Gini Coefficients*)
        *Source: As for Figures 2.6 and 2.8. 'Redistribution' is percentage point difference
        between Gini coefficients for market and disposable incomes.*

2.10   Taxes and benefits by household income group, 2010–11
        Source: Based on ONS (2013a). Benefits in kind exclude rail and bus subsidies.

2.11   Preferences for taxation and cash benefits, 2008
        *Source: European Social Survey Round 4, 2008. Countries are Belgium,
        Germany, Denmark, Spain, Finland, France, Greece, Netherlands, Portugal,
        Sweden and the UK (averages weighted by population). The shading indicates
        the potential degree of redistribution implied.*

2.12 The poor cost more? Benefits and taxes going to poorest fifth of all
households, 1979, 1996–97 and 2010–11
*Source: Own analysis of ONS series on the effects of taxes and benefits on
household income, using database of results from 1997 to 2010–11 using modified
OECD equivalence scale, and adjusted to 2010–11 prices using ONS expenditure
deflator for household sector.*

2.13 Net gain to poorest fifth of all and of non-retired households
as a percentage of average market income
*Source: Own analysis of ONS series on the effects of taxes and benefits on
household income, using database of results from 1997 to 2010–11 using modified
OECD equivalence scale. Net gain is difference between benefits in cash and kind
and total taxes. Percentages are of average original incomes for all households and
for non-retired households respectively.*

2.14 Shares of income going to each fifth of distribution,
1979 to 2010–11
*Source: DWP HBAI analysis. 1979 figures from Jenkins and Cowell (1993) for
UK. 1996–97 (GB) and 2010–11 (UK) figures from Adams et al (2012, Table
2.2ts). Incomes are for individuals based on household incomes after cash
benefits and direct taxes and adjusted for household size.*

Chapter 3

1   Average adult earnings grew by 3.5 times between April 1985 and April 2010. The numbers quoted here are based on those in Woolley and Le Grand (1990, Table 4 and p 23), as calculated from 1985–86 data, adjusted by that factor. The Osbornes' total is based on Stephen being contracted out of the state earnings-related pensions system (SERPS). The net gain to the Osbornes is based on the difference between total receipts and lifetime taxes allocated to them. The original numbers were simple totals for what the families would receive over their lifetimes, given entitlements in 1985–86. There is no discounting for amounts received and paid out at different ages, nor allowance for economic growth. The results are, in effect, what would result from the values of benefits and services growing in line with average incomes, but then applying a discount rate equal to the rate of growth.

2   Rowntree (1901, pp 170–1).

3   Part of the problem was that flat-rate contributions could never be set high enough to finance sufficient benefits to get people out of poverty (Glennerster and Evans, 1994). Another was that groups that were not in a position to make contributions were still seen as deserving of benefits – such as those already in old age when the new scheme came in, or mothers at home bringing up children (Hills, 2004b). Beveridge's model did not allow for those who were poor even when in paid work and with child allowances, and its assumption of a world of stable families with breadwinner husbands neglected what has become a growing risk.

4   Of what is technically known as the 'household reference person', or colloquially, 'head of household' – the person legally or financially responsible for the accommodation shared by the household (or the elder of two people equally responsible).

5   Note that the figure, and those that follow, show cross-sectional patterns of incomes by age. They therefore reflect two effects: changes as people themselves age, and differences between successive cohorts born at different dates.

6   The numbers used in this figure and in Figures 3.5 and 3.6 are not part of ONS's standard annual analysis, but were supplied to the House of Commons Library by the UK Statistics Authority in response to a Parliamentary Question by the Rt Hon David Willetts MP (*Hansard*, 11 June 2008, col 308W).

7   See Evans and Williams (2009) for a detailed examination of how components of the tax and benefit systems affect different kinds of family across their lives. They look at effects year by year on three archetypal families with different income levels – the 'Lowes', the 'Meades' and the 'Moores'. They also show how they were affected by changes in the structures of the systems between 1979, 1997 and 2008.

8   See Hills (2013a, Table A1). The figures are based on DWP statistics for spending on benefits and tax credits in Great Britain defined in a consistent way across the period, allowing for changes in the names and administration of benefits. Non-pensioner benefits were divided between those specifically related to children – such as Child Benefit, Child Tax Credit and Working Tax Credit for families with children, and their predecessors – and other transfers for the working-age population (such as the adult parts of Income Support or Jobseeker's Allowance or Housing Benefit for working-age families).

9   Poverty rates are drawn from the DWP's HBAI analysis, with each family member allocated an income based on that of the whole household (after direct taxes), adjusted for family size. The relative poverty rates shown in Figure 3.5 are the proportions with incomes below 60 per cent of contemporary median income, before allowing for housing costs. Poverty rates also converged when incomes are compared with an absolute threshold (based on 60 per cent of 1996–97 median income). When relative incomes are examined after housing costs, relative poverty remained higher for children (27 per cent) than for all individuals (21 per cent), but had fallen well below the national average for pensioners (14 per cent). For more details see Hills (2013a, Figure 9 and Table 4).

10 For more detailed discussion see Hills (2013a, Section 8).

11 Child Trust Funds were accounts into which the government paid an amount for each child (more for those on low incomes), which would build up – possibly with further payments in – until they could be withdrawn when a young person turned 18. They were established for children born between September 2002 and January 2011.

12 For more detailed discussion, see Hills (2011).

13 This is the result of simply adding up the amounts shown for each age group in Figure 3.5 at 2005–06 prices, without any allowance for future real growth or any discounting of later receipts. If the system actually grew at a real rate equal to the discount rate, this would be equivalent to the net present value of the future flows.

14 Hills (2004b).

15 See Falkingham and Hills (1995) for details of the model and its results.

16 From DWP (2012, Table 1). Earnings for all adults working full time rose 3.5 times, from £171.00 in April 1985 to £598.60 per week in April 2010.

17 Jim and Tracy Ackroyd's lifetime net gain of £200,000 was therefore a little higher than typical low-income households, while Stephen and Henrietta Osborne's net loss of only £140,000 was lower than typical high-income households (although it did take into account a wider range of services).

18 Falkingham and Hills (1995, Table 7.6b) shows an average net lifetime gain to women of £32,000 at 1985 prices, assuming that households share their incomes equally.

19 See Barr (2001) for a more general discussion of the welfare state's role as a 'piggy bank'.

20 Pensions Commission (2004, 2005).

21 Burchardt and Hills (1997); Burchardt et al (1999). For a more recent discussion on the limits to private insurance in the case of long-term care, see Commission on Funding of Care and Support (2011).

22 Lupton et al (2013, Table 5).

23 Hills (2013a, Table A1), drawn from DWP analysis using consistent definitions of spending over the period.

24 Hills et al (2010, p 50 and Figure 2G), based on ONS analysis of the effects of the tax and benefits systems on household incomes between 1997 and 2007–08.

25 In Evans and Williams's (2009) examination of differences in structures of tax and benefit systems between 1979, 1997 and 2008, they find that, 'Overall the median earner can be seen as having fairly constant outcomes overall throughout one of the periods of most radical change seen yet in British social policy' (p 312). The biggest change across the period for any of the different kinds of family they looked at was a substantial fall then rise in the lifetime state transfers received by a low-income family (the Lowes) measured as a proportion of their lifetime earnings. This fell from 43 to 34 per cent between the 1979 and 1997 systems, but then rose again to 47 per cent by 2008 (Evans and Williams, 2009, Table 4.1). The benefit system was doing more of a redistributive job at the end of the period than in 1997, but at the same time the rising importance of healthcare and education, outside that analysis, was boosting the life cycle redistribution effect.

26 Brewer et al (2012a, p 2).

27 Average receipts per member of the cohort are based on the aggregate received per member alive when aged 15–19.

Figure sources and notes

3.1 Seebohm Rowntree's 'cycles of want and plenty' in a labourer's life, York, 1899
   Source: Rowntree (1901).

3.2 Schematic effects of Beveridge's social insurance over the life cycle

3.3 Schematic effects of Beveridge's social insurance and short-term income changes

3.4 Market income by age of household, 2005–06
   Source: ONS, from its 'Redistribution of Income' series.
Note: Incomes are adjusted for household size (using estimated equivalisation factors by age based on adjustment to disposable incomes). Ages are those of 'household reference person'.

3.5 Taxes and benefits by age of household, 2005–06
   Source: ONS from 'Redistribution of Income' series (see also Figure 3.4).
Note: Benefits and services (such as education) for children are allocated to parental household. Taxes are direct and indirect taxes allocated to households. Incomes are adjusted for household size. Ages are those of 'household reference person'. State pensions include both retirement pensions (RP) and pension credit (PC).

3.6 Market and disposable incomes by age of household, 2005–06
   Source: ONS from its 'Redistribution of Income' series (see also Figure 3.4).
Note: Incomes are adjusted for household size (using estimated equivalisation factors by age for market incomes based on adjustment to disposable incomes). Ages are those of 'household reference person'.

3.7 Poverty rates for different population groups
   Source: DWP/Institute for Fiscal Studies (IFS) HBAI analysis (from IFS Poverty and Inequality spreadsheet, 2012).
Note: Figures show proportions of each group with incomes below 60 per cent of contemporary median income in each year.

3.8 Net incomes by age, 1997–98 and 2010–11
   Source: Hills (2013a), based on DWP analysis of HBAI dataset.
Note: Incomes are adjusted for household size and are before housing costs.

3.9 Difference in median net income for each age group from overall median, 1997–98 and 2010–11
Source: Hills (2013a), as Figure 3.8. 1997–98 figures are for GB; 2010–11 figures are for the UK.

3.10 Range of net incomes by age, 2010–11
Source: Based on DWP analysis of HBAI dataset used in Hills et al (2013a).
Note: Incomes are adjusted for household size and are before housing costs.

3.11 Overall balance of cuts and reforms after 2010 by age

3.12 Lifetime social benefits and taxes by income group
Source: Falkingham and Hills (1995, Table 7.6b,) adjusted by earnings growth to 2010 prices.
Note: Figures based on simulation of complete lifetimes using LIFEMOD model based on 1985 population, but using structure of taxes and benefits in 1991. Lifetime taxes are based on the proportionate share of lifetime incomes.

3.13 Projected lifetime receipts from health, education and social security, and taxes paid towards them by year of birth, 1901–1960, GB
Source: Hills (2004, Table 8.2).
Note: Based on actual spending and taxation by age to 2001 allocated by five-year age cohorts and then projected to 2051 with 2003 Government Actuary's Department projections using age-related spending patterns and policies as in 2001. Amounts shown as equivalent of totals in terms of GDP per capita in year of receipt per member of cohort (given its size when aged 15–19).

Chapter 4

1   Her weekly earnings put her in the top 30 per cent of women aged 30–34 at the time. She was paying 6.5 per cent pension contributions, deductible before calculating Income Tax (but not National Insurance) and was contracted out of the state second pension.

2   Using DWP's tax benefit model for 2010–11, with Gary working 35 hours at £9 per hour, rent of £149 per week and Council Tax of £22 per week, with one child aged four and no childcare costs, their after housing costs income allowing for Denise working 15 hours a week at £6.20 in 38 weeks of term time (but losing 65 per cent of that through reduced Housing Benefit) would be £264. Adjusting for household size gives equivalent income of £220, at the 22nd percentile of the 2010–11 income distribution (after housing costs).

3   See Hills et al (2006) for a detailed presentation of the results of this exercise. The survey was carried out by the National Centre for Social Research, with operational details described in Barnes et al (2004).

4   See Hills et al (2006, Sections 2 and 7) for more details. 2003–04 was a special year in two ways, as it was when the 'new tax credits' replaced the old Working Families' Tax Credit (WFTC). That meant that there was some disruption for a few weeks at the start of the year as the new system came in, and so tax credits fluctuated a bit more than normal then. On the other hand, during this year, there was no adjustment if the previous year's tax credits had not been based on the correct amount of income, as there was from 2004–05 onwards. For our respondents there was therefore *less* variation in tax credits of the kind that affected Denise and Gary and others like them in the middle of the year.

5   The incomes we recorded did not include Housing Benefit. This was often paid directly to landlords and so came in the form of a reduction in the net rent payable. However, some respondents did not know or report what their rent would have been in the absence of benefit. For consistency, we excluded Housing Benefit and Council Tax Benefit from the income patterns analysed.

6   It was harder to carry on collecting information from people who split up or re-partnered during the year, as these cases were more likely to drop out.

7   And apportioning out monthly incomes between four-week periods. This was necessary to smooth out fluctuations that resulted just from some incomes coming in on a weekly pattern and some on a monthly one.

8   That is, families with incomes staying within 15 per cent of their average for 11 or more of the 13 periods, and the others within 25 per cent of the average.

9   Hills et al (2006, Table 4.2).

10   Hills et al (2006, Table 6.5).

11   Hills et al (2006, Table 8.4).

12   Reported in *The Guardian*, 9 March 2014.

13   ONS (2014); not all of these contracts will be what is commonly called 'zero hours', however.

14   Standing (2011, 2014).

15   Shildrick et al (2012, p 2).

16   Gregg and Wadsworth (2011, p 26).

17   The figures are for unemployment on International Labour Organization (ILO) definitions (and so include those who are out of work and are seeking it, not just those receiving out-of work benefits). They are for the UK adults aged 16–64, and are seasonally adjusted, derived from data downloaded from the ONS's database (Table UNEM01) on 18 November 2013.

18   Long (2009, Figure 1), based on data from the British Household Panel Survey (BHPS).

19   DWP online tabulation tool (downloaded 25 January 2014). Figures relate to working-age claimants.

20   CSJ (2013, Figure 10).

21   EUROSTAT figures for long-term unemployment (for all adults) from Labour Force Survey, downloaded 31 May 2014.

22   DWP (2013b, Table 4). Includes claimants aged 18–59 of Jobseeker's Allowance, Income Support for lone parents, and those in the 'assessment phase' or put in the 'work-related activity' group of people receiving Employment and Support Allowance.

23   Gregg and Wadsworth (2011, Figure 5.3).

24   Chris Grayling, quoted in Macdonald et al (2014).

25   Macdonald et al (2014).

26   Macmillan and Gregg (2012), using data from the National Child Development Study (NCDS), 1970 British Cohort Study (BCS70) and BHPS.

27   Glennerster and Evans (1994).

28 Beveridge (1942, p 14 et seq). His calculations allowed an allowance of 56s (shillings) for a couple with two children, with average rents of 12s 6d.

29 Whiteford et al (2003).

30 HMRC figures for final assessments for 2003–04, quoted in Hills et al (2006, p 60).

31 NAO (2013b).

32 At 65 per cent of the rise in *net* income after allowing for tax, NICs and tax credits, and so reducing more slowly as a percentage of gross earnings.

33 The taper in the old Council Tax Benefit system was 20 per cent (continued by most local authorities) applied to net income after tax, National Insurance and tax credits. For Universal Credit recipients not paying tax, this 20 per cent would be applied to the net gain of 35 per cent, so adding 7 per cent to effective rates. Some councils are now applying steeper rates, up to 30 per cent, which would increase this in proportion (NAO, 2013b).

34 De Agostini and Brewer (2013, Table 3.6).

35 NAO (2013a).

36 DWP (2014b).

37 PAC (2013).

38 PAC (2013, Qn 38).

39 Bennett (2010).

40 Kempson and Whyley (2001).

41 Keohane and Shorthouse (2012).

42 Bennett (2011).

43 For instance, de Agostini and Brewer (2013) suggest that if the system replaced current arrangements in one go in 2014–15, with no transitional protection for losers, households would gain *on average* £2.16 per week. But single parents would *lose* £3.43 per week on average, while single out-of-work adults would *gain*. Within different household groups there would be gainers and losers.

44 Tarr and Finn (2012).

Figure sources and notes

4.1   Example case with regular weekly income: one-earner couple with two children and mortgage, 2003–04
Source: Hills et al (2006, Figure 3.1).

4.2   Example case with unchanging circumstances but varying income: lone parent with one child and mortgage, 2003–04
Source: Hills et al (2006, Figure 3.3).

4.3   Example case with changing circumstances: lone-parent tenant with one child, 2003–04
Source: Hills et al (2006, Figure 3.4).

4.4   Highly stable cases: incomes in four-week periods, 2003–04
Source: Hills et al (2006, Figure 4.1[a]).

4.5   Highly erratic cases: incomes in four-week periods, 2003–04
Source: Hills et al (2006, Figure 4.1[h]).

4.6   Income trajectories followed by 93 families, 2003–04
Source: Hills et al (2006, Table 4.1).
Note: Highly stable: income in all periods within 10 per cent of annual average; stable/broadly stable: families with at least 11 periods within 15 per cent of average; stable with blips: families with income in 10 periods within 15 per cent of average; rising/falling: higher/lower than average income in periods in second part of year and reverse in first part (with only one exception); erratic/highly erratic: all other cases.

4.7   Unemployment in the UK by duration
Source: ONS.
Note: Figures are for the third quarter of each year, seasonally adjusted, for adults aged 16–64. Figures are for durations of uncompleted spells of unemployment (using Labour Force Survey definitions).

4.8   Proportion of claimants remaining on Jobseeker's Allowance, spells starting in April 2007, 2009 and 2011
Source: Data kindly supplied by DWP from Work and Pensions Longitudinal Study (not seasonally adjusted).

4.9   Components of income for couple with one child, 2010–11
Source: DWP tax benefit model for 2010–11 (webarchive.nationalarchives.gov. uk/+/http://statistics.dwp.gov.uk/asd/index.php?page=tbmt).
Note: Calculations are for couple working 30 hours or more per week with rent of £149 and Council Tax of £22.

GOOD TIMES, BAD TIMES

4.10   Combined tax and benefit withdrawal rates for couple with one child,
       2010–11
       *Source: DWP tax benefit model for 2010–11 (webarchive.nationalarchives.gov.
       uk/+/http://statistics.dwp.gov.uk/asd/index.php?page=tbmt).*

4.11   Net income by hours worked under current system and Universal Credit,
       lone parent with two children
       Source: Brewer et al (2012b, Figure 3.2).

Note: Earnings of £6.50 per hour. Does not include housing costs or support.

Chapter 5

1   We learned that Tracy was pregnant again in the March 1991 'Beat the Taxman' programme.

2   All figures in this vignette are presented in 2010–11 earnings terms, for simplicity of exposition using the 2010–11 tax benefit system, and comparing resultant incomes with the 2010–11 (before housing costs) income distribution. Jim and Tracy Ackroyd's net income was £512 per week, equivalent after adjustment for family size to £275 for a couple with no children. This put them at the 21st percentile of the distribution (see Figure 2.5 in Chapter 2).

3   With Jim Ackroyd still taking home £338 per week and Tracy £123, but with Child Benefit and a small amount of the new Child Tax Credit that replaced WFTC for Paul, their net income was now £581 per week, equivalent to £379 for a couple with no children, and so at the 43rd percentile of the national distribution.

4   Their total income was up to £731 per week, including Michelle's Income Support and tax credit, giving them an equivalent income of £354, at the 38th percentile of the national distribution.

5   Equivalent to £446 for a couple with no children, and so, at the 55th percentile.

6   It came to £299 per week including Jim's Jobseeker's Allowance, full Child Tax Credit, Tracy's earnings, and the partial Housing and Council Tax Benefit they got. With Paul aged 15, this would be counted as equivalent to £225, at the 11th percentile of the distribution.

7   A total of £302, including EMA, Jobseeker's Allowance for a couple, Child Benefit (as Paul was still at school) and full Child Tax Credit, Housing Benefit and Council Tax Benefit, equivalent to £227 for a couple, inching them up to the 12th percentile of the distribution.

8   Stephen Osborne's net income fell to £85,000 in 2002 and £75,000 in 2003, including the insurance pay-out, while Henrietta's net earnings halved that year to £5,000. This left them with £2,050 per week in 2002 (with three in the household) and £1,780 in 2003 (with two of them at home).

9   The surviving BHPS sample has now been subsumed into a new and larger panel study, Understanding Society.

10   Jenkins (2011, Table 4.1).

11   For detailed analysis not just of what the BHPS shows, but also of the issues

and principles involved in understanding income mobility, see in particular Jenkins (2011). For a detailed survey of approaches to analysing income mobility between and within generations (as discussed in Chapter 7), see Jäntti and Jenkins (2014: forthcoming). DWP analysis of results from the data relating specifically to low income in particular can be found, for instance, in Barton et al (2013).

12   Movements were taken as substantive if they amounted to more than 15 percentiles of the *original* distribution in real terms, or 'quasi-percentiles'. 'Flat' trajectories remained within plus or minus 15 quasi-percentiles of the individual's mean. 'Blips' go outside this range for two periods, either together or separately. Rising or falling trajectories ended up at least 15 quasi-percentiles above or below the original position, and had a statistically significant time trend at the 10 per cent level. See Rigg and Sefton (2006) for more details.

13   Jenkins (2011, p 361).

14   Rigg and Sefton (2006, Tables 5 and 6).

15   Derived from Buck and Scott (1994, Table 3.5).

16   Clarke and McKay (2008, Table 4.4), based on BHPS waves 1–15.

17   Clarke and McKay (2008, Table 4.2), based on the Families and Children Survey (FACS) waves 3–7.

18   Derived from Table S204 for 2005/06 from the Communities and Local Government's Survey of English Housing (details of the survey are available at   www.gov.uk/government/publications/english-housing-survey-2011-to-2012-headline-report).

19   Disney et al (2009). For full results for public and private sectors and mid-level education, see Hills et al (2010, Figure 11.20).

20   Burchardt (2000).

21   See the report of one of the task groups for Sir Michael Marmot's review of health inequalities: Glennerster et al (2009, p 22).

22   Sainsbury et al (2008, p 151).

23   From April 2011 the system changed for those who had been receiving Incapacity Benefit, and cases started being reassessed for transfer to Employment and Support Allowance (or other benefits, if not judged eligible), which is why the numbers of those starting in April 2007 remaining on the old Incapacity Benefit drop more rapidly after 50 months.

24 Using more detailed data from Jenkins (2011, Figure 5.1).

25 Jenkins (2011, Figures 5.2 and 5.7).

26 Jenkins (2011, Figure 8.1).

27 Hills (2007, Figure 9.1), based on DWP's HBAI dataset. The 1979 figure is for the UK; the 2004–05 figure is for England only. Note that the proportion of *people* living in social housing was greater than the proportion of *households*.

28 Alzubaidi et al (2013, Table 3.6db). Proportion with incomes below 60 per cent of the median.

29 Alzubaidi et al (2013, Table 8.1) (before housing costs).

30 The Centre for Social Justice's Housing Dependency Working Group (2008) made some proposals of this kind, and the Coalition government consulted on doing this soon after it was elected (CLG, 2010). In 2013, Hammersmith and Fulham became the first London borough to offer new tenancies on this basis (*Inside Housing*, 6 March 2013).

31 See, for instance, Hills (2007, Figure 9.3).

32 See Hills et al (2010, Figure 11.11) for Department for Children, Schools and Families (DCSF) analysis showing the strong adverse association between having recently changed school and performance in GCSEs.

33 This was announced in the 2013 Budget, following an earlier consultation on 'Pay to Stay' proposals (CLG, 2012).

34 The other was to abolish Housing Benefit altogether for those aged under 25 (New Year economy speech by the Chancellor, 6 January 2014).

35 One of the housing ministers under the Labour government suggested this sort of approach (speech by the Rt Hon Caroline Flint to the Fabian Society, 5 February 2007).

36 Sefton (2007), based on analysis of BHPS data (for England).

37 For more discussion of this, see Hills (2007, Sections 17 and 18).

38 For more detailed discussion of the results presented in this section, see Hills and Richards (2012).

39 Fifty of the 52 universities with the greatest number of full-time undergraduates (two had not published information in January 2012, when students were applying), plus the two research-intensive Russell Group universities that did not fit into this category (Imperial College London and LSE). We restricted analysis to full-time students resident in England and

excluded several groups subject to special rules, including mature students, and those leaving public care, with partners, or not going to university for the first time. We focused on those living away from home and excluded foundation courses, foundation years, non-honours degrees, years abroad, and years in industry.

40 See www.russellgroup.ac.uk/our-universities

41 It excludes pension contributions eligible for tax relief and deducts an allowance (£1,130 in 2010–11) for each other financially dependent child apart from the student (but makes no other adjustment for family size).

42 Drawn from DWP's tax benefit tables as used in earlier chapters. The results are rescaled in terms of the 'residual income' that would be generated by income from earnings alone if one of the children remained at home and one went to university, deducting the allowance for one other child still at home.

43 We illustrate the position for £1,000 differences in residual income (for example, comparing someone with an income of £25,001 with their treatment if income was £24,001), avoiding showing the extreme marginal rates that would apply to small income variations around a particular threshold.

Figure sources and notes

5.1 Income-age trajectories for women born in 1966 from 1991 to 2007
Source: Jenkins (2011, Figure 7.2), based on BHPS.
Note: Figures are for women with A-levels or higher qualifications only, and are at January 2008 prices (logarithmic vertical scale).

5.2 Income trajectories in the first 10 years of BHPS compared to random patterns
Source: Rigg and Sefton (2006, Table 1), based on data from BHPS 1991–2000.

5.3 Age-earnings profiles by gender, private sector employees with high and low education, UK
Source: Hills et al (2010, Figure 11.20) based on Disney et al (2009), using Labour Force Survey data from 1994 to 2006.

5.4 Average hourly wage-age trajectories for men and women born before 1955 by qualifications
Source: Jenkins (2011, Figure 7.3).
Note: Original shown on logarithmic scale.

5.5   Proportion of claimants remaining on Incapacity Benefit or Severe
        Disablement Allowance, spells starting in April 2004 and April 2007
        *Source: Data kindly supplied by DWP from Work and Pensions Longitudinal
        Study (includes Severe Disablement Allowance).*

5.6   Positions in income distributions of 1992 and 2006 of those who started
        in top and bottom tenths of distribution in 1991
        Source: Jenkins (2011, Figure 5.1) (simplified and inverted).

5.7   Where people starting in different fifths of the income distribution spend
        their time over following years
        Source: Barton et al (2013, Tables 3.1 and 3.2).
Note: Income before housing costs.

5.8   Length of spell of poverty starting in one year
        Source: Jenkins (2011, Figure 8.8), based on BHPS 1991–2006.
Note: Poverty threshold is 60 per cent of median income, adjusted for
        household size.

5.9   Patterns of poverty persistence over nine-year periods
        Source: Jenkins (2011, Figure 8.4).
Note: Poverty line is 60 per cent of median income, adjusted for household size.

5.10   Persistent low income 1991–94 to 2005–08
        Source: Barton et al (2013, Table 6.1) (before housing costs).
Note: The proportion of the population with income (adjusted for household
        size) below 60 per cent of contemporary median before housing costs for
        three or more years of each four-year period.

5.11   Total effective marginal tax and withdrawal rates (%) on £1,000
        differences in parental income – average for 27 universities
        Source: Hills and Richards (2012).
Note: Figures are for single-earner families with one child going to university
        (first year) and one child still at home.

Chapter 6

1   That is, *all* of Stephen's current contributions, as his firm runs a 'salary sacrifice' scheme, where what would have been his own contributions are now counted as being employer contributions. Many employers – including the author's – now run schemes like this to minimise their National Insurance payments.

2   Although since 1997 pension funds have not been able to reclaim 'tax credits' for Corporation Tax already paid on the profits from which dividends are paid, so that could be counted as a partial tax on returns coming as dividends.

3   Henrietta's grandmother had left the money to her parents, but through a legal 'deed of variation' they had passed it straight on to Henrietta so it would not count towards any possible Inheritance Tax liability of their own.

4   Based on figures derived from the ONS Wealth and Asset Survey for 2008–10 (see ONS, 2012b), with methodolody for assessing pension rights revised in May 2014, updating those presented in Hills et al (2010, Table 11.6 for 2006–08). The data tables used here are available at www.ons.gov.uk/ons/about-ons/business-transparency/freedom-of-information/what-can-i-request/published-ad-hoc-data/econ/june-2014/index.html.   Within the £2.1 million total, a somewhat smaller proportion comes from pension rights than typical for the 90th percentile of higher professionals of this age (typically more than 40 per cent), as parts of Stephen's pension rights are on a 'defined contribution' basis, and so have not increased as much in current value as much from low long-term interest rates as those on a 'defined benefit' basis. On the other hand, their financial and physical assets are higher than the £500,000 typical for such households as a result of their high and tax-efficient levels of savings since the late 1980s.

5   Based on the ONS Wealth and Asset Survey for 2008–10 as revised in May 2014. Median total wealth for 55–64-year-old council tenant households was £16,000 excluding private pension rights, or £30,000 including them, but as things are described, the Ackroyds had not been in pension schemes. How they would have been treated as members is discussed below.

6   See Hills and Glennerster (2013, Section 8.3.1) for a more detailed discussion. Strictly speaking, the Council Tax Benefit and Housing Benefit the Ackyroyds were receiving in 2005 should have been cut back to reflect their savings over £3,000 at the time, but that was not taken into account in the calculations at the start of Chapter 5.

7   At the time the basic rate of income tax was 22 per cent and the withdrawal rate for tax credits (then the WFTC) was equivalent to 37.4 per cent of gross income, for those paying Income Tax and NICs. Under the tax credit system from 2003–04 the withdrawal rate became 37 per cent of gross income. For the full (gory) details of the net value of the tax and benefit treatment of pension savings for people in different circumstances, see Pensions Commission (2004, pp 237–9).

8   This chapter draws heavily on analysis carried out with colleagues and reported in Hills et al (2013b), where many of the issues it presents are discussed in more detail.

9   See Piketty (2014) for a comprehensive discussion of long-term trends in the importance of personal wealth and inequalities in it internationally. See also Rowlingson and McKay (2011) and Birmingham Policy Commission on Wealth (2013) for more discussion of the position in the UK.

10   In the survey used in Figure 6.1, 5.7 per cent of households said they had a personalised number plate, 'worth' an average of £1,300, giving a startling total of £1.8 billion (although that makes only a small contribution to the overall total, excluding pension rights, of £5.5 *trillion*).

11   A total of £8,965 billion in 2008–10, as revised by ONS in 2014, divided between 24.725 million households.

12   See Hills and Bastagli (2013b) for more detailed discussion.

13   Based on the age of the 'household reference person', as described in earlier chapters.

14   Hood and Joyce (2013, Figure 2.3b).

15   Hood and Joyce (2013, Figure 2.7).

16   Hood and Joyce (2013, Figures 3.12 and 3.9). Younger cohorts are much more likely to be in 'defined contribution' pension schemes from private employers, which are less valuable than the 'defined benefit' schemes that older generations were more likely to benefit from.

17   Willetts (2010); Howker and Malik (2010).

18   Hood and Joyce (2013, Figure 4.3), based on the ONS Wealth and Asset Survey.

19   This section draws heavily on joint work with Francesca Bastagli. See Bastagli and Hills (2012, 2013) for more detailed discussion.

20 See Dorling (2014) for a discussion of the wider effects of what has happened to house prices and inequalities in housing wealth.

21 See Bastagli and Hills (2013, Table 4.12), and associated discussion.

22 'Best buy' rates from leading providers according to the *Financial Times* website, downloaded on 15 January 2014 (www.ft.com/personal-finance/annuity-table). £100,000 would have bought an annual income of £3,746 on a joint-life basis (50 per cent for a survivor), with 3 per cent annual escalation to offset inflation.

23 DWP (2013c, p 22).

24 Pensions Commission (2005, p ix). The author was a member of the Commission.

25 Pensions Commission (2005, p 60).

26 Even after a significant increase between 1995 and 2009, the share of national income spent on state transfers for old age and survivors, at 6.2 per cent, was still the 18th lowest out of 30 OECD countries (Hills, 2013a, Table A2 based on OECD social expenditure database).

27 Pensions Commission (2005, p 117).

28 Figures for 2002–03 from Pensions Commission (2004, Figure 3.5).

29 Pensions Commission (2005, Figure Ex.2).

30 An alternative figure, 'period' life expectancy, is based on mortality rates at particular ages, assuming that they stay as they have been recently, and that improvements grind to a halt. For planning pensions policy and forecasting costs, cohort life expectancies are more useful – but they do require assumptions to be made about how and whether things continue to improve in the future, and so have uncertainty around them.

31 DWP (2013c, para 129).

32 DWP (2013c, Chart 6.5). The figure for women in 2012 would have been slightly higher, if the process of equalising men's and women's pension ages had not started in 2010.

33 Over the 24 years from April 1988 to April 2012, a formula of this kind would have meant pensions increasing by 8.8 per cent in relation to average earnings, with 8.3 percentage points of this occurring in the recession between April 2008 and April 2012 (using figures for the CPI and average earnings from DWP, 2012, Tables 1.1 and 1).

34 Pensions Commission (2004, Figure 1.9).

35 Pensions Commission (2005, Appendix D, Figure D28).

36 ONS (2012a, Figure 3.3). These figures are only available on a period basis, showing about 75 per cent of male life expectancy and 70 per cent of female life expectancy at 65 to be 'healthy' in both 1981 and 1999.

37 DWP (2013c, Chart 6.3).

38 Hills et al (2013a, Figures 9.2 and 4.2).

39 Cribb et al (2013a).

40 ONS (2012a, Figures 3.4 and 3.5).

41 See Vizard and Obolenskaya (2013) for a detailed discussion of these differences and trends in them between 1997 and 2010.

42 See Hills (2012, Chapter 7), for a discussion of the relative effectiveness of different approaches to tackling fuel poverty; Winter Fuel Payments have very little effect on the problem.

43 This section draws in particular on joint work with Howard Glennerster. For more detail of current treatment of different kinds of wealth accumulation see Chapter 8, and for reform possibilities (and difficulties with many of them), see Chapter 9 of Hills et al (2013b).

44 See Glennerster (2012).

45 This was the case made by the authoritative Mirrlees Review of the tax system, which argued that Council Tax should be explicitly transformed into a tax on housing services to balance the lack of VAT on them (Adam et al, 2011).

46 Hills and Glennerster (2013, Table 8.1).

47 Hills and Glennerster (2013, Figure 8.1).

48 HM Treasury (2014a, Table D3).

49 Echailer et al (2013).

50 Echailer et al (2013, Chart 1).

51 Echailer et al (2013, Chart 2).

52 See www.hmrc.gov.uk/statistics/tax-statistics/table2-1.pdf

53 These rules now put a limit of £40,000 per year (from 2014–15) on tax-deductible contributions, including an assessment of how much the effective value of someone's 'defined benefit' pension rights increase in value when

they are promoted (but not the sometimes very large increase in value, if their prospective life expectancy rises).

54 Talking to the BBC, 21 March 2014.

55 Pensions Commission (2005, Figure 1.42).

56 Hills and Glennerster (2013, p 171).

57 See Hills and Glennerster (2013, Section 8.3.1), for more details and discussion.

58 For pensioners claiming Pension Credit the rules are somewhat more generous, with savings up to £10,000 ignored, and an assumed return on any excess over that of 10 per cent.

59 In Scotland the rules are different, and 'personal' and 'nursing' care are free, regardless of means, but people have to contribute towards accommodation, if they have assets above £15,250 (in 2012).

60 Hills and Glennerster (2013, Figure 8.3).

61 Commission on Funding of Care and Support (2011, p 13).

62 DH (2013). The £72,000 lifetime cap excludes £12,000 per year for 'daily living costs' in residential care.

63 The ending of 'contracting out' from the state second pension, which led to some people and their employers paying lower NICs, but with lower eventual state pension rights.

64 See House of Lords Select Committee on Public Service and Demographic Change (2013) and Fabian Commission (2013).

65 Hills and Glennerster (2013, Section 8.5.1).

Figure sources and notes

6.1 Pen's parade of household wealth (excluding pensions), 2008–10
Source: Hills et al (2013b, Figure 2.1), based on ONS analysis of Wealth and Assets Survey, July 2008–June 2010 (as revised by ONS in May 2014).

6.2 Pen's parade of household wealth (including pension rights), 2008–10
Source: Hills et al (2013b, Figure 2.1), based on ONS analysis of Wealth and Assets survey, July 2008–June 2010 (as revised by ONS in May 2014).

6.3 Wealth by age of household, 2008–10
Source: ONS analysis of Wealth and Asset Survey, July 2008–June 2010 (as revised by ONS in May 2014).

6.4   Wealth in 1995 and 2005 by initial age of household
       Source: Bastagli and Hills (2013) based on 2,075 BHPS households for whom
       we have observations over the 10-year period.

Note: Age is that of the head of household in 1995. Wealth is the total of net
       financial assets and housing wealth, net of mortgages.

6.5   Projections for remaining years of life for men reaching 65 between 1955
       and 2055
       Source: DWP (2013c, Figure 6.1), based on ONS and Government Actuary's
       Department, period and cohort expectation of life tables (various issues).

Chapter 7

1   Social Mobility and Child Poverty Commission (2013, Figure 5.1), based on Dearden et al (2011), Figure 2. Figures show average percentile ranking by fifth of parental income.

2   The 2012 figures are from Social Mobility and Child Poverty Commission (2013, Appendix, p 36).

3   Hills et al (2010, Figure 3.6[a]) updated to 2010 results using analysis of the National Pupil Database. Figures are for pupils in England, with results categorised by areas according to Income Deprivation Affecting Children Index (IDACI).

4   2012 figures from Social Mobility and Child Poverty Commission (2013, Appendix, p 41).

5   For all those from state schools turning 18 in 2009, 18 per cent from the most deprived fifth of families went on to higher education, but 55 per cent of those from the least deprived fifth. If he ends up in private school, Edward's chances would be better than this (Blanden and Macmillan, 2014, Table 5, based on Crawford, 2012).

6   2010–11 figures of 63.7 and 23.8 per cent respectively from Social Mobility and Child Poverty Commission (2013, Appendix, p 46).

7   Gregg et al (2013), based on results from BCS70, using an average of family income at age 10 and 16 to reduce the effects of measurement error, yielding an intergenerational income elasticity of 0.457.

8   Given weekly earnings for men aged 35–39 working full time of £577 per week in 2010 (Hills et al, 2013a, Figure 6.3, based on Labour Force Survey data) and an elasticity of 0.457 (see Note 7).

9   Based on the ONS analysis of Wealth and Assets Survey 2008–10 as revised by ONS in May 2014; figures for median total wealth of households aged 55–64.

10 These are ONS's life expectancies on a *cohort* basis, taking account of projected future improvements in mortality rates at any given age. On this basis life expectancy for women born in 2013 was 94.1 for England as a whole, and 90.8 for men (ONS, 2013b). The ONS does not publish life expectancies by area on a cohort basis, but on the period basis, life expectancies for men born in Salford in 2010–12 were 3.1 years below the England average of 79.2, while those for men born in Stockport were 0.6 years above it (ONS, 2013c).

In the most favoured area (Purbeck in Dorset) the figures imply that a girl born in 2013 had a life expectancy around 98.

11 This chapter draws extensively from Chapter 11 of the report of the National Equality Panel (Hills et al, 2010), which gives more detail on many of the issues covered.

12 Figures from the 1912 official report on the disaster (Cmd 6352; www. anesi.com/titanic.htm). There is some uncertainty about whether one of the children in first class died; if so, only 87 per cent of children in first class survived.

13 'School readiness' is measured in terms of the Bracken School Readiness Assessment, which is the sum of correct responses on six sub-scales: colours, letters, numbers/counting, sizes, comparisons and shapes.

14 Waldfogel and Washbrook (2008).

15 See Feinstein (2013) for a discussion of the controversies around early differences in measured cognitive ability of children, and how they change as children from different backgrounds grow older, relating to some combination of measurement error in assessments, genetics, culture and environment, and the interactions between them.

16 Hills et al (2010), based on Goodman and Gregg (2010).

17 Hansen and Joshi (2008, Table 7.2).

18 The figure shows the factors that were significant at the 1 per cent level in the researchers' 'full model' (Cullis and Hansen, 2008, Table 5). Data are for England only.

19 Crawford et al (2011).

20 Cooper and Stewart (2013). From the 47,000 studies screened, 34 met the criterion of being based on randomised controlled trials, 'natural' experiments, instrumental variable techniques, or fixed effects approaches with longitudinal data. A further 58 studies were used for additional discussion. Most of the studies came from the US, with others from the UK, Canada, Norway, and Mexico.

21 Summary of Cooper and Stewart (2013, p 2.)

22 Only five of the studies found no evidence that money had an independent effect, but there were methodological reasons in four of those cases.

23 Summary of Cooper and Stewart (2013, p 3).

24 Social Mobility and Child Poverty Commission (2013, Figures 5.2 and 6.3).

25   Social Mobility and Child Poverty Commission (2013, Figures 6.2 and 6.3).

26   Social Mobility and Child Poverty Commission (2013, Appendix, p 45).

27   Lupton and Obolenskaya (2013, pp 39–41).

28   Social Mobility and Child Poverty Commission (2013, Figure 6.1).

29   Social Mobility and Child Poverty Commission (2013, p 175), based on PISA results for 2009.

30   Whitty and Anders (2014), based on Jerrim (2012).

31   The results are for the combined 'GCSE points score' in up to eight subjects, and show where children come as a percentile point in the overall national distribution. Neighbourhoods are classified by the IDACI.

32   Blanden and Macmillan (2014, Table 5), using results from Crawford (2012). Socio-economic status based on a combination of indicators including both free school meals status and characteristics of the neighbourhood in which people live.

33   Blanden and Macmillan (2014, Table 10). High status institutions are taken as those in the Russell Group and others with comparable research performance.

34   Social Mobility and Child Poverty Commission (2013, Appendix, p 46).

35   Hills et al (2010, p 364), based on analysis in Machin et al (2009).

36   Chowdry et al (2013, Tables 13 and 14). The individual characteristics allowed for as well as examination performance are ethnicity, whether English is a second language, whether they have special educational needs, and month of birth.

37   Chowdry et al (2013, Tables 16 and 17).

38   For more details, see Hills et al (2010, Figure 11.19), based on analysis in Machin et al (2009).

39   But not the individual university attended. Looking at earnings just six months after graduation, where this could be allowed for, the effects of higher social class and of attendance at private schools were reduced somewhat, but remained significant apart from the effect of having professional parents for men (Machin et al, 2009, Table 7).

40   Macmillan et al (2013).

41   For more details see Hills et al (2010, Figure 11.20), based on Disney et al (2009).

42   Cooper and Stewart (2013).

43   Mayer (1998).

44   By 2010, 10.6 per cent of men and women in their early thirties had a higher degree (and a further 22.6 per cent a first degree), but only 14.2 per cent of those in their early sixties had any kind of degree, 5.4 per cent having a higher degree, and 8.8 per cent a first degree only (Hills et al, 2010, Figure 3.8, updated using data from Labour Force Survey for the UK).

45   Social Mobility and Child Poverty Commission (2013, p 4).

46   As in the study by Atkinson et al (1983), that tracked down some of the children of the families that Seebohm Rowntree had interviewed in 1950.

47   See, for instance, Blanden and Machin (2007), summarised in Hills et al (2010, Table 11.1), for an earlier comparison of the relationship between sons' and daughters' earnings in their early thirties and family incomes. This suggests that at that age, the chances of women and men ending up in the bottom or top quarter of earners depend in a similar way on whether their families had higher or lower incomes. The chances of sons who grew up with low incomes themselves ending up with low wages were slightly greater than for daughters who also grew up with low incomes.

48   Although note that Atkinson et al (1983) found – from a particular sample from one area – an elasticity of 42 per cent between the earnings of parents in York in 1950 and their children in the 1970s.

49   Panel on Fair Access to the Professions (2009), summarised in Hills et al (2010, Figure 11.5). The relative family incomes of those born in 1970 who went on to become lecturers and professors, however, were lower than for their equivalents born in 1958.

50   Gregg et al (2013). It is the coefficient of 0.457 from this analysis that was used in the vignette at the start of this chapter.

51   Goldthorpe and Mills (2008), summarised in Hills et al (2010, Figure 11.3).

52   Corak (2013, Figure 1).

53   For instance, Kornrich and Furstenberg (2013) find that in the US parental spending focused on children increased in both real terms and as a share of parental income between the early 1970s and the late 2000s but, with growing overall income inequality, the gaps in spending between rich and poor grew.

54 Hills and Bastagli (2013, Table 2.2), updated using ONS analysis of the 2008–10 Wealth and Assets Survey and taking account of ONS's revisions to the survey results published in May 2014. Total wealth includes personal possessions, net financial assets, housing wealth (net of mortgages), and the valuation put by ONS on future private pension rights.

55 McKnight and Karagiannaki (2013).

56 Hills and Karagiannaki (2013, p 95).

57 Hills and Karagiannaki (2013, Table 5.1), based on figures from the BHPS.

58 Hills and Karagiannaki (2013, Table 5.2), based on figures from the BHPS.

59 See Hills and Karagiannaki (2013, Table 5.3), for raw differences between population groups, and Karagiannaki (2011a) for the differences in the chances of receipt and size of inheritance when controlling for other factors.

60 Hood and Joyce (2013, Figures 4.3 and 4.4).

61 Karagiannaki (2001b, Tables 6 and 7), summarised in Hills and Karagiannaki (2013, pp 115–16).

62. Speech to the Institute of Government, 9 September 2010.

63. Quoted in *The Guardian*, 23 November 2010.

64. Quoted in *The Guardian*, 14 November 2013.

65 John Smith Memorial Lecture, April 1996.

66. Quoted on BBC News website, 28 June 2008.

67 Aldridge (2001, para 70).

Figure sources and notes

7.1 Six-year survival rates (%) for men and women aged over 60 by wealth
Source: Based on Nazroo, et al (2008, p 267), using data from English Longitudinal Survey of Ageing 2001–06. Survival rates over six years, age-adjusted.

7.2 Differences in 'school readiness' (average position out of 100) by parental income
Source: Hills, et al (2010, Figure 11.6), drawn from Waldfogel and Washbrook (2008), based on MCS.

7.3 Factors related to differences in teachers' assessment of children entering primary school

Source: Hills, et al (2010, Figure 11.9), drawn from Cullis and Hansen (2008), based on FSP in MCS.

7.4   Children's test scores (aged 5–16 in 2004) by parents' socio-economic position and parents' test scores in childhood (aged 10 in 1980)
Source: Based on Crawford et al (2011, Figure 1 reordered).

7.5   Attainment gaps between children receiving free school meals (FSM) and other children at different ages
Source: Social Mobility and Child Poverty Commission (2013, Figure 6.3 and Appendix, p 45).

Note: Figures are for England; those for entry into higher education (HE) are for 2010–11. Measure at age 5 is 'good' level of development; at age 11, 'Level 4' in English and maths; at age 16, five or more GCSEs at A*–C; at age 19, 'Level 3' qualification or higher.

7.6   Trends in attainment gaps between children by background, by year of birth
Source: Blanden and Macmillan (2014, Figure 2, simplified).

Note: Based on composite of results of 59 observations of attainment gaps at different ages, education level, family background measures and date of birth.

7.7   GCSE results for girls (rank in national distribution) by area deprivation (England, 2010)
Source: Hills et al (2013a, Figure 2.3 simplified), based on National Pupil Database.

Note: Pupils ranked according to aggregate GCSE 'points score' in up to eight subjects. Areas ranked by IDACI.

7.8   University attended by background, UK-born students, UK universities
Source: Hills et al (2010, Figure 11.17), based on Machin et al (2009).

Note: Figures are for those completing higher education in 2002–03.

7.9   Class of degree achieved by background, UK-born students, UK universities
Source: Hills et al (2010, Figure 11.18), based on Machin et al (2009).

Note: Figures are for those completing higher education in 2002–03.

7.10   How much of the variation in children's earnings is associated with parental income?
Source: Gregg et al (2013).

Note: 1958 cohort results are based on the NCDS. 1970 cohort results are based on the BCS70. Parental incomes are based on single observation when children were 16. The vertical scale shows the elasticity between child's earnings and parental incomes.

7.11   The Great Gatsby curve

Source: Corak (2013, Figure 1).

Note: Income inequality is Gini coefficient for disposable household income
in mid-1980s. Intergenerational link in earnings mobility is association
(elasticity) between paternal and son's earnings for men born in the
early 1960s, with adult earnings in the mid to late 1990s. Results
from individual studies are adjusted for measurement error to give
comparability between nations.

7.12   Education earnings premiums and earnings mobility

Source: Corak (2013, Figure 4).

Note: Earnings premium is difference between men aged 25–34 with a college
degree compared to earnings of those with a high school diploma (in US
terms). Earnings mobility as described in notes to Figure 7.11.

Chapter 8

1   Applying the increase in the average earnings index projected by the Office for Budget Responsibility (OBR) from 2010 Q2 to 2014 Q2 (OBR, 2014, Economy Supplementary Table 1.6). That meant that Stephen had done a little better than the general rise in male full-time earnings for those at the 90th percentile (on the basis of figures from the Annual Survey of Hours and Earnings up to April 2013, at least), but he was still gaining a little in his pay from seniority.

2   Adjusting by the CPI as projected by the OBR (2014, Economy Supplementary Table 1.7).

3   The calculations in the text compare their tax liabilities with those that would have been due under the 2010–11 system simply adjusted for CPI inflation. Later in this chapter we discuss the differences between this kind of assumed benchmark and one that was uprated in line with income growth (which would have meant smaller increases in tax brackets over this particular period). The calculations assume that both Stephen and Henrietta Osborne make pension contributions of 7 per cent of gross pay, deductible in calculating Income Tax.

4   Their total Council Tax is £2,981, but £548 of this is made up of 'precepts' from other authorities that have not been frozen, and are assumed here to have risen with CPI inflation only.

5   Based on the proportion of disposable income (after Council Tax) estimated by the ONS to be paid in VAT by people in the top tenth of the income distribution of non-retired households on average in 2010–11 (ONS, 2013a).

6   This calculation assumes that her housing association rent had increased with CPI inflation from £71 in 2010–11 to £79.66 in 2014–15.

7   This is the rate for a Band B property, assuming that the other precepts contributing to the tax rose in line with CPI inflation over the period, and so were unchanged in real terms. After allowing for the 25 per cent single adult discount, her Council Tax was £16.95 per week in 2010–11, but would have been £19.01 if it had risen with inflation, compared to the £17.20 she is actually paying.

8   This is based on her spending half of her income after allowing for rent, Council Tax and £20 per week on fuel (on which VAT has not changed) on VAT-able goods and comparing with what she would have had to spend on them if other parts of the tax benefit system had been price-linked and the main VAT rate had stayed at 17.5 per cent.

9   See Power et al (2014) and O'Hara (2014) for evidence on the actual experiences of people being affected by 'welfare reform'.

10   What the scale of such an adjustment should be, and whether recent policies have attempted to do this too rapidly or at the right speed, is obviously one of the central issues in politics, but is well outside the scope of this book.

11   See Hills (2013b) for more discussion.

12   With the possible addition of the fifth, if in a particular case the effect of a crisis had borne proportionately more heavily on the better-off than on the worse-off.

13   Using the CPI measure of inflation, although that choice is in itself controversial, and the use of another index such as the RPI would lead to different results.

14   Adam and Browne (2010). Note that the income groups used are based on where households would have been placed in the income distribution under the 2005 system, that is, after the bulk of Labour's reforms. This places some of the larger gainers from the changes (such as pensioners and families with children) higher up the distribution than they would have been at the start, while some of those who did not benefit – such as low-income working-age households without children – remain at the bottom.

15   Phillips (2014, Slide 20).

16   UK Women's Budget Group (2013, Figures 6, 9, 12 and 16) (based on analysis by Landman Economics).

17   De Agostini et al (2013, Figure 7).

18   This section draws heavily on joint work with Holly Sutherland, Martin Evans, Ruth Hancock and Francesca Zantomio. See Sutherland et al (2008) for more discussion of these issues.

19   Earnings figures here and below taken from DWP (2012, Table 1), up to April 2011. Earnings growth since then to 2014 Q2 from OBR (2013b, Supplementary Table 1.4).

20   For instance, it would take 27 years for earnings growing at 1.5 per cent per year to reach the same level as with 20 years growing at 2 per cent.

21 The standard rules at the time included: uprating most benefits, tax credits and tax allowances in line with the RPI; uprating minimum income benefits such as Income Support with the 'Rossi' index, excluding housing costs; uprating the basic state pension with earnings (after 2012); uprating some parts of the tax credit system and Pension Credit thresholds with earnings for the periods pledged by the then government; and freezing benefits and tax allowances that are rarely or never adjusted. See Sutherland et al (2008, Section 5), for more details.

22 The figures are those based on ONS's principal projection based on its mid-2010 population estimates, as published in 2011. They will be revised taking into account the larger population revealed by the 2011 Census, increasing the total forecast for later years, but not necessarily increasing the proportion of it above particular ages.

23 See OBR (2013a, Chapter 3) for more details.

24 OBR (2012, pp 152–4).

25 House of Lords Select Committee on Public Service and Demographic Change (2013, para 20), based on research by Professor Carol Jagger of Newcastle University.

26 OBR (2013a, Annex A, Table A.6).

Figure sources and notes

8.1 Losses from general cuts in social benefits and services or general tax increases averaging £1,000 per household
Source: Derived from ONS series on effects of taxes and benefits in 2010–11, as in Figures 2.9(b) and 2.10.

8.2 Distributional effects of Labour's tax and benefit reforms from 1997 to 2009 compared to systems adjusted with prices or incomes
Source: Adam and Browne (2010, Figure 3.8).

8.3 Institute for Fiscal Studies estimates of effects of tax and benefit reforms, January 2010 to April 2015
Source: Phillips (2014, Slide 11).
Note: Households are ranked by disposable income under the January 2010 system. Includes effects of 'Bedroom Tax' and of Council Tax support reforms (using a national average minimum contribution of 10.4 per cent).

8.4   Institute for Fiscal Studies estimates of effects of tax and benefit reforms, January 2010 to April 2015, by household type
        Source: Phillips (2014, Slide 18).

8.5   HM Treasury estimates of distributional effects of tax, benefit and public service changes by 2015–16
        Source: Based on HM Treasury (2014b, Chart 2.I).

8.6   Distributional effects of direct tax and benefit changes in six countries, 2008–13
        Source: De Agostini et al (2014, Figure 3) (selected countries).
Note: Effects shown are those for simulated measures (excluding VAT). Vertical axes are on different scales, but gridlines are at same intervals.

8.7   Effects of fiscal drag and benefit erosion over twenty years, if real earnings grew by 2 per cent per year
        Source: Sutherland et al (2008, Figure 18).
Note: Base system is that in place in 2006–07, with indexation rules based on conventional practice at the time.

8.8   Effects of fiscal drag and benefit erosion if part of revenue used for tax cuts or benefit increases
        Source: Sutherland et al (2008, Figure 20).
Note: Base system is that in place in 2006–07, with indexation rules based on conventional practice at the time.

8.9   ONS projections for percentage of population in each age range, 2011 and 2051
        Source: ONS (2011).

8.10   OBR long-term public spending projections
        Source: OBR (2013a, Table 3.6).

Chapter 9

1   See Notes to Chapter 1 for their net 'equivalent' incomes allowing for household size in the way they are used in official DWP HBAI statistics.

2   Stiglitz (2012); Piketty (2014).

3   YouGov survey of 1,805 British adults, December 2012 (http://touchstoneblog.org.uk/2013/01/benefit-cuts-government-support-relies-on-keeping-people-in-the-dark and www.tuc.org.uk/social/tuc-21796-f0.cfm).

4   Taylor-Gooby and Hastie (2002, Table 4.11).

5   BSA survey results (www.britsocat.com). 'Don't know' and refused to answer included in the base.

6   Figures for Great Britain from DWP (2014a).

7   DWP (2014a, Table 2.1).

8   YouGov survey of 1,805 British adults, December 2012 (see Note 3 above).

9   BSA survey results (www.britsocat.com). 'Don't know' and refused to answer included in the base.

10   Baumberg et al (2012, Table 15).

11   The 27 per cent rate of fraud that is people's average belief for fraud of all benefits multiplied by the 41 per cent of the budget that is the average belief for the proportion going to unemployed people would imply that 11 per cent of the total would be the result of unemployment benefit fraud, but people are likely to believe that fraud is higher for these benefits.

12   Webster (2014, Figure 1).

13   Webster (2014, Figure 3).

14   One estimate is that by the end of 2013, 87 per cent of those appeals were being upheld, compared with only around 20 per cent in the 2000s (Webster, 2014, Figure 5).

15   Fenton (2011).

16   Wilcox (2014).

17   See www.trusselltrust.org.uk/stats

18   O'Hara (2014); Power et al (2014).

19   Roantree and Shaw (2014), Table 2.3. Those reporting receiving tax credits,

Income Support, Council Tax Benefit, Housing Benefit or Jobseeker's Allowance were 16.5 per cent in a single year, but 47.8 per cent over the years from 1991 to 2008. The numbers reporting receipt for many of these benefits was only two-thirds to three-quarters of actual payments, however (Table A.1).

20   For instance around 95 per cent of those surveyed by Eurobarometer disagreed with the statement that 'older people are a burden on society' in countries such as the Netherlands, Ireland and the UK, compared to only 70 per cent in the Czech Republic. Presentation of results from the New Dynamics of Ageing programme by Alan Walker, British Academy event on 'Benefit or burden?', London, 26 February 2014.

21   Taylor-Gooby (2013).

Figure sources and notes

9.1   Spending on the welfare state, 2014–15
      Sources: Main categories from HM Treasury (2014a, Chart 1); social security and tax credits from DWP (2013a).
Note: Housing spending based on percentage of total managed expenditure in 2012–13 from HM Treasury, *Public expenditure statistical analyses, 2013*; out-of-work tax credits based on number of out-of-work recipients and full entitlement from *HMRC Child and Working Tax Credit statistics, December 2013*, adjusted to GB basis; out-of-work benefits include Housing Benefit for recipient categories; figures exclude Council Tax support. Other working-age benefits include Child Benefit and tax credits for those in work, etc.

9.2   Agreement that 'social benefits and services make people lazy', 2008
      Source: European Social Survey, 2008.

9.3   Commitment to work and benefit levels in different countries
      Source: Esser (2009).
Note: Index of 'commitment' is based on the combined result from answers to questions whether people 'would enjoy work even if didn't need money' and whether 'job is just way of earning money'. The countries covered are: Australia, Belgium, Canada, Denmark, Germany, Ireland, Japan, New Zealand, Norway, Sweden, Switzerland, the UK and the US.

References

Adam, S. and Browne, J. (2010) *Redistribution, work incentives and thirty years of UK tax and benefit reform*, IFS Working Paper 10/24, London: Institute for Fiscal Studies.

Adam, S., Besley T., Blundell, R., Bond, S., Chote, R, Gammie, M., Johnson, P., Myles, G. and Poterba, J. (2011) *Tax by design: The Mirrlees Review*, edited by the Institute for Fiscal Studies and James Mirrlees, Oxford: Oxford University Press.

Adams, N., Carr, J., Collins, J., Johnson, G. and Matejic, P. (2012) *Households Below Average Income: An analysis of the income distribution, 1994/95 to 2010/11*, London: Department for Work and Pensions.

Aldridge, S. (2001) *Social mobility: A discussion paper*, London: Performance and Innovation Unit, Cabinet Office.

Alzubaidi, H., Carr, J., Councell, R. and Johnson, G. (2013) *Households Below Average Income: An analysis of the income distribution, 1994/95–2011/12*, London: Department for Work and Pensions.

Atkinson, A.B., Maynard, A.K. and Trinder, C. (1983) *Parents and children: Incomes in two generations*, London: Heinemann Educational Books.

Barnes, M., Hales, J. and Lyon, N. (2004) *Tracking Income: The family income study*, Report P2251, London: National Centre for Social Research.

Barr, N. (2001) *The welfare state as a piggy bank*, Oxford: Oxford University Press.

Barton, A., Drummond, R. and Matejic, P. (2013) *Low-income dynamics 1991–2008 (Great Britain)*, London: Department for Work and Pensions.

Bastagli, F. and Hills, J. (2012) *Wealth accumulation in Great Britain 1995–2005: The role of house prices and the life cycle*, CASEpaper 166, London: London School of Economics.

Bastagli, F. and Hills, J. (2013) 'Wealth accumulation, ageing and house prices', in J. Hills, F. Bastagli, F. Cowell, H. Glennerster, E. Karagiannaki and A. McKnight, *Wealth in the UK: Distribution, accumulation, and policy*, Oxford: Oxford University Press.

Baumberg, B., Bell, K. and Gaffney, D. (2012) *Benefits stigma in Britain*, Canterbury: Elizabeth Finn Care/University of Kent.

Bennett, F. (2010) *Universal Credit – Written evidence*, Briefing for House of Lords, December.

Bennett, F. (2011) 'Universal Credit: The gender impact', *Poverty*, vol 40, pp 15–18.

Beveridge, W.H. (1942) *Social insurance and allied services*, Cmd 6404, London: HMSO.

Birmingham Policy Commission on Wealth (2013) *Sharing our good fortune: Understanding and responding to wealth inequality*, Birmingham: University of Birmingham.

Blanden, J. and Machin, S. (2007) *Recent changes in intergenerational mobility*, Report for the Sutton Trust, London: Sutton Trust.

Blanden, J. and Macmillan, L. (2014) *Education and intergenerational mobility: Help or hindrance?*, Social Policy in a Cold Climate Working Paper 08, London: London School of Economics.

Brewer, M., Browne, J. and Jin, W. (2012b) *Benefit integration in the UK*, ESRI Research Series 28, Dublin: Economic and Social Research Institute.

Brewer, M., Costas Dias, M. and Shaw, A. (2012a) *A dynamic perspective on how the UK personal tax and benefit system affects work incentives and redistributes income*, IFS Briefing Note 132, London: Institute for Fiscal Studies.

Buck, N. and Scott, J. (1994) 'Household and family change', in N. Buck, J. Gershuny, D. Rose and J. Scott (eds) *Changing households: The British Household Panel Survey 1990–1992*, Colchester: ESRC Research Centre on Micro-Social Change.

Burchardt, T. (2000) *Enduring economic exclusion: Disabled people income and work*, York: Joseph Rowntree Foundation.

Burchardt, T. and Hills, J. (1997) *Private welfare insurance and social security: Pushing the boundaries*, York: Joseph Rowntree Foundation.

Burchardt, T., Hills, J. and Propper, C. (1999) *Private welfare and public policy*, York: Joseph Rowntree Foundation.

Chowdry, H., Crawford, C., Dearden, L., Goodman, A. and Vignoles, A. (2013) 'Widening participation in higher education: Analysis using linked administrative data', *Journal of the Royal Statistical Society A*, vol 176, no 2, pp 431–57.

Clarke, H. and McKay, S. (2008) *Exploring disability and family formation: Reviewing the evidence*, Research Report 514, London: Department for Work and Pensions.

CLG (Communities and Local Government) (2010) *Local decisions: A fairer future for social housing*, London: CLG.

CLG (2012) *High income social tenants: Pay to Stay consultation paper*, London: CLG.

Commission on Funding of Care and Support (2011) *Fairer care funding: The report of the Commission on Funding of Care and Support*, London: Department of Health.

Cooper, K. and Stewart, K. (2013) *Does money affect children's outcomes? A systematic review*, York: Joseph Rowntree Foundation.

Corak, M. (2013) 'Income inequality, equality of opportunity and intergenerational mobility', *Journal of Economic Perspectives*, vol 27, no 3, pp 79–102.

Crawford, C. (2012) *Socioeconomic gaps in higher education attainment: How have they changed over time?*, IFS Briefing Note, November, London: Institute for Fiscal Studies.

Crawford, C., Goodman, A. and Joyce, R. (2011) 'Explaining the socio-economic gradient in child outcomes: The inter-generational transmission of cognitive skills', *Longitudinal and Life Course Studies*, vol 2, no 1, pp 77–93.

Cribb, J., Emmerson, C. and Tetlow, G. (2013a) *Incentives, shocks or signals: Labour supply effects of increasing the female state pension age in the UK*, IFS Working Paper 13/03, London: Institute for Fiscal Studies.

Cribb, J., Hood, A., Joyce, R. and Phillips, D. (2013b) *Living standards, poverty and inequality in the UK: 2013*, IFS Report 81, London: Institute for Fiscal Studies.

CSJ (Centre for Social Justice) (2013) *Signed on, written off: An inquiry into welfare dependency in Britain*, London: CSJ.

CSJ Housing Dependency Working Group (2008) *Housing poverty: From social breakdown to social mobility*, London: CSJ.

Cullis, A. and Hansen, K. (2008) *Child development in the first three sweeps of the Millennium Cohort Study*, Research Report DCSF-RW077, London: Department for Children, Schools and Families.

De Agostini, P. and Brewer, M. (2013) *Credit crunched: Single parents, Universal Credit and the struggle to make work pay*, London: Gingerbread.

De Agostini, P., Paulas, A., Sutherland, H. and Tasseva, I. (2014) *The effect of tax-benefit changes on income distribution in EU countries since the beginning of the economic crisis*, Social Situation Monitor Research Note 02/2013, Brussels: European Commission Directorate-General for Employment, Social Affairs and Inclusion.

Dearden, L., Sibieta, L. and Sylva, K. (2011) 'The socioeconomic gradient in early childhood outcomes: Evidence from the Millennium Cohort Study', *Longitudinal and Life Course Studies*, vol 2, no 1, pp 19–40.

DH (Department of Health) (2013) *Caring for our future: Consultation on reforming what and how people pay for their care and support*, London: DH.

Disney, R., Emmerson, C. and Tetlow, G. (2009) 'What is a public sector pension worth?', *Economic Journal*, vol 119, no 541, F517–F535.

Dorling, D. (2014) *All that is solid: The great housing disaster*, London: Allen Lane.

DWP (Department for Work and Pensions) (2007) *Ready for work: Full employment in our generation*, Cm 7290, London: The Stationery Office.

DWP (2012) *Annual abstract of statistics 2012*, London: DWP.

DWP (2013a) *Benefit expenditure and caseload tables, 2013*, London: DWP.

DWP (2013b) *Duration on working-age benefits, Great Britain, April 2013*, London: DWP.

DWP (2013c) *The single tier pension: A simple foundation for saving*, Cm 8528, London: The Stationery Office.

DWP (2014a) *Fraud and error in the benefit system: 2012/13 estimates (Great Britain)*, London: DWP.

DWP (2014b) *Universal Credit – Experimental official statistics to January 2014*, April, London: DWP.

Echailer, M., Adams, J., Redwood, D. and Curry, C. (2013) *Tax relief for pension saving in the UK*, London: Pensions Policy Institute.

Esser, I. (2009) 'Has welfare made us lazy? Employment commitment in different welfare states', in A. Poole, J. Curtis, K. Thomson, M. Phillips and E. Clery (eds) *British Social Attitudes: The 25th report*, London: Sage.

Evans, M. and Williams, L. (2009) *A generation of change, a lifetime of difference? Social policy in Britain since 1979*, Bristol: Policy Press.

Fabian Commission (2013) *2030 vision: The final report of the Fabian Commission on future spending choices*, London: Fabian Society.

Falkingham, J. and Hills, J. (eds) (1995) *The dynamic of welfare: The welfare state and the lifecycle*, Hemel Hempstead: Prentice Hall/Harvester Wheatsheaf.

Feinstein, L. (2013) 'Social mobility: Delusions and confusions', in Centre for Analysis of Social Exclusion, *Annual report 2012*, London: London School of Economics.

Fenton, A, (2011) *Housing benefit reform and the spatial segregation of low-income households in London*, Cambridge: Department of Land Economy, University of Cambridge.

Glennerster, H. (2012) 'Why was a wealth tax for the UK abandoned?: Lessons for the policy process and tackling wealth inequality', *Journal of Social Policy*, vol 41, no 2, pp 233–49.

Glennerster, H. and Evans, M. (1994) 'Beveridge and his assumptive worlds: The incompatibilities of a flawed design', in J. Hills, J. Ditch and H. Glennerster (eds) *Beveridge and social security: An international retrospective*, Oxford: Oxford University Press.

Glennerster, H., Bradshaw, J., Lister, R. and Lundberg, O. (2009) *Reducing the risks to health: The role of social protection. Report of the Social Protection Task Group for the Strategic Review of Health Inequalities in England post 2010*, CASEpaper 139, London: London School of Economics.

Goldthorpe, J. and Mills, C. (2008) 'Trends in intergenerational class mobility in modern Britain: Evidence from national surveys, 1972–2005', *National Institute Economic Review*, vol 205, no 1, pp 83–100.

Goodman, A. and Gregg, P. (2010) *Children's educational outcomes: The role of attitudes and behaviours, from early childhood to late adolescence*, London and Bristol: Institute for Fiscal Studies and Centre for Market and Public Organisation, University of Bristol.

Gregg, P. and Wadsworth, J. (eds) (2011) *The labour market in winter: The state of working Britain*, Oxford: Oxford University Press.

Gregg, P., Macmillan, L. and Vittori, C. (2013) 'Lifetime intergenerational economic mobility in the UK', Presentation to Social Mobility and Child Poverty Commission Seminar on 'Intergenerational mobility and social gradients in children's life chances', London, 20 November.

Hansen, K. and Joshi, H. (2008) *Millennium Cohort Study Third Survey: A user's guide to initial findings*, London: Centre for Longitudinal Studies, Institute for Education.

Hedges, A. (2005) *Perceptions of redistribution: Report on exploratory qualitative research*, CASEpaper 96, London: London School of Economics.

Hills, J. (2004a) *Inequality and the state*, Oxford: Oxford University Press.

Hills, J. (2004b) 'Heading for retirement? National Insurance, state pensions, and the future of the contributory principle in the UK', *Journal of Social Policy*, vol 33, no 3, pp 347–71.

Hills, J. (2007) *Ends and means: The future roles of social housing in England*, CASEreport 34, London: London School of Economics.

Hills, J. (2011) 'The changing architecture of the UK welfare state', *Oxford Review of Economic Policy*, vol 27, no 4, pp 589–607.

Hills, J. (2012), *Getting the measure of fuel poverty*, CASEreport 72, London: London School of Economics.

Hills, J. (2013a) *Labour's record on cash transfers, poverty, inequality and the lifecycle 1997–2010*, Social Policy in a Cold Climate Working Paper 05, London: London School of Economics.

Hills, J. (2013b) 'Safeguarding social equity during fiscal consolidation: Which tax bases to use?', in S. Princen and G. Mourre (eds) *The role of tax policy in times of fiscal consolidation*, European Economy Economic Papers 502, Brussels: European Commission.

Hills, J. and Bastagli, F. (2013) 'Trends in the distribution of wealth in Britain', in J. Hills, F. Bastagli, F. Cowell, H. Glennerster, E. Karagiannaki and A. McKnight, *Wealth in the UK: Distribution, accumulation, and policy*, Oxford: Oxford University Press.

Hills, J and Glennerster, H. (2013) 'Public policy, wealth and assets: A complex and inconsistent story', in J. Hills, F. Bastagli, F. Cowell, H. Glennerster, E. Karagiannaki and A. McKnight, *Wealth in the UK: Distribution, accumulation, and policy*, Oxford: Oxford University Press.

Hills, J. and Karagiannaki, E. (2013) 'Inheritance, transfers and the distribution of wealth', in J. Hills, F. Bastagli, F. Cowell, H. Glennerster, E. Karagiannaki and A. McKnight, *Wealth in the UK: Distribution, accumulation, and policy*, Oxford: Oxford University Press.

Hills, J. and Lelkes, O. (1999) 'Social security, selective universalism and patchwork redistribution', in R. Jowell, J. Curtice, A. Park and K. Thomson (eds) *British Social Attitudes: The 16th report, who shares New Labour values?*, Aldershot: Ashgate.

Hills, J. and Richards, B. (2012) *Localisation and the means test: A case study of support for English students from Autumn 2012*, CASEpaper 160, London: London School of Economics.

Hills, J. and Sutherland, H. (1991) *The Ackroyds, the Osbornes and the tax system*, Welfare State Programme Research Note 23, London: London School of Economics.

Hills, J., Smithies, R. and McKnight, A. (2006) *Tracking income: How working families' incomes vary through the year*, CASEreport 32, London: London School of Economics.

Hills, J., Cunliffe, J., Gambaro, L. and Obolenskaya, P. (2013a) *Winners and losers in the crisis: The changing anatomy of economic inequality in the UK 2007–2010*, Social Policy in a Cold Climate Research Report 2, London: London School of Economics.

Hills, J., Bastagli, F., Cowell, F., Glennerster, H., Karagiannaki, E. and McKnight, A. (2013b) *Wealth in the UK: Distribution, accumulation, and policy*, Oxford: Oxford University Press.

Hills, J., Brewer, M., Jenkins, S.P., Lister, R., Lupton, R., Machin, S., Mills, C., Modood, T., Rees, T. and Riddell, S. (2010) *An anatomy of economic inequality in the UK: Report of the National Equality Panel*, CASEreport 60, London: London School of Economics.

HM Treasury (2014a) *Budget 2014*, London: HM Treasury.

HM Treasury (2014b) *Impact on households: Distributional analysis accompanying Budget 2014*, London: HM Treasury.

Hood, A. and Joyce, R. (2013) *The economic circumstances of cohorts born between the 1940s and the 1970s*, IFS Report 89, London: Institute for Fiscal Studies.

House of Lords Select Committee on Public Service and Demographic Change (2013) *Ready for ageing*, London: The Stationery Office.

Howker, E. and Malik, S. (2010) *Jilted generation: How Britain bankrupted its youth*, London: Icon.

Jantti, M. and Jenkins, S.P. (2014: forthcoming) 'Income mobility', IZA Discussion Paper 7730, Berlin: IZA (prepared as a chapter for the *Handbook of income distribution, Volume 2*, edited by A.B. Atkinson and F. Bourguignon, Elsevier-North Holland).

Jenkins, S.P. (2011) *Changing fortunes: Income mobility and poverty dynamics in Britain*, Oxford: Oxford University Press.

Jenkins, S.P. and Cowell, F. (1993) *Dwarfs and giants in the 1980s: Trends in UK income distribution*, Department of Economics Working Paper 93–03, Swansea; University of Swansea.

Jerrim, J. (2012) 'The socio-economic gradient in teenagers reading skills: How does England compare with other countries?', *Fiscal Studies*, vol 53, no 2, pp 159–84.

Karagiannaki, K. (2011a) *Recent trends in the size and the distribution of inherited wealth in the UK*, CASEpaper 146, London: London School of Economics.

Karagiannaki (2011b) *The magnitude and correlates of inter-vivo transfers in the UK*, CASEpaper 151, London: London School of Economics.

Kempson, E. and Whyley, C. (2001) *Payment of pensions and benefits: A survey of social security recipients paid by order book or girocheque*, DWP Research Report 146, London: Department for Work and Pensions.

Kenworthy, L. (2011) *Progress for the poor*, Oxford: Oxford University Press.

Keohane, N. and Shorthouse, R. (2012) *Sink or swim: The impact of Universal Credit*, London: Social Market Foundation.

King, D. (1995) *Actively seeking work? The politics of unemployment and welfare policy in the United States and Great Britain*, Chicago, IL: University of Chicago Press.

Kornrich, S. and Furstenberg, F. (2013) 'Investing in children: Changes in parental spending on children, 1972–2007', *Demography*, vol 50, pp 1–23.

Korpi, W. and Palme, J. (1998) 'The paradox of redistribution and strategies of equality: Welfare state institutions, inequality, and poverty in the Western countries', *American Sociological Review*, vol 63, no 5, pp 661–87.

Le Grand, J. (1982) *The strategy of equality*, London: Allen & Unwin.

Long, K. (2009) 'Unemployment durations: Evidence from the British Household Panel Survey', *ONS Economic and Labour Market Review*, vol 3, no 10.

Lupton, R. and Obolenskaya, P. (2013) *Labour's record on education*, Social Policy in a Cold Climate Working Paper 03, London: London School of Economics.

Lupton, R., Hills, J., Stewart, K. and Vizard, P. (2013) *Labour's social policy record: Policy, spending and outcomes 1997–2010*, Social Policy in a Cold Climate Research Report 1, London: London School of Economics.

Macdonald, R., Shildrick, T. and Furlong, A. (2014) 'In search of "intergeneratioanl cultures of worklessness": Hunting the Yeti and shooting zombies', *Critical Social Policy*, vol 34, no 2, pp 199–220.

Macmillan, L. and Gregg, P. (2012) '"Never working families" – a misleading sound-bite', 21 February (inequalitiesblog.wordpress.com).

Macmillan, L., Tyler, C. and Vignoles, A. (2013) *Who gets the best jobs? The role of family background and networks in recent graduates' access to high status professions*, Department of Quantitative Social Science Working Paper 13–15, London: Institute of Education.

McKnight, A. and Karagianniaki, E. (2013) 'The wealth effect: How parental wealth and asset holdings predict future outcomes', in J. Hills, F. Bastagli, F. Cowell, H. Glennerster, E. Karagiannaki and A. McKnight, *Wealth in the UK: Distribution, accumulation, and policy*, Oxford: Oxford University Press.

Machin, S., Murphy, R. and Soobedar, Z. (2009) *Differences in the labour market gains from higher education participation*, Report for the National Equality Panel, London: Centre for Economic Performance, London School of Economics.

Marx, I. and van Rie, T. (2014) 'The policy response to inequality: Redistributing income', in W. Salverda, B. Nolan, D. Checchi, I. Marx, A. McKnight, I. Tóth, and H. van de Werfhorst (eds) *Changing inequalities and societal impacts in rich countries: Analytical and comparative perspective*, Oxford: Oxford University Press.

Mayer, S.E. (1998) *What money can't buy: Family income and children's life chances*, Cambridge, MA: Harvard University Press.

NAO (National Audit Office) (2013a) *Universal Credit: Early progress*, HC621 (2013–14), London: NAO.

NAO (2013b) *Council Tax support*, HC882 (2013–14), London: NAO.

Nazroo, J., Zaninotto, P. and Gjonca, E. (2008) 'Mortality and healthy life expectancy', in J. Banks, E. Breeze, C. Lessof and J. Nazroo (eds) *Living in the 21st century: Older people in England. The 2006 English Longitudinal Study of Aging (Wave 3)*, London: Institute for Fiscal Studies.

OBR (Office for Budget Responsibility) (2012) *Fiscal sustainability report, July 2012*, London: OBR.

OBR (2013a) *Fiscal sustainability report, July 2013*, London: OBR.

OBR (2013b) *Economic and fiscal outlook, December 2013*, London: OBR.

OBR (2014) *Economic and fiscal outlook, March 2014*, London: OBR.

O'Hara, M. (2014) *Austerity bites*, Bristol: Policy Press.

ONS (Office for National Statistics) (2011) *Mid-2010 based population projections*, 26 October, London: ONS.

ONS (2012a) *Pension trends Chapter 3: Life expectancy and healthy ageing*, London: ONS.

ONS (2012b) *Wealth and Assets Survey for 2008–10*, London: ONS.

ONS (2013a) *The effects of taxes and benefits on household income 2010/11, reference tables*, London: ONS.

ONS (2013b) *Historic and projected mortality data from the period and cohort life tables, 2012-based, UK, 1981–2062*, 11 December, London: ONS.

ONS (2013c) *Life expectancy at birth and at age 65 for local areas in England and Wales*, 24 October, London: ONS.

ONS (2014) *Analysis of employee contracts that do not guarantee a minimum number of hours*, 30 April, London: ONS.

PAC (Public Accounts Committee) (2013) *Universal Credit: Early progress, Thirtieth report of Session 2013–14, Report, together with formal minutes, oral and written evidence*, HC619, London: House of Commons.

Panel on Fair Access to the Professions (2009) *Unleashing aspiration: The final report of the Panel on Fair Access to the Professions*, London: Cabinet Office.

Pearce, N. and Taylor, E. (2013) 'Government spending and welfare: Changing attitudes towards the role of the state', in *British Social Attitudes: The 30th Report*, London: NatCen Social Research.

Pensions Commission (2004) *Pensions: Challenges and choices. The first report of the Pensions Commission*, London: HMSO.

Pensions Commission (2005) *A new pension settlement for the 21st century. The second report of the Pensions Commission*, London: HMSO.

Phillips, D. (2014) 'Personal tax and welfare measures', Institute for Fiscal Studies Seminar Presentation, March, London: Institute for Fiscal Studies.

Piketty, T. (2014) *Capital in the twenty-first century*, Cambridge MA: Harvard University Press.

Power, A., Provan, B., Herden, E. and Serle, N. (2014) *The impact of welfare reform on social landlords and tenants*, Report by LSE Housing and Communities for the Joseph Rowntree Foundation, York: Joseph Rowntree Foundation.

Rigg, J. and Sefton, T. (2006) 'Income dynamics and the life cycle', *Journal of Social Policy*, vol 35, pp 411–35.

Roantree, B. and Shaw, J. (2014) *The Case for taking a life-cycle perspective: Inequality, redistribution and tax and benefit reforms*, IFS report R92, London: Institute for Fiscal Studies.

Rowlingson, K. and McKay, S. (2011) *Wealth and the wealthy: Exploring and tackling inequalities between the rich and poor*, Bristol: Policy Press.

Rowlingson, K., Orton, M. and Taylor, E. (2010) 'Do we still care about inequality?', in A. Park, J. Curtice, E. Clery and D. Bryson (eds) *British Social Attitudes: The 27th report: Exploring Labour's legacy*, London: Sage.

Rowntree, S. (1901) *Poverty: A study of town life*, London: Macmillan. [Reissued by Policy Press in 2000.]

Sainsbury, R., Irvine, A., Aston, J., Wilson, S., Williams, C. and Sinclair, A. (2008) *Mental health and employment*, Research Report 513, London: Department for Work and Pensions.

Sefton, T. (2005) 'Give and take: Attitudes to redistribution', in A. Park, J. Curtis, K. Thomason, C. Bromley, M. Phillips and M. Johnson (eds) *British Social Attitudes: The 22nd report: Two terms of New Labour: The public's reaction*, Aldershot: Ashgate.

Sefton, T. (2007) *Using the British Household Panel Survey to explore changes in housing tenure in England*, CASEpaper 117, London: London School of Economics.

Sefton, T. (2009) 'Moving in the right direction? Public attitudes to poverty, inequality and redistribution', in J. Hills, T. Sefton and K. Stewart (eds) *Towards a more equal society? Poverty, inequality and policy since 1997*, Bristol: Policy Press.

Shildrick, T., Macdonald, R., Webster, C. and Garthwaite, K. (2012) *Poverty and insecurity: Life in low pay, no pay Britain*, Bristol: Policy Press.

Skinner, C. and Main, G. (2013) 'The contribution of child maintenance payments to the income packages of lone mothers', *Journal of Poverty and Social Justice*, vol 21, no 1, pp 47–60.

Social Mobility and Child Poverty Commission (2013) *The state of the nation: Social mobility and child poverty in Great Britain*, London: HMSO.

Standing, G. (2011) *The precariat: The new dangerous class*, London: Bloomsbury Academic.

Standing, G. (2014) *A precariat charter: From denizens to citizens*, London: Bloomsbury Academic.

Stiglitz, J. (2012) *The price of inequality*, New York: Norton.

Sutherland, H., Evans, M., Hancock, R., Hills, J. and Zantomio, E. (2008) *The impact of tax and benefit reforms on incomes and poverty*, York: Joseph Rowntree Foundation.

Tarr, A. and Finn, D. (2012) *Implementing Universal Credit: Will the reforms improve the service for users?*, York: Joseph Rowntree Foundation.

Taylor-Gooby, P. (2013) *The double crisis of the welfare state and what we can do about it*, Basingstoke: Palgrave Macmillan.

Taylor-Gooby, P. and Hastie, C. (2002) 'Support for state spending: Has New Labour got it right?', in A. Park, J. Curtice, K. Thomson, L. Jarvis and C. Bromley (eds) *British Social Attitudes: The 19th report*, London: Sage.

Tonkin, R. and Thomas, N. (2012) *The effects of taxes and benefits on household income, 2010/11: Further analysis and methodology*, London: Office for National Statistics (www.ons.gov.uk/ons/dcp171766_268392.pdf).

UK Women's Budget Group (2013) *The impact of the Coalition government's spending record 2013*, July, London: Women's Budget Group.

Vizard, P. and Obolenskaya, P. (2013) *Labour's record on health*, Social Policy in a Cold Climate Working Paper 02, London: London School of Economics.

Waldfogel, J. and Washbrook, E. (2008) 'Early years policy', Paper presented at Carnegie Corporation of New York and Sutton Trust Conference on 'Social mobility and education', New York, June.

Webster, D. (2014) 'The DWP's Jobseeker's Allowance sanctions statistics release, 19 February 2014', Glasgow: Department of Urban Studies, University of Glasgow (mimeo).

Whiteford, P., Mendelson, M. and Millar, J. (2003) *Timing it right? Tax credits and responding to income changes*, York: Joseph Rowntree Foundation.

Whitty, G. and Anders, J. (2014) *(How) did Labour narrow the achievement and participation gap?*, LLAKES Research Paper 46, London: Institute of Education.

Wilcox, S. (2014) *The bedroom limits: The impact of the Housing Benefit size criteria for social sector tenants and options for reform*, York: Joseph Rowntree Foundation.

Willetts, D. (2010) *The pinch: How the baby-boomers took their children's future – and why they should give it back*, London: Atlantic.

Woolley, F. and Le Grand, J. (1990) 'The Ackroyds, the Osbornes and the welfare state: The impact of the welfare state on two hypothetical families over their life-times', *Policy & Politics*, vol 18, no 1, pp 17–30.

Young, M. (1958) *The rise of the meritocracy, 1870–2033*, Harmondsworth: Penguin Books.

INDEX

Page references for figures are given in italics; those for notes are followed by n

A

Ackroyds 6–7, 9
  economic crisis, cuts, growth and
    ageing 216, 217, 219–21, 230,
    241, 247–8, 257, 258
  high frequency living 74, 76–8, 83,
    86, 95, 97, 98, 99, 108, 252, 253
  life chances 180, 181–3, 195, 205,
    256, 257
  redistribution and the welfare
    state 14, 17–18, 19, 39, 44, 250
  social policies and the life cycle
    46, 47–8, 61, 64, 73, 251
  wealth and retirement 144, 147–8,
    149, 155, 255
  year-to-year variations 110, 111–13,
    117, 128–9, 143, 253
Adam, Stuart 225–6, 226
ageing population 5, 13, 179, 232,
  241–7, 248, 258, 267
annuities 173
asset-based welfare 177–8
Atkinson, Tony 43–4
austerity 12–13, 227–33, 247–8
  fairness 20, 221–4
  international comparison 233–6
  Osbornes and Ackroyds 216–21
Australia 27, 31, 96

B

baby-boomers 156–7, 166–7, 178,
  254–5
Baumol, William 246
Baumol effect 246
'Beat the Taxman' 7, 287n
Bedroom Tax 61, 106, 220, 228, 265
benefit erosion xii, 238–41, 239, 240,
  248
benefits
  Coalition government 19, 61,
    219–20, 223–4, 224, 227–33,
    229, 231, 232, 265–6
  disability 123–4, 123, 288n
  economic crisis, cuts and growth
    219–20, 236–41, 258
  fraud 1, 263–4
  high frequency living 86, 87,
    88–94, 105–6
  and life cycle 54–5, 55, 66–7, 66,
    69, 72–3
  making people lazy 1, 261–2, 262
  New Labour 225–7, 226
  pensioners 162
  public opinion 261, 262
  and redistribution 16, 17, 19, 23,
    28–35, 44–5
  sanctions 220, 229, 265
  and savings 147–8, 174–5
  spending on 259–61, 260

them and us 1–3, 19, 249–50, 266
Universal Credit 97–103, 108–9
see also cash benefits; Incapacity
Benefit; Jobseeker's Allowance;
unemployment benefits
benefits in kind 29, 30–1, 63–4
see also education; NHS
Beveridge, William 4, 50–2, *51*, 94–5
Birmingham 92
Blair, Tony 4
Blanden, Jo 193–4, *194*, 197
Brewer, Mike 69
British Household Panel Survey
(BHPS)
disability 122–3
family circumstances 119–20
house prices 158–9, *159*
income mobility 124, *125*, 126–7, *126*
income trajectories 115–18, *116*, *117*
wage-age trajectories 121–2, *122*
British Social Attitudes (BSA) survey
19–24, *20*, *21*, *22*, *23*, 259, 270n
Brown, Gordon 95, 213
Browne, James 225–6, *226*
budgeting 77, 87–8, 104–5, 108–9, 253
Burchardt, Tania 122–3
Bush, George W. 213
Business Expansion Scheme 146

C
Cameron, David 212
capital gains tax 146, 174
cash benefits
and life cycle 46, 47, 54, 55, *55*,
63–4
public opinion 36–7, *37*
and redistribution 14, 28, 29, 33, *34*
cash transfers xii, 56–7
see also cash benefits; tax credits
Centre for Social Justice 92

Child Benefit 16, 17, 47, *98*, 99
Coalition government 61, 219, 228
and income variation *80*, 81, *81*,
82, *82*
Child Tax Credit 16, 17, 95, 97, 98, *98*,
219, 270n
and income variation 76, 81, 82
Child Trust Funds 61, 177, 278n
children
early development 180, 181,
185–90
outcomes and low income 190–1
poverty 56–7, *57*, 58, *58*, 59, *59*,
129–32, *130*, *131*, 142
tax and benefit changes 61, 62, *63*,
231–2, *231*
see also education
Chowdry, Haroon 199
Clegg, Nick 212
Coalition government 1–2, 3–4
and different age groups 61–2,
63, 73
Inheritance Tax 176
long-term care 176–7
pensions 166, 173
redistribution 21
social housing 133, 134, 289n
social mobility 212
student finance 136, 137
tax and benefit changes 19, 223–4,
227–33, *229*, *231*, *232*, 241, 247,
265–6
Universal Credit 11, 97, 101–7,
108–9
Conservative Party 20
Cooper, Kerris 190–1
Corak, Miles 207, *208*, *209*
council housing 133, 136, 148, 177, 255
Council Tax 16, 17, 76–7, 145, 171, 218,
220, 295n

Coalition government 228
Council Tax Benefit 17, 25, 97, 98–9,
    98, 140
    cuts 61–2, 140, 219, 228, 266
    and Universal Credit 101–2, 106,
    284n
Crawford, Claire 199
Cullis, Andy 188–9, 188

D

de Agostini, Paola 233–5, 235
decile group xii
deduction rate see effective marginal
    tax rate
defined benefit pensions xii, 162, 293n
defined contribution pensions xii,
    162–3, 293n
delayed action means test 136–41
demography
    and income change 86, 118–20, 141
    and welfare state 241–7
    see also life expectancy
Denmark 38
Department for Work and Pensions
    (DWP)
    benefit fraud 263
    Households Below Average Income
    24, 26
    Incapacity Benefit 123–4, 123
    income mobility 126, 127–8
    persistent low income 131–2, 131
    Universal Credit 98, 101, 102–3, 104
dependency culture 1, 3, 4, 19, 261–2
Dilnot, Andrew 175–6
direct taxes xii, 29, 30, 33, 34
    see also capital gains tax;
    Income Tax; Inheritance
    Tax; National Insurance
    Contributions
disability 252

benefits 62, 220, 228, 265–6, 288n
    and income variation 122–4
Disney, Richard 120, 121
disposable income xii, 29, 30, 32
    life cycle 54–5, 56
Duncan Smith, Iain 2, 3–4, 93

E

earnings 120–2, 237
    mobility 182, 200–9
earnings-related benefits 36–7, 37
economic crisis 247
    Coalition impacts 227–33
    and fairness 20, 221–4
    international reactions 233–6
    New Labour 226–7
    Osbornes and Ackroyds 216–21
education
    Coalition government 61
    and family background 180, 181–2,
        191–6, 206, 214
    and life cycle 46, 48
    spending 33, 34, 54, 55, 68–9, 73,
        260, 261
    see also higher education
Education Maintenance Allowances
    (EMAs) 61, 112
effective marginal tax rate xii,
    99–100, 100, 138
    student finance 137, 138, 139–41,
        139, 143
employment
    in-work support 94–7
    and income variation 88–94
Employment and Support Allowance
    (ESA) 97–8, 265, 288n
equality of opportunity 5, 6, 12, 183–4,
    214–15, 256–7
    background and life chances
        184–5

child development 185–90
and earnings 200–9
higher education 196–9
income and children's outcomes
190–1
Osbornes and Ackroyds 180–3
policy 212–14
scale of intergenerational links
203–7
school years 191–6
and wealth 38, 152, 209–11
equivalised income xii, 25
Esser, Ingrid 261–2, 263
European Social Survey 261, 262

F
fairness 21, 221–4
Family Credit 95
Family Income Supplement 95
fiscal drag xii, 238–41, 239, 240, 248
Fitzgerald, F. Scott 207
flat-rate benefits 36–7, 37
France 27, 31, 234, 235
fraud 1, 263–4
free school meals 17, 181, 191–3, 192
fuel poverty 170, 295n
Furlong, Andy 93

G
gender see men; women
generations 6, 268
fairness 222
wealth inequalities 152, 153, 154–7,
178
and welfare state 69–72
see also equality of opportunity
Germany 27, 31, 234, 235
Gini coefficient xiii, 26–7, 27

Glasgow 93
granny tax 62, 170
Great Gatsby curve 207–8, 208, 214
Gregg, Paul 93, 203–4, 204

H
Hain, Peter 4
Hansen, Kirstine 188–9, 188
healthcare see long-term care; NHS
Hemingway, Ernest 207
Hewer, Nick 2
higher education
and social class 180, 182, 196–9,
197, 198
student finance 6, 48, 62, 136–41,
142–3, 177–8
HMRC 96, 97, 102–3
Hood, Andrew 156, 211
House of Lords Select Committee on
Public Service and Demographic
Change 245–6
Households Below Average Income
(HBAI) 24, 26
housing
Beveridge 94–5
and redistribution 33, 34
spending 260, 261
stamp duty 171–2
and wealth inequalities 153, 154,
158–61
see also owner occupation; social
housing
Housing Benefit 25, 77, 95, 97, 98, 98,
99, 134, 140, 282n
limits 61, 106, 219, 220, 228, 265
paid to claimants 104
Howker, Ed 156

I

Incapacity Benefit 123–4, *123*, 252, 288n
income
 and children's outcomes 185–95,
  214
 see also earnings; income
  variation; market income
income inequality 10, 15, 24–8, *31*, 45
 and earnings mobility 207–8, *208*,
  209
 and income mobility 124–8, 141
 public opinion 21–2
 and social mobility 215, 257
 and tax and benefit changes 230,
  247–8
 top 1 per cent 42–4, *43*
 and welfare state 28–33
 see also redistribution
income mobility 124–8, 141
Income Support 17, 82, *82*, 94, 95, 97
Income Tax 78, 99–100
 allowances 236–7, 238
 Coalition government 61, 62, 218,
  227
 savings 174
 tax forestalling 44, 272n
income variation 5–6
 demography 118–20
 disability 122–4
 earnings 120–2
 high frequency living 11, 74–88,
  108
 and life cycle 49–55
 Osbornes and Ackroyds 74–7,
  110–14
 persistent poverty 128–32
 year to year 11, 110–32, 141–3,
  253–4
indexation xiii, 228, 231, 236, 237

indirect taxes xiii, 16, 17, *29*, 30, 33, *34*
 see also VAT
inequality *see* equality of opportunity;
  income inequality; wealth
  inequalities
inheritance 157, 178, 183, 210–11
Inheritance Tax 171, 176
Institute for Fiscal Studies 69
intergenerational links *see*
  generations
International Social Survey
  Programme 261–2, *263*
internships 202
Ireland *27*, *31*, 234, 235, *235*
ISAs (Individual Savings Accounts)
  75, 146, 147, 174
Italy
 earnings mobility 207, 208, *208*,
  209
 inequality *27*, *31*
 tax and benefit changes 234, 235,
  235

J

Jenkins, Stephen 115, 118, 121–2, *122*,
  124, *125*, 126–7
jilted generation 156–7, 178, 254
Jobseeker's Allowance 97, 112, 147
 fraud 263, 264–5
 and income variation 82–3, *82*, 87
 indexation 236, 237
 length of time claimed 90–2, *91*,
  107, 252
 sanctions 265
Joyce, Robert 156, 211

K

Karagiannaki, Eleni 210
Keillor, Garrison 26

Kenworthy, Lane 38
Korpi, Walter 37–8
Krueger, Alan 207

L

Labour Force Survey 120, *121*
Labour Party *see* New Labour
Le Grand, Julian 269n
life chances *see* equality of
  opportunity
life cycle 6, 10–11, 49, 72–3, 251–2,
  253–4, 268
  Coalition policies 61–3
  and incomes 52–6
  intergenerational equity 69–72
  New Labour policies 56–61
  Osbornes and Ackroyds 46–9
  want and plenty 49–52
  wealth inequalities 178
  wealth and saving 152
  and welfare state 63–9
life expectancy *163*, 164, 168, 243
  inequalities 183, 184–5, *185*
  see also ageing population
Liverpool 92
London 193
long-term care 148, 175–7, 244–5,
  296n
long-term unemployment 90–2
low pay, no pay cycle 88–9
LSE, Personal Social Services
  Research Unit 244

M

Macdonald, Robert 93
McKnight, Abigail 210
Macmillan, Lindsey 93, 193–4, *194*,
  197, 201, 203–4, *204*
Malik, Shiv 156

market income xiii, 40
  inequality 28, *29*, 31–3, *31*, 45
  and life cycle 52–6, *56*
Marx, Ive 38–9
Mayer, Susan 202
means-tested benefits 36–7, *37*, 38
median xiii, 26, *26*
men
  earnings 120, *121*, *122*, 200–1,
    203–5, *204*, 214–15
  incomes 53–4
  life expectancy *163*, 164, 168, 169,
    184–5, *185*
  retirement age 168
  state pension age 165, 166
meritocracy 213–14
migration 243, 246
Millennium Cohort Study (MCS)
  185–7, *186*
Mountford, Margaret 2

N

National Employment Savings Trust
  (NEST) 167
National Insurance Contributions
  (NICs) 78, 176–7, 217–18, 227
National Scholarship Programme
  (NSP) 137, 138
net income xiii, 25
  age-related variations 59–60, *59*,
    60
  inequality 24–6, *26*
New Labour 4
  free nursery places 16
  Inheritance Tax 171
  life cycle redistribution 56–60,
    72–3
  long-term care 175
  Pension Credit 162
  redistribution 18, 20–1

social mobility 213
state pension 237
tax and benefit changes 18, 223–4, 225–7, 226, 247
tax credits 11, 95–7
NHS
    and ageing population 244–6, 248
    Coalition government 62
    and life cycle 46, 47–8, 73
    and redistribution 16, 17, 33, 34
    spending 68, 260, 261
Norway 27, 31, 262

O

occupational mobility 206–7
Office for Budget Responsibility (OBR) 243–5
Office for National Statistics (ONS)
    income inequality 28, 29
    indirect taxes 16
    life expectancy 243
    market incomes 52–3, 53
    redistribution 39, 40
    Wealth and Assets Survey 158, 211, 292n
older people
    life expectancy 184–5, 185
    long-term care 148, 175–7, 244–5, 296n
    poverty 41, 56–7, 57, 58, 58, 59, 59, 132
    tax and benefit changes 62, 63, 231, 231, 247
Osborne, George
    Inheritance Tax 171
    pensioners 170
    social housing 134
    welfare state 1–2
Osbornes 6–7, 8
    economic crisis, cuts, growth and

ageing 216, 217–18, 230, 247–8
high frequency living 74, 75, 78, 108, 252
life chances 180, 181–3, 205, 256
redistribution and the welfare state 14, 15–16, 18, 19, 35, 44, 250
social policies and the life cycle 46, 47–9, 60–1, 64, 73, 251
wealth and retirement 144, 145–7, 155, 172, 254–5
year-to-year variations 110, 113–14, 117–18, 127, 143, 253
'others' 249–50
owner occupation 15, 145, 148
    house prices 158–61, 159
    stamp duty 171–2

P

Palme, Joakim 37–8
paradox of redistribution 37–9
Paulus, Alari 233–5, 235
Pen, Jan 24, 25
Pen's parade xiii, 24
    incomes 24–6, 26
    wealth 149–51, 150, 151
Pension Credit 162, 296n
pensioners see older people
pensions
    tax relief 145–6, 148, 172–3
    wealth inequalities 145–6, 148, 150–1, 151, 153, 155, 156, 179, 293n
    see also state pension
Pensions Commission 161, 162–3, 165–6, 167
Pensions Policy Institute 172
percentile xiii
Personal Independence Payment 266
Phillips, David 228–32, 229, 231
Piketty, Thomas 43–4

Pinch, The (Willetts) 156
PISA (Programme for International
    Student Assessment) tests 194–5
population ageing 5, 13, 179, *232*,
    241–7, 248, 258, 267
poverty
    and life cycle 49, *50*, 56–7, *57*, 278n
    persistent 128–32, 141–2, 254
    and redistribution 39–42
poverty trap xiii, *98*, 99–100, 133–4,
    141
precariat 88
progressive taxation xiii, 30
    public opinion 36–7, *37*, 45
proportional taxation 69
    public opinion 36–7, *37*, 45
Public Accounts Committee 104

Q
quintile group xiii

R
redistribution 5, 7, 10, 44–5, 250–1
    and life cycle 56–61, 65–9
    mechanics 33–5
    Osbornes and Ackroyds 14, 15–18
    over lifetime 251–2
    paradox 37–9
    public opinion 18–24, 35–7
    scale of 39–42
    and tax and benefit changes 225–7,
        226, 238–41, *239*, *240*
    see also income inequality
regressive taxation xiii, 30
    public opinion 36–7, *37*
retirement *see* pensions
Richards, Ben 137
Rigg, John 116–17, 118–19
Right to Buy 133, 136, 148, 177, 255

Roantree, Barra 266
Romney, Mitt 3
Rowntree, Seebohm 10, 49–50, *50*, 55,
    119, 253

S
Saez, Emmanuel 43–4
sanctions 220, 229, 265
savings 145, 146, 147–8, 149
    life cycle pattern 152
    tax treatment 174–5
    see also pensions
Savings Gateway 177
Scandinavia 207, 208, *208*, *209*
school readiness 186, *186*, 299n
Scotland 175, 296n
Sefton, Tom 116–17, 118–19
self-employment 88, 106
Shaw, Jonathan 266
Shildrick, Tracy 88 *9*, 93
sickness 51
    see also disability
social care *260*, 261
    see also long-term care
social housing 5, 17, 132–6, 142
    Right to Buy 133, 136, 148, 177, 255
social insurance 35, 50–2, *51*
social mobility 5, 6, 12, 214–15, 257
    earnings 200–9
    policy 212–14
Social Mobility and Child Poverty
    Commission 197, 202
social security *see* benefits; Incapacity
    Benefit; Jobseeker's Allowance;
    state pension
social wage *see* benefits in kind
Spain 27, *31*, 234, 235, *235*
'Spongers' 6, 269n
squeezed middle 42, *43*, 45, 251
stamp duty 171–2

Standing, Guy 88
state pension 236, 243
    age addition 236
    Beveridge 51
    and life cycle 46, 54, 55, *55*, 68–9, 73
    and life expectancy 163–70, *163*
    policy and problems 161–3
    public opinion 36–7, *37*
    and redistribution 33, *34*, 62
    spending on 259, 260, *260*
    triple lock xiv, 62, 166, 228, 237,
        243
state pension age 5, 62, 165, 166, 179,
    243, 244, 248
Stewart, Kitty 190–1
student finance 6, 136–41, 142–3, 177–8
Sutherland, Holly 233–5, *235*
Sweden
    income inequality *27*, *31*, 32, *32*
    redistribution 38

T

Tasseva, Iva 233–5, *235*
tax credits 18, 95–7, 109, 282n
    Coalition government 61, 228
    and income variation 5, 11, 76,
        80–3, 86–7
    and pension savings 148, 173
    spending on 259–61, *260*
    and student finance 137, 139–40
    and Universal Credit 97–103, 107
    see also Child Tax Credit; Working
        Tax Credit
taxes
    on capital assets 170–2
    Coalition government 217–19,
        223–4, 227–33, *229*, *231*, *232*
    economic crisis, cuts, and growth
        217–19, 223–4, *224*, 234–41, *235*,
        257–8

international comparison 234–6,
    235
and life cycle 46, 48, 54–5, *55*, 64,
    66–7, *66*, 69, 72–3
New Labour 225–7, *226*
pension saving 145–6, 172–3
public opinion 35–7, *37*
and redistribution 14, 15–16, 28–33,
    34–5, 44–5
on savings 146, 147, 174–5
see also direct taxes; indirect taxes
Taylor-Gooby, Peter 267
Titanic 184
Treasury 232–3, *232*
triple lock xiii, xiv, 62, 166, 228, 237,
    243
tuition fees 62, 136, 178
Tyler, Claire 201

U

underclass 11, 128
unemployment 107–8, 252
    Beveridge 51
    and income variation 88–94
    and redistribution 42
    social tenants 135
unemployment benefits
    and commitment to work 261–2,
        263
    public opinion 36–7, *37*
    spending on 259, 260–1, *260*
Universal Credit 5, 11, 97, 101–7, *101*,
    108–9, 228, 229, 252–3
    and pension contributions 173
US
    earnings mobility 207, 208, *208*,
        209
    equality of opportunity 215
    inequality *27*, *31*
    redistribution 38

social mobility 213
welfare xiv, 62, 259
welfare state 3, 62

V
van Rie, Tim 38–9
VAT 218, 220, 225, 228
Vignoles, Anna 201
Vittori, Claudia 203–4, *204*

W
wages *see* earnings
wealth accumulation 5, 12, 170, 179
    asset-based welfare 177
    long-term care 175–7
    pension saving 172–3
    savings 174–5
    and student finance 177–8
    taxes on capital assets 170–2
Wealth and Assets Survey (ONS) *150,
    151, 153,* 158, 211, 292n
wealth inequalities 11–12, 24, 27–8,
    149–52, *150, 151,* 178–9, 254–6
    and age 152, *153,* 154–5
    baby-boomers versus the jilted
        generation 156–7
    and equality of opportunity 183,
        209–11, 215
    housing 158–61
    Osbornes and Ackroyds 144–9
    pensions and changing lives
        163–70
    pensions policy and problems
        161–3
Webb, Steve 173
welfare xiv, 19, 62, 259
    see also benefits; welfare state
welfare state xiii, 19, 249, 259
    economic crisis, cuts, growth

    and ageing 12–13, 216–48,
        257–8
    equality of opportunity 12,
        180–215, 256–7
    fraud 1, 263–4
    high frequency living 11, 74–109,
        252–3
    life cycle 10–11, 46–73, 251–2
    making people lazy 1, 261–2, *262*
    myths and consequences 13,
        264–6
    Osbornes and Ackroyds 6–7, 8, 9
    redistribution 7, 10, 14–45, 250–1
    spending 259–61, *260*
    static or active 3–6
    them and us 1–3, 249–50, 266–8
    wealth and retirement 11–12,
        144–79, 254–6
    year-to-year variations 11, 110–43,
        253–4
Willetts, David 156
Winter Fuel Payments 62, 169, 170,
    295n
women
    annuities 173
    earnings 120, *121, 122,* 200, 201
    incomes 53–4
    life expectancy 164, 168, 169,
        184–5, *185*
    retirement age 168–9
    state pension age 165, 166
    tax and benefit changes 233
Working Families' Tax Credit
    (WFTC) 95
Working Tax Credit 17, 76, 81, 95, 97,
    98, 100
working-age population
    benefits 57, *63,* 93
    income *53,* 54, 55, *55, 56*
    poverty 57, *57*

tax and benefit changes 61–2, *63*,
     228, 231, *231*
World in Action 6–7
World Values Survey 264

Y
Yeti 93
YouGov 259
Young, Michael 214

Z
zero hours contracts 88, 103, 108